The Business of Life and Death

Volume II: Politics, Law, and Society

Collected Philosophical Essays

by

Giorgio Baruchello, PhD

NORTHWEST
PASSAGE
Books

Gatineau, Quebec, Canada

The Business of Life and Death
Volume 2: Politics, Law, and Society

Collected Philosophical Essays

by Giorgio Baruchello, PhD

Copyright © 2018 by Giorgio Baruchello. All rights reserved.

ISBN: 978-0-9939527-8-4

Published by
Northwest Passage Books
Gatineau, Quebec, Canada

Cover photo: Arch doorway, formerly of a bank in downtown Ottawa, Canada, installed in the Mackenzie-King Estate, Gatineau Park, Quebec, Canada. Photo by Brendan Myers.

To my parents

Table of Contents

Preface and Acknowledgments v

Introduction vi

Original publication credits xii

PART I – Socialist and Conservative Perspectives 1

   Chapter 1: Einstein's Socialism 2

   Chapter 2: Cornelius Castoriadis and "The Crisis of Modern Society" 15

   Chapter 3: Martha Nussbaum and John McMurtry 24

   Chapter 4: Giulio Tremonti's Exit Strategy: Ending the Tyranny of Finance 50

   Chapter 5: Arthur Fridolin Utz's Economic Ethics 65

   Chapter 6: Hans Jonas qua Political Thinker 121

PART II – Contemporary legal and social issues 139

   Chapter 7: The ICESCR qua Civil Commons 140

   Chapter 8: Europe's Constitutions qua Civil Commons 176

   Chapter 9: Iceland and the Crises 203

   Chapter 10: Eight Noble Opinions and the Economic Crisis: Four Literary-philosophical sketches à la Eduardo Galeano 214

Endnotes 248

Preface and Acknowledgments

The present volume is the fourth instalment in my ongoing collaboration with Northwest Passage Books and the second to be entitled *The Business of Life and Death*. As to these identically entitled two volumes, the first one dealt with life-and-death issues within the contexts of value theory and economics and, as the latter discipline is concerned, with special regard to the history of economics and economic history. This second volume, instead, deals primarily with political conceptions that are capable of identifying the literally lethal problems with, and likely ways out of, mainstream liberal categories of thought and economic praxes (hence "Politics" in the subtitle), as well as with features of existing international and national legal systems that can serve the same purposes, notably human rights legislation and financial regulation (hence "Law"), the ultimate legitimate function of which must be to serve, protect and promote societal wellbeing (hence "Society").

Once again, I must thank Dr Brendan Myers, chief consultant at Northwest Passage Books, who has been relentless in his encouragement and most generous in his professional advice. Without him, the very notion of a series of collected essays of mine would have probably never arisen, and no such volume as the present one would be available to the reading public. Also, I wish to express my gratitude towards two legal scholars, Ágúst Þór Árnason and Rachael Lorna Johnstone, who co-authored with me three of the five texts that, duly revised, appear in the second part of the present book. Their knowledge and professionalism informs my own appreciation and assessment of legal matters. If, however, any imprecision or error is going to be found in the pages that follow, the responsibility lies solely with me. Though certainly in dire need of other people's assistance whenever exploring culture and expanding understanding, I am fully capable of making mistakes by myself alone.

Introduction

As far as my generation is concerned, the single greatest geopolitical shake-up witnessed until now has been, without any doubt, the collapse of the Union of Soviet Socialist Republics (USSR) in 1991. This collapse marked the conclusion of a century-defining confrontation between East and West started with the Western Powers' military involvement in the Russian Civil War, peaked with the invasion of Soviet Union by Nazi Germany and its allies, and continued by way of a prolonged arms race between the United States of America (US) and their former anti-Nazi Soviet ally. Triumphantly, liberals, whether progressive or conservative, celebrated the "end of history" so confidently announced by Francis Fukuyama (b. 1952), according to whom the entire world was now going to become essentially liberal in all chief legal and business aspects,[1] whilst economic gurus such as Milton Friedman (1912–2006) advised the leaders of the world's nations, and especially those that had experienced communism, "to imitate Margaret Thatcher and Ronald Reagan; free markets in short... The fall of the Berlin Wall did more for the progress of freedom than all of the books written by myself or Friedrich Hayek or others."[2]

Today, we stand in a world displaying all the achievements—and all the disruption—that a liberal conception of the human being and of human affairs is capable of in concrete reality. On the one hand, international economic integration has never been so widespread and so deep. Not even the self-proclaimed socialist and isolationist Republic of North Korea is insulated from for-profit transnational financial and commercial transactions, especially with regard to its gigantic, and growing, Chinese neighbour.[3] Similarly, traditionally liberal civil and political rights have extended to the citizens of most countries on our planet. Emblematically, lesbian, gay, bisexual and transgender (LGBT) rights are today the new frontier for the recognition of all individuals' rights to self-determination, choice of lifestyle and free pursuit of happiness, analogously to what women campaigned and fought for one hundred years ago, or Europe's and the Americas' common men long before them.

However, what is the meaning of two men or two women marrying today, if they can have no economic security, if they have no trade union that is capable of protecting them, if the provision of healthcare when ill is costlier and poorer in quality than it was twenty years ago, if their old-age pensions are at the mercy of financial vagaries upon which these men and women have no control whatsoever, if their meaningful employment is at risk or non-existent, if the price-tag for the care and education of their children is beyond their ability to pay, or if the environment that they all need to survive is in grave peril while carcinogenic pollutants and stressors abound all around them?

Though saluted by its sycophants as the source of limitless bounty, today's liberalism and the profit-centred criteria that it assumes *qua* only rational path of human behaviour are also, as experienced by our forefathers in the 19th and 20th century, the source of deflationary spirals—the gold standard back then, the Eurozone today—, disastrous market collapses—the panics and crashes of old, today's meltdowns and credit crunches—, prolonged slumps—the Great Depression of the 1930s, today's Great Recession —, enormous inequalities—the Gilded Age or Belle Époque dissected by Thorstein Veblen (1857–1929), the 21st-century patrimonial capitalism dissected by Thomas Piketty (b. 1971)—and severe ecological calamities—the thousands killed by the Great Smog of London, the abandoned ancestral homes of the Alaskan Inuit swallowed by melting permafrost.

All civilisations have their ills. Ours, which is liberal, has got liberal ills. As amply discussed in my third volume for Northwest Passage Books, Canadian value theorist John McMurtry (b. 1939) has diagnosed these ills as tantamount to a cancer—indeed, to "the cancer stage of capitalism", as reads the title of his most famous book. In light of these ills, it can only be sensible to investigate other, alternative conceptions, so as to retrieve different approaches; identify aspects hidden, twisted or neglected by the application of liberal concepts; remember aims, methods and values that are either alien or secondary to liberalism; and seek correctives, constrictions and compromises that liberalism, by its own devices, would not easily generate or quite simply be oblivious to.

Historically, both socialism and conservatism have, in many ways, contributed to integrate, impede and innovate liberal institutions in life-enabling modes. Among them, human rights jurisprudence is a major example. Often confused with the fundamental freedoms of the individual defended by liberals since at least the days of John Locke (1632–1704), the notoriety of human rights—the rights of "man", "woman" and "infants"—originates in the 18th century with so-called "radicals" such as Thomas Spence (1750–1814), Mary Wollstonecraft (1759–1797), Robert Burns (1759–1796) and, above all, the Jacobins leading the most extreme wave of political and socio-economic reforms of the French Revolution. As to the concept itself of human rights, earlier scholastic thinkers such as Francisco de Vitoria (1483–1546) and Bartolomé de las Casas (1484–1566) should be credited as its likeliest fathers, as also reflected in our century by the staunch defence of jusnaturalism by the Catholic Church, traditionally a champion of conservatism, and by Thomist thinkers like Jacques Maritain (1882–1973) and Arthur Fridolin Utz (1908–2001), whose vast oeuvre informs, enriches and symbolises the Social Doctrine of the Church and its focus upon human rights.

Socialists, on their part, played historically a crucial role in making economic, social and cultural rights recognised, enshrined formally in constitutions, justiciable in actual legal practice, and funded by means of progressive taxation of both income and wealth. It is also, if not primarily, because of the pressure exercised, and the actions taken, by socialists of various streaks and sorts that, say, tax-funded public hygiene programmes and infrastructures, public schools, public works and public hospitals, all of which were among the dreams concocted by the French Jacobins back in the 1790s, became a widespread reality in the 20th century. In the last quarter of the 20th century, however, many countries started witnessing a gradual retrenchment from the secured provision of these rights, as inaudibly but poignantly flagged out by the recent drop in life expectancy rates, for the first time in decades, in post-industrial countries such as the US and the United Kingdom (UK).

The old right-wing powers of landed aristocrats and clergymen are long gone, and with them whatever paternalistic attention to the plight of the most vulnerable members of society that these patricians may have paid. The Roman Popes continue to issue articulate, reasoned and well-meaning warnings about the deplorable condition of the poor and the dramatic state of the Earth's environment, but it is unclear whether such warnings can change the conduct of the world's ruling elite and, along with it, humanity's fate. The 20th-century pressure of left-wing socialism and trade-unionism is perhaps not entirely spent. Nonetheless, it has been certainly weakened dramatically by the collapse of the USSR and, with it, the rhetorical, political and ideological bargaining power that, at least in the liberal countries, the sheer existence of the Warsaw Pact granted to workers, trade unions and socialists, including those who opposed Soviet communism, abhorred armed revolution, or refused to seek the abolition of capitalism as a desirable goal.

In essence, contemporary liberalism rules, by and large, unrestrained. Even the current alleged threat to it that goes under the name of "Islamic fundamentalism" does very little in terms of stopping actual for-profit trade between the seemingly threatened nations (e.g. France and the UK) and the nations whence most fundamentalists are born, trained, and their organisations funded (e.g. Saudi Arabia). Moreover, as a result of liberalism's unrestrained rule and its attendant accruing of both wealth and power into the hands of a small interest group, wealth is no longer successfully taxed to the extent required in order to secure the widespread provision of the social, economic and cultural rights enshrined in most countries' constitutions, as denounced *inter alia* by leading thinkers of the Frankfurt School, i.e. Jürgen Habermas (b. 1929) and Axel Honneth (b. 1949). Even in Europe, where some of the most extensive achievements have been reached in terms of both *de iure* and *de facto* entrenchment of human rights, liberalism's money-based partiality and elitist drive has recently been shown by, and showered upon, the Republic of Greece, where wealthy creditors' interests took priority over poorer and poorer swaths of the population, with dire consequences in terms of nutrition, health, and survival. (I provided an articulate ethical assessment of the effects of austerity in post-2008 Greece in my first volume for Northwest Passage Books.)

As the great 20th-century Greek polymath Cornelius Castoriadis (1922–1997) had feared and denounced in the 1980s, the loss of both nationalist and socialist restrains upon liberal politics and policies has meant that high finance enjoys once more that freedom of movement, predation and devastation that only the stringent legal constraints of the 1930s and post-bellic Bretton Woods had been able to choke. Castoriadis called it a "vast financial casino".[4] Unsurprisingly for people capable of historical memory, i.e. those who remember why those constraints had been put in place, the 20th century ended with a series of financial collapses that were greater and greater in both frequency and gravity, turning quickly many a celebrated "tiger" into a sacrificial lamb, no matter whether the big cat in question was Asian, Baltic, Celtic or Viking. Evidently, this sort of historical memory is in short supply, if it is not short as such. As John Kenneth Galbraith (1908–2006) declared in 1987: "History may not repeat itself, but some of its lessons are inescapable. One is that in the world of high and confident finance little is ever really new. The controlling fact is not the tendency to brilliant invention; the controlling fact is the shortness of the public memory, especially when it contends with a euphoric desire to forget."[5]

The continued result of such an amnesia *vis-à-vis* the rationale for potent financial regulation is that the 21st century has witnessed too several additional instances of self-inflicted financial mayhem, which is largely accepted as the new normal and somewhat akin to the erratic inescapability of bad weather, rather than as an avoidable and unpleasant state of affairs brought about by human agency. Reflecting on conservative and socialist alternatives, perhaps, can help us understand that it is neither new nor normal and that, above all, it does not have to be accepted, for other paths are open to human societies.

Specifically, in the first part of this book, I explore the socialist perspectives of Albert Einstein (1879–1955; chapter 1), Cornelius Castoriadis (chapter 2), Martha Nussbaum (b. 1947) and John McMurtry (both in chapter 3). Then I tackle the intellectual vistas provided by conservative thinkers Giulio Tremonti (b. 1947; chapter 4), Arthur Fridolin Utz (chapter 5) and Hans Jonas (1903–1993; chapter 6). In the second part of the book, I integrate the theoretical apparatus offered in the first part by means of concrete examples of opposition and redirection of liberal economic principles and practices, i.e. human rights law (chapters 7 & 8) and Iceland's boom-bust cycle and recovery in the early 21st century (chapter 9), to which the concluding musings of mine also relate, at least in good part (chapter 10).

The sources that, in this book, were revised, partially redrafted and updated, do differ considerably in both length and character, some being extensive articles or book chapters, others being reasoned book synopses, conference proceedings or review essays. Once again, as in my previous collections for Northwest Passage Books, the term "essay" has been understood and used in a broad sense. Therefore, the chapters of this book are markedly uneven too. Nevertheless, they all share my concern with and for the fate of the life-support systems upon which we all stand to survive and, if possible, live well. Life-value onto-axiology, which I tackle explicitly in chapters 3 and 7, informs implicitly the whole book.

Original publication credits

As done already in the second and third volumes published with Northwest Passage Books, all the included bibliographic information is provided in the endnotes; there is no separate bibliography.[6] Original publication dates, authors' full first names, translators' names and edition numbers are stated only when available and/or relevant. Equally, as done throughout the book series, no analytical indices are included. Cited thinkers' dates of birth and death were kept, when available, and inserted already in the introduction, while bracketed translations of foreign phrases were dropped. This economy of information allows the present book to be much more slender than it would otherwise be, considering also its target audience, which is not the same as the one of the original texts. Readers looking for a bulkier and more detailed bibliographic apparatus can refer to the original published texts, which are listed below. Whenever the chapter titles of the present book differ significantly from the original texts' titles, such a difference signposts that substantial redrafting occurred in this volume (e.g. deleted sections, paragraphs renaming and rearrangement, etc.).

PART I – Socialist and conservative perspectives

Chapter 1
On Einstein's Socialism, in C. Tandy (ed.), *Death and Anti-Death Volume 13. 60 Years After Albert Einstein*, Palo Alto: Ria University Press, 2015, 25–42.

Chapter 2
Reflections on Castoriadis' "The Crisis of Modern Society", *Nordicum-Mediterraneum: Icelandic E-journal of Nordic and Mediterranean Studies*, 9(4), 2014, http://nome.unak.is/wordpress/09-4/c75-conference-paper/reflections-on-castoriadis-the-crisis-of-modern-society/

Chapter 3
Your Money or Your Life: John McMurtry and Martha C. Nussbaum on the For-profit Assault on Life-capabilities, *Journal of Philosophy of Life*, 1(1), 2011, 13–48.

Chapter 4
A review essay of Giulio Tremonti's *Uscita di sicurezza*, *Nordicum-Mediterraneum: Icelandic E-journal of Nordic and Mediterranean Studies*, 8(1), 2013, http://hdl.handle.net/1946/14545

Chapter 5
The *Economic Ethics* of Arthur Fridolin Utz, *Nordicum-Mediterraneum: Icelandic E-journal of Nordic and Mediterranean Studies*, 11(3), 2016, http://nome.unak.is/wordpress/volume-11-no-3-2016/conference-proceeding-volume-11-no-3-2016/the-economic-ethics-of-arthur-fridolin-utz/

Chapter 6
Gnosticism, Sustainable Development and Racism: Re-appraising Hans Jonas as a Political Thinker, *Appraisal*, 7(2), 2009, 13–20; and Hans Jonas: A short biography and bibliography, *Appraisal*, 7(2), 2009, 3.

PART II – Contemporary legal and social issues

Chapter 7
Rights and Value: Construing the International Covenant on Economic, Social and Cultural Rights as Civil Commons (with Dr R.L. Johnstone), *Studies in Social Justice*, 5(1), 2011, 91–126; and Comment on "Rights and Value": The Committee on Economic, Social and Cultural Rights Assesses the Environment (with Dr R.L. Johnstone) *Studies in Social Justice*, 7(1), 2013, 175–9.

Chapter 8
Europe's Constitutional Law in Times of Crisis: A Human Rights Perspective, (with Á.Þ. Árnason), *Nordicum-Mediterraneum: Icelandic E-journal of Nordic and Mediterranean Studies*, 10(3), 2016, http://nome.unak.is/wordpress/volume-10-no-3-2016/conference-paper-10-3/europe-s-constitutional-law-in-times-of-crisis-a-human-rights-perspective/

Chapter 9
The Picture – Small and Big: Iceland and the Crises, *Nordicum-Mediterraneum: Icelandic E-journal of Nordic and Mediterranean Studies*, 9(3), 2014, http://nome.unak.is/wordpress/09-3/c73-conference-paper/the-picture-small-and-big-iceland-and-the-crises/

Chapter 10
Eight Noble Opinions and the Economic Crisis: Four Literary-philosophical Sketches *à la* Eduardo Galeano, *Nordicum-Mediterraneum: Icelandic E-journal of Nordic and Mediterranean Studies*, 5(1), 2010, http://hdl.handle.net/1946/14223

PART I – Socialist and Conservative Perspectives

Chapter 1: Einstein's Socialism

Introduction

Prompted by worried letters of self-perceiving patriotic informants, the Federal Bureau of Investigation (FBI) had intelligence gathered about Albert Einstein since at least 1932, when he sought admission into the US and, a few years later, naturalisation. His dubious associations with "anarchist" and "communist" individuals in Continental Europe, his questionable participation in the initially left-leaning German Democratic Party, his outspoken interest in the socio-economic and cultural developments of Bolshevik Russia, and his even louder objections to post-war McCarthyism made him a highly suspicious character during his life, capable of "un-American activities", in spite of his mathematical genius.[7] Sternly and unmercifully, the Official Memorandum prepared by the agency on the 27th of July 1955, soon after Einstein's death, concluded that he had indeed "sponsored entry into U.S. of numerous individuals with pro-Communist backgrounds" and "affiliated... with literally hundreds of pro-Communist groups".[8] However, "[n]o evidence of CP membership developed" and so neither prosecution nor expulsion could ever be justified.[9]

Quite the opposite, Einstein received considerable public recognition in the US, not solely for his contribution to the sciences, but also for his role in furthering the development of the atomic bomb, by which the war with Japan was brought to a close and military supremacy was gained over all nations, including the US' former allies, Joseph Stalin's (1878–1953) USSR *in primis*. Throughout the years that he spent working in the US, Einstein gave repeated proof of the highest academic ability and instructed a generation of American minds, who went on to make the US the leading power in modern physics and, either directly or indirectly, its military applications. Special awards and honorary doctorates were showered on him by prestigious US universities, including Princeton and Harvard.[10] Like Galileo (1564–1642), Newton (1642–1726) and

Darwin (1809–1882) before him, Einstein became an icon of intellectual achievement, transcending the borders of academia and reaching far and deep into popular consciousness.

What were Einstein's political views, though? Was he actually an "anarchist" or "communist", as the FBI's informants feared, even if he never joined such political organisations or parties? How could he be a trustworthy sponsor of Roosevelt's (1882–1945) Manhattan Project, given the subversive leanings the FBI attributed to him?

Pacifism and Zionism

Most non-scientific articles, speeches and letters written by Albert Einstein, primarily in German, are kept and catalogued at the *Albert Einstein Archives* of the Jewish National and University Library in Jerusalem, Israel. Together with other original sources, they have been studied and assessed by scores of biographers, among whom should be cited the comprehensive 21st-century works by Thomas Levenson[11] and Hubert Gönner.[12] After a 9-year-long process of digitalisation, the materials contained in the archives were released online in 2012.[13] Upon this basis, yet further integrated, translated into English, and aimed at both printed publication and digitalisation, the *Collected Papers of Albert Einstein* have been made available as well by Princeton University Press and, following a two-year delay on each printed volume, by the California Institute of Technology, which sees to the management of the *Digital Einstein* project.[14] So far, fourteen of the planned twenty-five volumes have been issued, covering Einstein's writings and correspondence from his youth to 1925.

A review of the vast critical literature on Einstein's political views shows no palpable disagreement as concerns the notion that he had two chief open ideological aims throughout his life *qua* engaged intellectual: pacifism and Zionism. On the one hand, given the far-from-uncommon shock at the sight of World War I's brutality and devastations, Einstein devoted much of his non-scientific literature, pleas and activism to the goal of international peace. The historical context and specific issues did vary, ranging from Wilson's (1856–

1924) plans for European reconciliation[15] to Cold-War appeasement.[16] Nonetheless, the overall aim of peace, i.e. the avoidance of physical violence and murderous agency within and among nations, is as unambiguous as it is recurrent. Even the controversial atomic bomb, the development of which he undoubtedly promoted to President F.D. Roosevelt, was justified as *extrema ratio* against the modern barbarity of German National Socialism. Hitler's (1889–1945) regime seemed interested in developing novel weaponry of this kind and, most ominously, willing to use it for the sake of military conquest.[17]

As to Zionism, Einstein started campaigning for a Jewish Palestine in 1921, after witnessing the vast post-war migrations of Eastern European Jews, the abrupt resurgence of unashamed anti-Semitism in Central European politics and societies, and the growing imperative of developing a Jewish consciousness among European Jews that, until then, had regarded themselves as fully integrated and legal equals of the non-Jewish populations. The worsening plight of such ill-treated European citizens in the 1920s and 1930s, not to mention the horrible fate suffered by millions of them during World War II, strengthened Einstein's support for the establishment of a Jewish Palestine in which Jews and Arabs could co-exist peacefully. He went so far along this line of thought and personal commitment as to blame the growing tensions between the local population and the Zionist settlers onto the "treachery" of "the English" administering that region after the end of the second global conflict.[18]

Whereas there are many public statements of support and several self-descriptions proffered by Einstein *vis-à-vis* both pacifism and Zionism, none can be found on either anarchism or communism as such. Many references are made by Einstein to "communism" and "communist" in connection with Soviet Russia and Eastern Europe, much interest is shown by him with respect to the novel experiments taking place in those societies, but no genuine self-commitment to that specific ideology or its incarnation in the Soviet political system can be found in an unequivocal manner. It is actually much easier to come across critical remarks, especially during the 1930s, once the idealistic internationalist hopes of Lenin (1870–1924) and Trotsky (1879–1940) had been definitively supplanted by Stalin's pragmatic State-building cruelty.[19] Though not interested *per se* in scholarly assessment, the FBI itself, after decades of close scrutiny on the mathematically gifted yet potentially subversive Albert Einstein, discovered no damning evidence to have him either prosecuted or expelled. On this point, even the following incriminating piece of evidence briefed in the Internal Security Report of the 30th of January 1950 was regarded as inadequate:

> [T]he 'Monthly Review,' 66 Barrow Street, New York City, self proclaimed [sic] 'an independent Socialist magazine' made its initial appearance in May of 1949. The first issue contained articles by [Albert Einstein] and others. This report stated further that a study of the articles contained in a background check of the editors and contributors revealed that this magazine was Communist inspired, and followed the approved Communist Party line.

What kind of article by Einstein was ever published in it? As stated above, and as subsequent events manifestly revealed, it was not enough to cause Einstein to face charges or have serious problems with the US authorities. Nevertheless, it may well be the clearest statement of Einstein's political views available to us.

Why Socialism?

"Why Socialism?" was issued in May 1949 by the *Monthly Review*, republished in 1998 to celebrate the review's fiftieth year of life, and again in May 2009 for the article's own sixtieth anniversary.[20] In it, a mature Albert Einstein explains why, all things considered, *socialism*—not anarchism, communism or, for that matter, liberalism—is the best option on the table.

The article opens with some epistemological considerations. Writing first of all as a practicing scientist, Einstein argues that, unlike physics, economics cannot easily proceed to the "discovery of general laws" because of two main reasons.[21]

On the one hand, the phenomena that economics studies "are often affected by many factors which are very hard to evaluate separately".[22] Unlike specialists in the hard sciences, economists cannot credibly abstract, isolate and assess individual parameters within concrete economic phenomena. On the other hand, these phenomena have been "largely influenced and limited by causes which are by no means exclusively economic in nature", such as "conquest", the violent self-establishment of "the privileged class", their consequent enjoyment of "a monopoly of the land" and of "education", thus making "the class division of society" a firmly rooted feature of human relations over generational time and creating "a system of values" guiding "social behavior" consistently with such class division and related privileges.[23]

In this connection, Einstein cites the one and only economist, indeed the one and only expert, whom he finds worth quoting in the whole article, namely Thorstein Veblen. Known to most contemporary economists for a handful of insightful notions (i.e. conspicuous consumption and conspicuous leisure, ceremonial and instrumental institutions, the conflict between business and industry, and the fundamental instincts of emulation, predation, workmanship, parental bent and idle curiosity), Veblen has been commonly saluted as the father of evolutionary economics, for he rejected the physics-inspired conception of neoclassical economics *qua* abstract system of *equilibria* among depersonalised atomic agents, and replaced it with the biology-inspired conception of economic life *qua* historical network of adaptive behaviours ingeniously developed by members of our species and socially institutionalised over time.[24]

As modern economies are concerned, Einstein refers to Veblen's claim that it still reflects the second stage in the history of our species, i.e. "'the predatory phase' of human development".[25] In this phase, strong individuals prey upon the weak as a matter of course and upon each other as a matter of honour. Business conglomerates, like industrialists, entrepreneurs, merchants, conquerors and tribal chieftains before them, operate according to this barbaric logic, which is "the real purpose of socialism" to "overcome and advance beyond".[26] Accordingly, as Einstein concludes, "economic science in its present state" is limited in its potential knowledge to the "predatory phase" of human associations and whatever tentative economic laws we can derive therefrom; *a fortiori*, today's economists "can throw little light on the socialist society of the future."[27]

What is more, "socialism is directed towards a social-ethical end", which lies beyond the purview of science.[28] Science, at best, "can supply the means by which to attain certain ends", but the ends themselves are the product of political innovators, prophets, preachers, poets, philosophers and popular writers: these are "personalities with lofty ethical ideals" that can inspire "many human beings" and, indirectly, "determine the slow evolution of society."[29] As a result, economists cannot claim any special expertise on socialism nor, for that matter, can any other breed of scientists: "we should be on our guard not to overestimate science and the scientific methods when it is a question of human problems; and we should not assume that experts are the only ones who have a right to express themselves" on socio-political matters.[30]

Confronted with the horrors of the 20th century, as well as with the disillusionment and the nihilistic despair of many, Einstein proceeds to delineate a basic philosophical anthropology. According to him, the human being is both "a solitary being and a social being."[31] As the former, the human being seeks self-preservation and self-gratification. As the latter, the human being seeks approbation and acceptance by her peers, with whom she is willing to coexist cooperatively and empathise. If there is any "equilibrium" that matters in economic and socio-political affairs, then it is the one between these two aspects of human nature.[32]

Moreover, for the individual to come into existence and grow, she must rely entirely upon a functioning society's past, present and future being. We are inextricably social animals, "just as in the case of ants and bees."[33] Unlike these animal species, however, the human one is not determined solely by its biological make-up, but also by its cultural make-up, which can be even modified, albeit to a small extent, by the individual's "conscious thinking".[34] That is the ground for human freedom, which, unfortunately, has been used for all kinds of horrible ends.

As concerns the fundamental root of all characteristically modern horrors, it is to be found in the excessive emphasis placed upon the "solitary" aspect of human nature by the predominant liberal traditions and institutions. The classical economists' self-serving atom contains highly destructive potential. Specifically, because of the excessive emphasis on the "solitary" aspect of human nature, human beings no longer think of themselves primarily as members of a human community and no longer focus their personal efforts upon social improvement *qua* social beings, but rather upon self-centred, self-maximising aims dictated by "egotism".[35] This is reflected chiefly in the "economic *anarchy* of capitalist society", which allows by law, culture and economic practice the selfish expropriation of other people's labour and fruits thereof for the sake of self-aggrandisement.[36]

Einstein singles out and attacks the capitalist institutions of "private property" and the only nominally "free" labour contract between powerful employers and powerless individual employees.[37] Upon such bases, the governing individualistic logic of predatory "competition" and self-aggrandising deprivation favours the few that "share in the ownership of the means of production" and can therefore keep at ransom the other allegedly "free" members of society, who depend on the former élite for work, wages, housing, bread—in essence, for survival.[38] This basically barbaric élite is nothing but an "oligarchy of private capital the enormous power of which cannot be effectively checked even by a democratically organized political society", no matter whatever parliamentary, multi-party system may be in place, since institutions of this ilk are all too easily "selected… financed… [and] influenced" by "private capitalists", who also "control… the main sources of information" and therefore shape the collective consciousness in accordance with the élite's desiderata.[39] It is mostly if not uniquely trade unions, which were established after prolonged and arduous struggles, that offer "the workers" opportunity for independent thought, a modicum of bargaining power, protection from the capitalists' worst excesses, and some degree of self-direction.[40]

Pivotal in its negative character is, within such a sorry state of affairs, capitalism's mental "crippling of individuals", who learn already at school that they must be "competitive" and "worship acquisitive success".[41] Therefore, Einstein argues that in a proper socialist society, in addition to a "planned economy" that is duly run for the benefit of the people rather than of an "all-powerful and overweening… bureaucracy", there should be an "educational system" that is "oriented towards social goals".[42] The social side of the human being needs nurturing, so that it may be the prime source of meaning in people's lives: no other truly constructive and comprehensive existential meaning can be given, according to Einstein.

Which Socialism?

The FBI's informants had reason to worry about Albert Einstein. In "Why Socialism?", capitalism is criticised adamantly and forcefully in its historical origins, institutional articulations and socio-cultural effects. Especially, the liberal constitutions' sacred right to own property privately is condemned as an institution that validates and maintains ancient conquests, extortions and brutalities.[43] The attendant competitive business and labour relations are similarly criticised, insofar as they further the inequality and oppression established by such ancient conquests, extortions and brutalities. The educational and, more broadly, the value system of capitalist societies are equally blamed for legitimising, entrenching and advancing them, as well as an individualistic, dog-eat-dog mentality that ruins most people's chances of finding any fulfilment in life, since the meaningful inter-personal social aims that can offer true fulfilment to most people are severely neglected, if not completely removed from view. Only the privileged, property-owning few can benefit from the individualistic ethos replacing such positive social aims.

According to Einstein, a planned economy and, *above all*, a renewed emphasis on social goals and the social self-understanding of the human person are the alternative to be pursued. This alternative is the only one that makes sense to Einstein, lest we wish to remain within the predatory phase of human development. Still, this alternative is not tantamount to "anarchism", which, in all of its manifestations, would do away with planning institutions and, in many of its manifestations, would stress the solitary side of the human being over the social one.[44] The word "anarchy" does appear in Einstein's text, but in connection with the socially and existentially destructive individualistic emphasis of capitalism. Could it be "communism" then? Yes, it could; possibly, that is, but not plausibly. Einstein's qualifications on the pivotal role of a truly socialist education and the potentially self-serving excesses of the bureaucracy presiding over a planned economy are a not-so-implicit attack against the Soviet model, Stalin's cult of personality, and the communist camp in general, in which predatory behaviour was still rife. Any reader of the *Monthly Review* would have easily grasped it back in 1949.

Above all else, Einstein speaks of "socialism" *tout court*. He does so both in the article's title and in its main text. Open-ended, perhaps vague, positively capable of many non- and anti-communist declinations in its long life as a political ideology (e.g. Saint-Simonianism, Fourierism, Proudhonism) as well as in Einstein's lifetime (e.g. German revisionist Marxism, British Fabianism, Scandinavian social-democracy), "socialism" is the term that Einstein chose. *Pace* the FBI's informants, he opted neither for "anarchism" nor for "communism". It would be uncharitable not take Einstein's word for it. Not even the FBI's top echelons did it, despite being suspicious of him for longer than two decades. What kind of socialism is it, though?

A few of Einstein's key concepts are patently of Marxian origin (e.g. "class", the "ownership of the means of production", the dismal account of the early stages of capitalism i.e. primitive accumulation). Even so, Marx himself is never cited. On the contrary, the Norwegian-American economist Thorstein Veblen is the only explicitly quoted authority, and one that does not figure among the most famous champions of socialism, which Veblen actually conceived of *in primis* as "an animus of dissent" symptomising capitalism's inherent malaise[45] and, *in secundis*, as the inevitable future form of rational economic engineering brought about by the eventual collapse of intrinsically unstable capitalist institutions.[46] Was Einstein then a socialist *à la* Veblen—a Veblenite?

Einstein's archives contain loads of references to, and exchanges with, a "Professor Veblen", but it is Oswald Veblen (1880–1960), the noted mathematician, Thorstein's nephew. Apart from the citation in "Why Socialism?", Thorstein Veblen openly resurfaces only in Einstein's "Remarks on Bertrand Russell's Theory of Knowledge", where he is commended as follows: "I owe innumerable happy hours to the reading of Russell's works, something which I cannot say of any other contemporary scientific writer, with the exception of Thorstein Veblen."[47] However, the text is about Lord Russell (1872–1970), the British Nobel-laureate philosopher and Labour activist with whom Einstein shared many campaigns for international peace and nuclear disarmament, and nothing can be derived from it as regards Einstein's assessment of Veblen's political views but generic appreciation.[48]

Upon a review of Einstein's writings on socialism, as pursued for example by Rowe and Schulmann in 2007, and of his essay "Why Socialism?" in particular, I believe it impossible to determine along specific party- or theory-lines what sort of socialist Einstein could have been. Verily was he a "socialist", but in as open-ended and as broad a way as this term allows for and along the specifications available to us in "Why Socialism?", which I have summarised and highlighted in the previous section. A master of theoretical physics, Einstein was not prone to lengthy, hair-splitting theoretical speculation on human, social and political matters, even if he wrote often about these issues and regarded them as paramount. His die-hard liberal colleague at the Keiser Wilhelm Institute in Berlin, the great Hungarian chemist Michael Polanyi (1891–1976), was certainly much more so inclined than Einstein ever was.[49]

Furthermore, Einstein had not always been a socialist, or at least not as clearly as he declared himself to be in 1949. As a young man, Einstein had grown up in a classically liberal Swiss milieu and the political writings of his youth show him to be a compassionate liberal, who felt deeply for the less fortunate, but also took for granted many liberal institutions, e.g. wage relations, and feared novel, unorthodox socialist plans. For example, reasoning along liberal lines, he condemned the Austrian proto-Zionist Josef Popper-Lynkeus' (1838–1921) projects for a compulsory national labour service, which, in his view, would affect negatively individuals' crucial incentives, such as "the effort of striving for an improved existence as a wage earner" and the shame of being among "those who are not gainfully employed".[50]

Similarly, whilst Einstein did salute Lenin as an honourable "man, who in total sacrifice of his own person has committed his entire energy to realizing social justice", he did "not find his methods advisable".[51] Even though he followed with keen interest the developments in Bolshevik Russia, Einstein adamantly rejected their being founded upon "bloody terror".[52] To Bolsheviks and revolutionaries, Einstein—the pacifist indeed—much preferred "the most courageous fighters against militarism… the Quakers."[53]

Albeit never abandoning peace or Zionism as cherished socio-political and moral goals, Einstein was willing to change his economic and political views in the face of new evidence.

The Great Depression proved to be the watershed for Einstein, much more so than the horrors of the First World War or the tumultuous yet intriguingly novel Russian experiment that ensued thereof. Given the self-inflicted collapse of capitalism and the seemingly endless turmoil that followed it, Einstein believed the remedies to have to be found in non-capitalist forms of socio-political and economic agency. Writing in 1932, Einstein argued that "the unrestrained lust for profit" that had brought down the liberal economic architecture could not plausibly rescue it from itself.[54] Besides, liberal institutions had had a considerable time to prove themselves worthy: they had fared poorly and failed miserably.[55]

Echoing the plight of Veblen's revolutionary engineers, who get frustrated by the repeated sabotage of productive efficiency caused by businesspersons for the sake of pecuniary gain (e.g. snuffing new technologies threatening established monopolies, restricting production in quantity and/or quality to control supply and/or demand, wasting time and resources on advertising unnecessary goods and services), Einstein suggested that an international "Council of the Wise" comprising a number of top-notch experts should be created in order to deal effectively with the "social and economic" woes of the planet.[56]

Veblen aside, such a technocratic suggestion recalls Saint-Simon's (1760–1825) influential pre-Marxian socialism[57] and the positivist tektology (or "tectology") of Russian revolutionary and science-fiction author Alexander Bogdanov (1873–1928).[58] In any case, as reminiscent of other forms of socialism as it may be, Einstein's advice at that point was no longer "liberal", i.e. a notion that, as he lamented in 1948, "has become so watered down as to cover the most diverse views and attitudes".[59] Most importantly, in the same year and document, Einstein also asserts: "socialism, as I understand it, does not exist anywhere today."[60]

Einstein's socialism was of his own stripe: the one that he presents in "Why Socialism?". That is, in short, the answer to this section's opening interrogative.

Concluding Remarks

It is not possible to align Einstein's stripe of socialism with any other in a clear-cut manner. There is simply no sufficient theoretical articulation in his writings to perform such an intellectual operation. What is more, any careful study of the various schools of thought comprised within the socialist camp is absent therein. This may be disappointing for the political partisan, the keen scholar, and the pedant. However, it is not disappointing for those who find Einstein's stance enlightening, inspiring, or insightful.[61]

For one, I believe that it is beneficial to recall the crucial circumstances that led him to gradually abandon the liberal beliefs of his youth and embrace a socialist conception in its place. It was after the 1929 crash of Wall Street and the ensuing years of economic decline—not to mention the resulting worldwide armed conflagration—that it became clear to Einstein, as it became to many intellectuals of his generation, that capitalism was hopelessly flawed and in need of replacement. As Karl Polanyi (1886–1964) and John Maynard Keynes (1883–1946) had also loudly acknowledged in Einstein's day, dreadful socio-political nightmares are the outcome of deep economic slumbers, especially financial ones.

Staring at rapacious and life-disabling historical manifestations of liberalism such as the Great Depression, Einstein eventually saw the error of the liberal doctrines of his youth and, rather than being wilfully blind to the facts or committing himself to *ad hoc* exculpations of the doctrines themselves, he moved on; that is, he gave an answer to the question "Why Socialism?"—rather than liberalism.[62] The answer was not going to be changed later; socialism was his conclusion. It was the outcome of a lifetime's wisdom of experience and reflection upon the circumstances that history had presented him with.

Chapter 2: Cornelius Castoriadis and "The Crisis of Modern Society"

It was May 1965, longer than 50 years ago, when Paul Cardan, one of Cornelius Castoriadis' many pseudonyms, gave a talk at Tunbridge Wells, Kent, entitled "The Crisis of Modern Society". The talk was published one month later in the *Solidarity* pamphlet number 23.[63] By no means does this talk alone cover all the relevant reflections by Castoriadis on either the notion of crisis as such or on the specificities of the modern age.[64] Even less does it constitute Castoriadis' final word on socio-political, economic and axiological matters, given that he was active and productive for three decades following the talk hereby discussed. Still, this talk is as forceful a document on what Castoriadis understood to be crises and, specifically, modern crises, as there can ever be found in his vast legacy of published materials, interviews and private memoirs. In particular, the liberal ills of modern capitalist societies are identified therein and systematically scrutinised, in the attempt to further the ideal of libertarian socialism as a better option in view of societal wellbeing.

The first and most obvious element of crisis retrievable in modern society is the contradiction that Castoriadis individuates between ever-growing techno-scientific abilities (e.g. generating "energy from matter") and augmenting socio-political inabilities (i.e. the "tremendous chaos and sense of impotence" of modern communities).[65] While human ingenuity gives rise to more and more complex technological applications of scientific knowledge, our capacity to steer human society towards full employment, genuine well-being, long-term political and economic stability, individual as well as collective harmony and happiness appears to decrease more and more. "Progressive changes" in society are not denied, e.g. "so-called prosperity", "spreading of culture", "expanding society", "better health", "apparently... less cruel living conditions for most of the people".[66] Yet, according to Castoriadis, "people are dissatisfied... grumbling... protesting, constant conflicts exist", more "than most other societies we have known in history".[67]

Looking "a bit deeper" for the "roots" of this unprecedented dissatisfaction, Castoriadis retrieves five crises or dimensions of the modern crisis that can be characterised as follows: (1) axiological; (2) productive; (3) political; (4) familial; and (5) educational.[68]

While Castoriadis discusses the notion of crisis in other works of his, he focuses therein on one or two of these five specific elements, e.g. (1) in "The Crisis of Culture and the State", (1) and (3) in "Un monde à venir", and (5) in "Entretien avec Cornelius Castoriadis".[69] Thus, what makes this 1965 talk unique is its broader, perhaps more superficial, but undoubtedly more comprehensive scope. It is the one and only synthetic picture of what Castoriadis understood as crisis, and particularly as modern crisis. Also, whilst Castoriadis revised his assessment of (4) in his later essay "The Crisis of the Identification Process", which reduces considerably the relevance of this element as regards the troubles faced by modern societies, his later assessments of (1)–(3) and (5) do not differ from what he stated in 1965.[70]

Axiology

There exists a "crisis of social and human values" that Castoriadis does not intend to dismiss as an issue of mere "superstructure", like "traditional Marxists" would do, for shared values are necessary for social "cohesion" across class divisions: fear and oppression alone cannot suffice to keep a society together; "*positive* motives" are required as well, whether reducible to false consciousness or not.[71] In modern societies, "religious values are out" and so are "moral values", if it makes sense to separate them from the religious ones in which they have been traditionally embedded and cultivated.[72] If we think of integrity, honesty, rectitude, propriety, at the official level there is little more than a veneer of formal respect for such ethical values, but it is so thin as to be, for Castoriadis, nothing but a rather transparent form of "hypocrisy" that fuels "widespread cynicism", to the point that "the general idea is that you can do anything and that nothing is wrong, provided you can get away with it, provided that you are not caught."[73] Morality, in essence, becomes a matter of self-interested calculation. Not even nationalism, which in the past had replaced to some extent the religions of old, is any "longer an accepted value" today, capable of holding society together and legitimise moral behaviour amongst the masses.[74] The disenchantment of the world famously proclaimed by Max Weber (1864–1920) has reached its final stage. Modernity is here, but its rational instrumentality and the secular abandonment of mystical beliefs come with strings attached.

On the elitist end of the social spectrum, "knowledge and art are important or have meaning… [but] for only very limited strata of the population", who alone can derive existential value thereof; moreover, even in the "Renaissance" or "ancient Greece", art was a means of expressing shared values, rather than establishing them.[75] As for knowledge, scientists today are no longer seeking to read out "the eternal book of nature or of God's creation", but producing "three lines in a history of this experiment" that allows for the production of "theory X… later superseded by… theories Y and Z."[76] On top of that, "there is no longer any scientific community with a common language", due to the hyper-specialisation of contemporary science. Men and women of knowledge are not separated by mutual ignorance in just two cultures, one scientific and another humanistic, as C.P. Snow (1905–1980) had famously argued, but in a plethora of sub- and sub-sub-fields of expert study. The world of science too is disenchanted, primarily by fragmentation, according to Castoriadis.

In this general void, "[t]he only value that survives today is *consumption*" as a way "to fill people's lives, to orient their effort, to make them stick to work", despite the evident and recurrent inadequacy of such a consumption, which is fostered by extensive marketing manipulation, but "does not express organic human needs" and therefore falls eventually flat and insufficient, growing "absurd" and de-humanising—"the rat race" that US parlance captures poignantly.[77]

Production

Concerning "work as a meaningful activity", it too has been destroyed more and more "since the beginning of capitalism", the corrosive power of which has been studied by Marx (1818–1883) and the Marxist school under the category of "alienation" and by Weber under that of "bureaucracy".[78] *Via* alienation and "bureaucratization", the meaningfulness of work has been erased both on the "*subjective*" side (i.e. the externally decided, planned and managed process of production, which the worker does not steer or perceive at all as her own, its resulting wealth being also accrued to others but her) and on the "*objective*" side (i.e. workers no longer make any complete objects; rather they produce sheer parts of an often unknown final commodity that is assembled, sold, consumed and experienced elsewhere).[79]

Insofar as capitalist production is possible only by teams of workers, there should emerge group or collective identity, which could give some meaning to their work. However, such a path to meaningfulness is closed to most, for it is opposed vehemently by owners and managers, who fear profit- and/or power-reducing unionisation, workers' democracy and/or coordinated industrial action by self-aware labour. Self-managed workers' cooperatives, though certainly existed and existing, have been the exception, rather than the norm, in both the capitalist countries of the West and the socialist countries of the East where, according to Castoriadis, "the Russian Revolution had led to the instauration of a new type of exploitative and oppressive regime in which a new ruling class, the bureaucracy, had formed around the Communist Party… [i.e.] total and totalitarian bureaucratic capitalism."[80]

Politics

Political "apathy" is a fairly well-known "crisis" of the modern age.[81] Castoriadis claims it to be a symptom of a deeper malaise, since disaffection *vis-à-vis* political agency is caused by the "bureaucratization" of State institutions, political parties and trade unions: "people [are] excluded from their own affairs", which are left in the hands of small groups of mediators for capitalists' interests and/or self-serving political experts and career politicians.[82] As a consequence, people lose faith in the institutions that could give them a voice, and this loss of faith furthers the bureaucratisation process into a "vicious circle" reinforcing the afore-mentioned "widespread cynicism" *vis-à-vis* society's official values, hence reducing politics, party- and trade-union life to yet another form of top-down marketing or "advertising".[83] Professionalised and professionally conducted, even democracy is reduced to the level of consumption.

Family

Castoriadis' longest analysis concerns the "crisis" in "family relationships."[84] According to him, "the authority of the man" and the "traditional standards" of "the patriarchal family" have eclipsed together with their religious and moral cocoons, as exemplified most notably in "sex morals" and the "more and more disrupted… relations between parents and children", while "nothing is put in their place."[85] It may be correct to say that the old patriarchal standards were "absurd, inhuman, alienated", but it is also true that "society cannot function harmoniously unless relations between men and women and the upbringing of children are somehow [socially] regulated" so as to foster society's reproduction and prevent unending inter-generational conflict.[86] Over millennia, patriarchy, matriarchy, polygamous families allowed for social reproduction and limited conflict levels through a web of deeply rooted institutions, whether "legal… economic… sexual… deeper psychological [or…] Freudian."[87] Modern societies have removed them and left no clearly discernible alternative, thus inducing "the breaking up of families, the homeless children, the tremendous problem of youth… the… mods and rockers", i.e. juvenile gangs of the 1960s, "and so on."[88] This is essentially not a matter of siding with liberal morals or progressive ideals, but of determining whether "the reproduction of personalities having a certain relation to their environment" is possible under such changed conditions, i.e. "the continuation of society" itself.[89]

Castoriadis observes that there are no clear gender and generational roles any more. The old ones may have been "inhuman... barbaric" but, as the continuation of society is concerned, they were "coherent".[90] The demolishing of old traditions creates "uncertainty" that translates into the "crisis" of women's "status" and "personality", as well as men's "complete disorientation".[91] This is a problem not only for the adults involved, but also and above all for the children, who can no longer "cho[o]se out of the[adults] what correspond[s] to [their] own nature", i.e. whether they are men or women and what sort of men or women to be.[92]

On the one hand, there endure forms of patriarchy that often lead to conflicts within families, whose children have been exposed to the new freedom of some peer of theirs. On the other hand, a common result of this critical freedom is the "disintegration" of long-established family structures: "children just grow up. The parents play no significant role whatsoever, except perhaps providing pocket money, shelter, and food."[93] "In the majority of instances conditions are somewhere in between", namely a pendulum between the two extremes just described: "They are 'liberal' one day. And the next day they are shouting, 'This is enough'".[94] That means a conflict-ridden family life, which is likely to become even more conflict-ridden as "the children of today will have to produce and bring up children of their own."[95]

Education

The crisis in family structures is mirrored by a crisis in "education".[96] No longer do societies take for granted the vertical relationship between "master" and "pupil", though "the adult is necessary for the education of the children"; hence "the relationship must be shaped in a completely new way", but what?[97] When Castoriadis delivered his talk, he could not envision any clear new way to reshape this relationship.

The problem of education is also a problem of "content", though, i.e. what exactly to teach.[98] The humanities, in today's educational setting, teach us how disconnected we are from each other and our own past. They have a negative function. They can only tell us what a lack of harmony there is in our society and Castoriadis does not hint at any new way in which their relevance could be recovered. On its part, "technical-scientific" education seems a more obvious candidate for the modern curriculum, since a society with a high rate of techno-scientific development requires sophisticated technical competences from its members.[99] However, Castoriadis observes three contradictions that emerge from focusing upon technical-scientific education:

(i) starting early with technical specialisation is "extremely destructive for the personality of the children", who desire ardently something far less arid and narrow-focused;

(ii) today's specialisation will be useless tomorrow, hence you must continually re-educate people, i.e. establish "a 'permanent educational process'"; and

(iii) in order to let re-education occur so frequently, "you must have as general a grounding as possible", which is what too "narrow" a starting point makes impossible to attain.[100]

Privatisation

Castoriadis wraps up his talk by stating that, "[a]t the *personal* level", there is no longer any clear "meaning of life" and only highly uncertain "human motives" remain, apart from mass-marketed inane consumption, which is too poor a substitute for the religions of old or nationalism.[101] At the "*social*" level, the result of such a widespread meaninglessness results "in the destruction and disappearance or responsibility" or the phenomenon of "privatization: people are… withdrawing into themselves."[102] Yet, the need for "positive socialization" endures, as expressed in "youth gangs"; and so does endure "the feeling that what is going on at large is, after all, our own affair", which engenders forms of "struggle" or the seeds for "new forms of life and social relations."[103] The cases of women's movements and the youth's rebellions are examples of such struggles and possibilities for new forms of life, where individuals have much more room for self-direction than before; the same is true of "informal groups and organizations" on the workplace,[104] where "people refuse to be dominated and... manifest a will to take their lives into their hands".[105]

Although undoubtedly critical, "the crisis of modern society... contains the seeds of something new" i.e. something that could supersede it, resolve it, or maybe make the experienced crises acceptable and accepted as the price to be paid for increased autonomy.[106] However, "the new will not come about automatically"; unless "the mass of the people" engages in promoting this new reality as "a conscious action", the new reality may never "complete" or "establish itself as a new social system".[107] Meanwhile, according to Castoriadis, consumption persists as the one and only value left that allows capitalist societies to cohere positively. Apart from fear of unemployment and oppression on the workplace, i.e. apart from negative motives for social cohesion, people consume:

(i) in order to give meaning to their lives (e.g. in the context of the prosperous Nordic countries, owning a gold Rolex watch or a fancy Porsche as a mode of supreme social statement and self-realisation);

(ii) have a consistent aim in life (e.g. amassing enough money so as to buy such a watch or car); and

(iii) be committed to their work (e.g. pursuing a corporate career that may lead one to the kind of remuneration needed in order to get hold of the much-desired watch or car without resort to outright crime, whether blue-collar [e.g. stealing the watch or car] or white-collar [e.g. embezzling corporate funds for the purchase of said watch or car]).

Castoriadis acknowledges that people are bamboozled since childhood into internalising the mode of self-realisation that translates into a lifetime of actual or attempted consumption. What his 1965 talks highlights is, rather, how such a lifetime is the one that people seem to adhere to by and large, and how it fails to deliver the goods. The very same people participating most eagerly in the consumerist rat race cannot avoid perceiving at some point the futility of such a life. The perception of this futility is manifested acutely in the neuroses and psychoses of modern men and women, whose choice of consumption *qua modus vivendi* proves pointless when confronted by the awareness of mortality, which most consumers try to ignore for as long as possible.[108]

A Concluding Remark

According to Castoriadis, consumption *qua* pivot of human behaviour leads to mental pathologies. Under capitalism, consumption is no longer aimed at survival and/or actual life-enhancement. It is consumption removed from genuine needs—as distinguished from, and opposed to, artificially created wants—at least as much as it is from any articulate understanding of what really matters in human life to let individuals mature and flourish *qua* unique individuals. It is the kind of consumption fostered by mass consumerism, the origins, development and characteristics of which had been studied in the classic works of institutional economists such as Veblen and Galbraith, both of whom were known to Castoriadis.[109]

In his view, the cure to such modern malaises is to be found in democratic emancipatory autonomy, i.e. the masses' conscious, wilful and actual ability "to take their lives into their hands" and reshape the institutions under which they live, economic ones *in primis*.[110] It has been now longer than half a century since Castoriadis depicted the crisis of modern society and prospected the path for its overcoming. I leave it to the reader to determine whether we have made use of autonomy or, rather, we keep being mired in the inane rat race that for-profit consumerist production spurs ceaselessly and promotes all around.

Chapter 3: Martha Nussbaum and John McMurtry

> *"[T]he 'human condition' has been transforming... In the old days religion told us that we were all sinners because of the original sin. Today it is our planet's ecology that accuses all of us of being sinners because of the overexploitation of human ingenuity. Back in the old days, religion terrified us with the Last Judgment at the end of times. Today our tortured planet predicts the coming of that day without any divine intervention. The final revelation... is the silent scream emerging from things themselves, those things that we must endeavour to resolve to rein in our powers over the world, or we shall die on this desolate Earth which used to be the Creation."*[111]

Such a grim picture of the human condition might appear extreme. Most ingenuous science-technology would seem to have contributed enormously to the enhancement of life-expectancy rates, agricultural productivity and other important dimensions of organised human existence. Besides, in many parts of the planet, most people have no problem whatsoever breathing fresh air, eating nourishing food, and walking fearlessly under the sun. Why accuse "human ingenuity" in this way?

One reason may be that in spite, or maybe because, of humanity's science-technology, many human beings do in fact encounter difficulty in accessing unpolluted air,[112] uncontaminated or genuine food,[113] and face an increased risk of developing melanoma because of excessive solar irradiation.[114] Analogously, "human ingenuity" does pose a threat to human survival in at least two major and well-known potential forms, to which testifies an extensive body of agreements aimed at binding the world's nations: nuclear annihilation and overexploitation of natural resources. Finally, heed should be paid to the fact that the man who depicted the human condition in these unpleasant terms was no suspect "radical", but a conservative German-born British and Israeli war hero, a pupil of Martin Heidegger (1889–1976) and Rudolf Bultmann (1884–1976), a long-time Alvin Johnson Professor of Philosophy at the New School for Social Research in New York City, a devout Jew, and one of the esteemed fathers of modern bioethics: Hans Jonas. In truth, his worried statement about the transformed human condition and "the silent scream emerging from things themselves" could be regarded as his spiritual testament, for it was uttered in 1993, the year of his death.

The United Nations

Since the 1990s, the scientific community has been at least as adamant as Hans Jonas. The Union of Concerned Scientists—to name one representative group of eminent researchers—asserted back in 1997: "Human activities inflict harsh and often irreversible damage on the environment and on critical resources. If not checked, many of our current practices put at serious risk the future that we wish for human society and the plant and animal kingdoms".[115]

Once again, words like these may sound hyperbolic. Yet, to date, there has been literally *no* fundamental aspect of our planet's environment that has been left unspoiled by those very ingenuous means of financing, extraction, production, transportation, consumption and disposal of the items traded for profit in the global free market.[116] If we look at the economic roots and fruits of late-modern scientific and technological enterprises, many of the very goods that should lead to growth and wellbeing have been rife with bad outcomes (including the existential anomie lamented by Einstein and Castoriadis and discussed in the previous two chapters of this book).[117] These have varied enormously, from recurrent oil spills, massive pollution and pollution-induced pathologies in a great variety of ecosystems,[118] to global-insecurity-creating securisation packages in the realm of finance.[119] Invariably and without exception, the planet's ozone layer, its boreal and tropical forests, oceanic planktons and corals, biosphere-wide hydrologic cycles, fresh water aquifers, humus-rich land, and the diversity of both vegetal and animal populations have *all* been affected negatively, whether by one of the for-profit processes mentioned above, or by several of them jointly.[120]

As a result of the current economic crisis, doubts have begun to emerge in high-level political bodies about the belief that growth should be pursued in the way in which it has been pursued over the past few decades. Hence, whilst massive life-depletion has been recognised by official emanations of the United Nations (UN) on a number of occasions,[121] the failure in the received conception of economic growth has been denounced by Ban Ki-moon (b. 1944) himself as UN Secretary-General: "the economic and financial turmoil sweeping the globe is a true wake-up call, sounding an alarm about the need to improve upon old patterns of growth and make a transition to a new era of greener, cleaner development."[122]

Statements like the one above reveal that something crucial is amiss, albeit in rather general terms. Precisely, what lies behind such expressions of concern is the etiological connection between the pursuit of profit-driven growth defining today's global free-market economy and multi-level bio-ecological loss. Cautiously avoided by political leaders and mainstream economists, this etiological connection has been debated in the works of "green" thinkers such as John McMurtry,[123] David Korten (b. 1937),[124] Jennifer Sumner[125] and Tim Jackson (b. 1957),[126] but above all it is unmasked in ordinary public life each time the business community or its political representation resist environmental and/or health-and-safety regulation, and/or their effective enforcement.

Typical reasons for this resistance are money-measured "costs", "fiscal unfriendliness", increased "rigidity", or "competition".[127] Whichever reason is preferred, this kind of resistance displays *de facto* blindness and/or eventual indifference to non-money-measured losses and considerations, such as physical and mental health, work- and unemployment-related suicides, long-term environmental viability, and children's present and future welfare. Competitiveness for profits is of ultimate value; vital parameters are not.

Unless restraints are forced upon the very ingenuous means of financing, extraction, production, transportation, consumption and disposal of the items traded worldwide, there is nothing intrinsic within such a profit-oriented mechanism that can overcome the merely instrumental attribution of value to life, so as to acknowledge either the unique requirements of the living or life's intrinsic worth.[128] This is shown manifestly whenever members of the business community bypass existing regulation by illicit behaviour and/or outsourcing of productive activities to nations that have comparably less stringent life-protective measures.[129] Once more, competitiveness for profits is signalled to be of ultimate value, not vital parameters.

Equally significant is the fact that, following the 2008 collapse of Wall Street, nearly all the countries affected by it have been busy rescuing with public money the profit-driven financial institutions that were responsible or co-responsible for the crisis in the first place.[130] Often created by central-bank *fiat*, these public resources had been long denied to, and are now not being utilised to fund, life-protecting and life-enhancing institutions, such as ambulance services, public hospitals, old-age pensions, university research, international aid, or primary schools.[131]

Quite the opposite, in most countries, public investments have been reduced across the board in order to secure the money-measured value of existing assets, keep treasury bonds attractive to institutional investors, and prevent inflation from mounting upwards.[132] *Pace* all relevant Keynesian economic wisdom on the subject, protecting existing money-measured wealth has been proved thereby to concern governments, their economic advisers and leading business elites much more than preventing further environmental degradation, not to mention securing the progressive realisation of economic, social and cultural rights, to which most governments are legally bound (e.g. the UN's International Covenant on Economic, Social and Cultural Rights (ICESCR)). Again, competitiveness for profits is of ultimate value; vital parameters are not, even if they are enshrined in international covenants and charters.[133]

To counter well-established life-destructive trends and assist governments in the fulfilment of their international obligations, UNESCO has been operating since 2002 the world's largest repository of information on sustainable development, *The*

Encyclopedia of Life Support Systems (EOLSS). These "systems" are defined as follows:

> *A life support system is any natural or human-engineered (constructed or made) system that furthers the life of the biosphere in a sustainable fashion. The fundamental attribute of life support systems is that together they provide all of the sustainable needs required for continuance of life. These needs go far beyond biological requirements. Thus life support systems encompass natural environmental systems as well as ancillary social systems required to foster societal harmony, safety, nutrition, medical care, economic standards, and the development of new technology. The one common thread in all of these systems is that they operate in partnership with the conservation of global natural resources.*[134]

By defining "life support systems" in this manner, UNESCO acknowledges that human life on Earth depends not solely on natural systems, but also on socially created and maintained ones. Actually, if Jonas' opening assessment is correct, then the natural systems themselves might depend on us too, for humanity has the power to keep at their destruction, or to cease it. In the following pages, the works of John McMurtry and Martha Nussbaum are presented in order to clarify how, in recent decades, the power of "human ingenuity" has relentlessly achieved the former end and how, instead, it could attain the latter.

John McMurtry's Life-value Onto-axiology

Consistently with Jonas' assessment, UNESCO's Honorary Theme Editor John McMurtry connotes *all* planetary life support systems as "civil commons" i.e. "social constructs which enable universal access to life goods".[135] The adjective "civil" is meant to highlight the social character and the social aims of these commons, namely life support systems conceived as such by the human mind.

McMurtry revokes the distinction between natural and socially created-and-maintained life support systems. If the Earth's natural life support systems are recognised and conceived of *qua* life support systems, then humankind must somehow organise itself in order to protect and/or restore them. Therefore, natural life support systems are turned into socially created—insofar as we create conceptions—and maintained—insofar as we get organised for their protection or rescue—life support systems, i.e. civil commons.

The revocation of the distinction between natural and socially created-and-maintained life support systems by the use of the adjective "civil" implies as well that McMurtry is not thinking of the commons *qua* resources available to all the members of a community without any form of regulation or conscious guardianship. They are not the perplexingly canonical unregulated commons of textbook economics, such that their invariably tragic doom justifies their convenient appropriation for private ends. Rather, McMurtry thinks of the commons *qua* resources that the community administers in order to support and possibly enhance the life of its members across time.

McMurtry identifies and explores three known modes of life's being: "thought", "experience" (also "feeling" or "felt being"), and "action" (also "biological movement" or "motility"); no ontological dualism or sharp separation is implied: "Although we can distinguish the cognitive and feeling capacities of any person, this does not mean dividing them into separate worlds as has occurred in the traditional divisions between mind and body, reason and the emotions. Life-value onto-axiology begins from their unity as the nature of the human organism."[136]

As a consequence of this synthetic approach to the phenomenon of life, genuine civil commons are therefore those institutions that protect and enhance life in these three modes of being, that is to say, as action (e.g. publicly subsidised provision of nourishing food and guaranteed access to potable water), felt being (e.g. freedom from fear *via* collective bargaining of employment contracts and/or legally enforced standards for job security) and thought (e.g. increased access to higher education by tuition waivers, extensive scholarship programmes, or direct public provision of educational services).

With his comprehensive approach to life, McMurtry operates in line with UNESCO's definition of "life support systems" and the much older UN's ICESCR. Yet, there is much more to civil commons/life support systems than their institutionalisation and instantiation by the UN. Historically, whether conceived of as civil commons or not, humankind has set up a vast number of life-protective and life-enabling social institutions, which step beyond the sole field of 20th-century international legislation. McMurtry's 1999 *The Cancer Stage of Capitalism* contains an exemplary two-page inventory of just such life-protective and life-enabling social institutions:

> *[U]niversal health plans, the world wide web, common sewers, international outrage over Vietnam or Ogoniland, sidewalks and footpaths, the Chinese concept of jen, the Jubilee of Leviticus... water fountains, Robin Hood of Sherwood Forest... effective pollution controls... music... old age pensions, universal education, Sweden's common forests... the second commandment of Yeshua... the rule of law, child and women shelters, parks, public broadcasting, clean water... the UN Declaration of Human Rights, occupational health and safety standards, village and city squares, the Brazilian rainforests, inoculation programmes, indigenous story-telling, the Ozone Protocol, the Tao, the peace movement, death rituals, animal rights agencies, community fish-habitats, food and drug legislation, garbage collection, the ancient village commons before enclosures.*[137]

As a keener look at the etymology of common parlance can reveal, several of the institutions listed above underpin "*civil* coexistence", "*civil*isation" and "*civil*ity", i.e. that which makes human life possible in societies and social life possibly humane. Together, these civil commons determine the scope of "the life ground", which McMurtry describes as follows: "Concretely, all that is required to take the next breath; axiologically, all the life support systems required for human life to reproduce or develop."[138]

The technical context within which the notion of life ground is cast is value theory (or axiology), for McMurtry attempts to demonstrate that all values rely ultimately upon the life ground and derive their value from it: "Life support systems - any natural or human-made system without which human beings cannot live or live well - may or may not have value in themselves, but have *ultimate* value so far as they are that without which human or other life cannot exist or flourish."[139]

Nevertheless, McMurtry's conception has ample implications and applications outside axiology, such as the revision of forestry governance,[140] the historical interpretation of democratic institutions as civil commons,[141] or the life-grounded understanding of human rights and their implementation.[142] In the perspective of an unusual "applied axiology", McMurtry has been developing since 2002 a "Well-Being Index" (WBI) comprising all fundamental "means of life" or "vital need[s]… for none can be deprived without reduction of vital life capability."[143] In its most recent formulation, the WBI lists seven vital goods that refer to as many vital needs:

(1) The atmospheric goods of breathable air, open space and light;
(2) The bodily goods of clean water, nourishing food, fit clothing, and waste disposal;
(3) The home and habitat goods of shelter from the elements;
(4) The environmental good of natural and constructed elements all contributing to the whole;
(5) The good of care through time by love, safety and health infrastructures;
(6) The good of human culture in music, language, art, play and sport; and
(7) The good of human vocation and social justice - that which enables and obliges all people to contribute to the provision of these life goods consistent with each's enjoyment of them.[144]

If these goods are not provided, then vital needs are not met; and if these needs are not met, then human capabilities dissipate, to the eventual point of individual and/or social non-existence. If instead these needs are met, then human capabilities do not only continue to be: they can "flourish" into the good life, individual as well as social.[145]

Grounding the WBI in "need" as a fundamental criterion, McMurtry has always had to be clear and strict about what may count as genuine need and what, upon closer examination, appears to be nothing but sheer desire. Thus, he builds the WBI upon a vast collection of empirical data from all the sciences and a precise definition: "*'n' is a need if and only if, and to the extent that, deprivation of n always leads to a reduction of organic capacity.*"[146] Only that without which life capacity is harmed counts as need; the rest does not. We can live, and possibly live well, without motorcycles and videogames, but we cannot live, and certainly not live well, if nourishing food, shelter, rest, meaningful self-expression and social interaction are denied to us.[147]

McMurtry's WBI is his most ostensible contribution to the development of standards for the measurement of human wellbeing, so that growth and decline may be interpreted in ways that mainstream economic criteria neglect or fail to ascertain.[148] The importance of determining novel standards and indicators is considerable. First of all, it has already been highlighted how the type of growth conceptualised and pursued in today's global market reality has had systemic negative implications upon life at many levels, such as human health, social cohesion, and the environmental conditions of planetary survival.[149] Secondly, in the wake of the post-2008 global economic crisis, the same reality has also been proved unable to attain stable growth even on its own, narrowly defined, pecuniary terms.[150]

Regarding the systemic negative implications of this global reality, McMurtry's *Cancer Stage of Capitalism* is famous for analysing the causal connection between late-modern for-profit economic activity and life-depletion, both natural and social, as *cancerous*:

1. In their defining, endless quest for ever-growing gains, life-disconnected pursuits of profit replicate themselves across Earth's societies through sequences of investment and returns that should proceed theoretically *ad infinitum*. *Homo economicus*' desires are non-satiable by textbook definition: according to standard economic theory, each sentient economic agent is a self-maximising pleasure-machine (non-sentient ones self-maximise too, but for the sake of their shareholders' pleasure). In their pattern of action, life-disconnected pursuits of profit mimic the life-disconnected self-replication of cancerous cells within a host body. McMurtry scholar and UK's Green-Party politician John Barry (b. 1966) speaks in this respect of "growthmania".[151]

2. The effects of this theoretically endless, non-satiable self-replication are analogous in practice too. As any oncological record can illustrate, the sprawling of cancerous cells leads eventually to loss of organic capacity, down to the very point of killing the host, whose demise implies also the demise of the cancerous cells within it. Similarly, the profit-pursuing sequences of investment and returns in the global economy have been producing life-losses on a massive scale by stripping the Earth's life support systems and societies' civil commons, such as: agribusiness' contamination of underground aquifers;[152] cuts to cultural,[153] educational[154] and healthcare provision;[155] less-inclusive privatised policing[156] and pension schemes;[157] and longer working hours.[158]

3. Finally, many of societies' long-established protective civil commons (e.g. democratic governments, universities, central banks *qua* socially responsible monitoring bodies) have been blind and unresponsive to the ongoing assault upon life-capabilities. Regularly, they have not even recognised it for what it is, that is to say, an assault on life-capabilities. On the contrary, they have pro-actively cooperated with its diffusion, e.g. by treating public investments in healthcare as costs, abolishing or marginalising ethics in the curricula of business schools, dismantling currency

trade regulations, and fostering the privatisation of public banks and other public assets that guaranteed a steady flow of revenues to public bodies.[159] By this sort of recurrent behaviour, many of societies' long-established protective civil commons have acted analogously to the immune defences of a living organism that failed to individuate its cancerous cells as harbingers of death and kept facilitating their replication.

As far as this cancerous pathology is concerned, political scientist David Humphreys argues that David Korten and John McMurtry are the only scholars who have taken the carcinogenic paradigm beyond the level of mere metaphor or analogy.[160] Using it as a powerful hermeneutical perspective, McMurtry's *Cancer Stage of Capitalism* is said to have applied it thoroughly and coherently to contemporary economic reality, in order to ascertain its multi-level life-destructiveness and the lack of recognition and defensive response by public institutions, including academic ones. As other commentators have also acknowledged, McMurtry's work exemplifies philosophy *qua* civil commons of Socratic questioning of received views, empirically backed critical reflection, and creative envisioning of alternative understandings, especially as economic theory and the economy are concerned.[161]

Martha Nussbaum's Capabilities Approach

Humphreys' correct observation notwithstanding, it is interesting to read the opening lines of Martha Nussbaum's 2010 book—significantly entitled *Not for Profit*—and discover that she too refers to the ongoing "world-wide crisis in education" as "a cancer".[162] Possibly unaware of McMurtry's work, Nussbaum shows that the social body is capable of pathology recognition *via* its immune system of historically evolved civil commons. Such are in fact the public educational system and the humanities, out of which Nussbaum's own work originates, and which she wishes to defend and revive in their life-serving social functions.

According to Nussbaum: "the humanistic aspects of science and social science—the imaginative, creative aspect, and the aspect of rigorous critical thought—are… losing ground as nations prefer to pursue short-term profit… and skills suited to profit-making."[163] The emphasis on money-returns for private investors is so strong in today's educational and academic environment that, in Nussbaum's view, what is at stake is the very survival of humanistic education in all of its complex forms, given their regular, growing, and prolonged underfunding, marginalisation and outright "fear" in the world's schools and universities.[164]

Social mores and attitudes reflect too the dominant axiology. As Nussbaum notes, many parents are worried and sometimes even ashamed if their children decide to pursue soul-enriching humanistic studies; whilst much rarer is to encounter parents who are worried about, or ashamed of, children that have opted for a wallet-enriching career in the notorious world of high finance. Thus, "at a time when nations must cut away all useless things in order to stay *competitive* in the global market, they [the humanities] are rapidly losing place in curricula, and also in the minds and hearts of parents and children."[165]

Nussbaum's chief preoccupation is not about the perception of humanistic studies, though; nor is it primarily with the composition of the curricula of universities either. Rather, Nussbaum thinks that human life is going to suffer immensely if this long-lived educational tradition perishes. As she remarks over and over in her latest book, humanistic education is not an ivory-tower endeavour, but an eminently civil one, for humanistic education has sustained for centuries "citizenship… employment and… *meaningful lives*".[166] Humanistic education has played an essential role in "cultivating humanity"—the title of a 1997 book by her—within sufficiently cohesive national communities delivering "health, education, a decrease in social and economic inequality… political liberty… democracy."[167]

In particular, the humanities and the humanistic component of education at large nurture "skills that we all badly need to keep democracies vital, respectful, and accountable"[168] and "provide a useful foundation for the public debates that we must have if we are to cooperate in solving major human problems".[169] According to Nussbaum's analysis of Western intellectual and socio-political history, humanistic education has contributed in a fundamental way to those emotional and intellectual elements expressed by institutions looking after the community-wide, long-term protection and enhancement of life capabilities. In her view, "[a]chievements in health and education, for example, are very poorly correlated with economic growth."[170] Life-beneficial progresses of this kind depend primarily upon the culture and dispositions that emerge from the cultivation of proper "moral emotions" across the community's youth.[171]

In contrast, today's pervasive profit-driven ethos offers merely "thin norms of market exchange in which human lives are seen primarily as instruments for gain."[172] If the youth's mental horizon and heart are deprived of those sympathetic sentiments that Adam Smith (1723–1790) himself depicted in his 1759 *Theory of Moral Sentiments* as the healthy counterforce to capitalism's inherent callousness, then it is inevitable that human communities become— and according to both McMurtry and Nussbaum have already become— more unequal, more brutal, and filled with "greedy desire, aggression... narcissistic anxiety... enslavement and subordination... fear and hate".[173]

In Smith's century, it was thought that a society based upon for-profit trade would foster politeness, civility and human solidarity. The martial ethos and policies of early-modern Europe would wane, replaced by the much milder ethos and policies of persons preferring the merchant's quieter competition for material gains to the conqueror's bloody warfare. Instead of pitting man against man, "commerce" would actually "get man closer to man".[174] In the 21st century, Nussbaum testifies to a subtle, unforeseen recrudescence of cruelty that had not been envisioned in the age of Enlightenment.

Politeness, civility and human solidarity may have been fostered centuries ago by for-profit trade, as unlikely as this notion may have sounded to the ears of the indigenous populations subdued or exterminated worldwide by 18th-century Western trading companies and settlers, but only as instruments of for-profit trade. If more profit can be made today by impoliteness, incivility and pitilessness, then humanity itself can be discarded, especially if no counterforce (e.g. religious self-restraint, trade unions, popular protest) intervenes to halt trade and its accessory political and military means of affirmation.

Even the conqueror's bloody warfare has been increasingly privatised in recent years so as to generate conspicuous profits.[175] This is no life-serving commerce, it should be noted, but rather life serving commerce—and life's obliteration in particular. Under these emblematic circumstances, for-profit trade's possible function *qua* civil commons is forgotten and betrayed, for it is lost in the most dramatic instantiation of for-profit life-blindness: intentional killing of human beings benefiting maximally money investors and/or managers, as also mathematically signalled by the regularly increasing value on Western stock exchange markets of the shares of arms manufacturers whenever conflicts take place in sufficiently distant foreign countries.

Norman Roessler criticises Nussbaum's 2010 dramatic assessment as the "jeremiad" of an anachronistic elitist academic.[176] On his part, Troy Jollimore connotes it as the true picture of the sad state of the university system of the US, in which the vast majority of students are being offered worse and worse higher education.[177] However, Nussbaum's 2010 book sounds much more like the outraged forewarning of an honest believer in human liberty, which all communities ought to cherish. What Nussbaum calls "the collapse of the Socratic ideal", i.e. the humanistic cultivation of open-minded inquiry and inclusively constructive dialogue, is in fact observable worldwide, not just in the US.[178]

From Canada to Singapore, over the last three decades, governments and corporate sponsors have been pursuing incessantly the transformation of public universities and research centres into means for the eventual generation of profit for private money investors and/or managers. In an egregious case of self-contradiction, even the world's leading Finnish educational system has been criticised of late by the Organisation for Economic Cooperation and Development (OECD) for not being adequately efficient, i.e. conducive to higher profits, as though that were the essential aim of education.[179]

Given the premises, today's OECD should be pleased with the record of many other countries, despite their much lower educational achievements, at least according to the internationally adopted, OECD-established PISA standards.[180] The policies implemented worldwide within academic settings over the past three decades display unvaryingly a prolonged tendency to make these settings profitable, as recorded by both McMurtry and Nussbaum. The former is particularly clear on the relentless corporate takeover of educational institutions, insofar as so-called public-private "partnerships" in research and teaching have been promoted as a way to: facilitate exchanges between universities and the business world; get students closer to potential employers and vice versa; and externalise the research costs of private enterprises onto public institutions and, ultimately, tax-payers. Sometimes, governments have proceeded to the outright privatisation of educational institutions, whether *in toto* or selectively (e.g. management, teaching, research positions, catering).

Less blatant but even more pervasive has been the market-oriented selection of research programmes and curricula; as well as the inculcation and implementation of top-down corporate command structures, both mental and administrative (e.g. no bottom-up consultation in faculty restructuring, increased pay for top management and decreased free access to education, faculty's ability to attract private sponsorships as promotion criterion). Within such mental and administrative command structures, scholars, schools, campuses and their inhabitants are seen as business opportunities and/or costs. They are no longer perceived *qua* civilising forces, centres of human excellence, or foundational rocks of democratic liberty—all of which are things that scholars, schools, campuses and their inhabitants have been able to instantiate in their long history, from Giordano Bruno's (1548–1600) defiance of religious dogmatism to young students' protests against the Vietnam War, the North America Free Trade Agreement (NAFTA), or the Iranian autocracy.

As to Nussbaum's 2010 book, she reports that in the UK, despite its long-established academic and parliamentary traditions, educational institutions have been required to "justify themselves to the government... by showing how their research and teaching contribute to economic profitability."[181] According to Nussbaum, any profit-driven assessment of the sort introduced in Great Britain and Northern Ireland fails completely to see how democracy and, probably, the economy's own profits have been made possible by an underlying layer of emotional and intellectual learning evolved by, and enshrined within, humanistic education.

This is no novel insight, nor a politically radical one. The celebrated thinker of reference for traditional British conservatives, Edmund Burke (1729–1797), had already observed long ago: "Even commerce, and trade, and manufacture, the gods of our economical politicians, are... themselves but effects, which as first causes, we choose to worship. They certainly grew under the same shade in which learning flourished. They too may decay with their natural protecting principles."[182]

Nussbaum's worried remarks upon the fate of humanistic learning and its function in promoting life-capabilities are part of her broader study of authentic human life and substantive freedom, i.e. the public provision of resources and opportunities for the actual enjoyment of the formal freedoms applying to each citizen of a liberal democracy. In this, Nussbaum follows a traditional liberal conception, which found a powerful expression in the words of 20th-century liberal champion Isaiah Berlin (1909–1997): "It is true that to offer political rights, or safeguards against intervention by the state, to men who are half-naked, illiterate, underfed, and diseased is to mock their condition... What is freedom to those who cannot make use of it? Without adequate conditions for the use of freedom, what is the value of freedom? [...] First things come first... individual freedom is not everyone's primary need."[183]

Although Berlin was never as exact as Nussbaum on the liberticidal implications of for-profit activities, he was familiar with enough economic history as to note: "[T]he minority who possess it [liberty] have gained it by exploiting, or, at least, averting their gaze from, the vast majority who do not... [Hence] [i]f my brothers are to remain in poverty, squalor, and chains—then I do not want it [liberty] for myself... To avoid glaring inequality or widespread misery I am ready to sacrifice some, or all, of my freedom... I should be guilt-stricken, and rightly so, if I were not."[184]

Analogous positions have been articulated in recent decades by Nobel-laureate Indian economist Amartya Sen (b. 1933), with whom Nussbaum co-edited a book in 1993 that established firmly in both human and social sciences what is "now widely known as the '*capabilities approach*'... [Whereby] we should focus on... What are the people of the group or country in question actually able to do and be?" rather than "opulence (say, GNP per capita)".[185] The capabilities approach considers people individually and reflects an ancient Aristotelian spirit, since it wonders about the "activities characteristically performed by human beings [that] are... definitive of a life that is truly human".[186] The capabilities approach wishes to ascertain not solely those "changes or transitions... compatible with the continued existence of a being as a member of the human kind", but also the "functions... [that] must be there if we are going to acknowledge that a given life is human".[187]

In connection with this twofold focus, Nussbaum lists a set of life-capabilities to be protected and/or promoted:

> *1. Life. Being able to live to the end of a human life of normal length...*
> *2. Bodily health and integrity. Being able to have good health... being adequately nourished; being able to have adequate shelter*
> *3. Bodily integrity. Being able to move freely from place to place; being able to be secure against violent assault... having opportunities for sexual satisfaction and for choice in matters of reproduction*
> *4. Senses, imagination, thought. Being able to use the senses; being able to imagine, to think, and to reason... in a 'truly human way', a way informed and cultivated by an adequate education... in ways protected by guarantees of*

freedom of expression... being able to have pleasurable experiences and to avoid nonbeneficial pain

5. Emotions. Being able to have attachments to things and persons outside ourselves; being able to love those who love and care for us; being able to grieve at their absence... to experience longing, gratitude, and justified anger; not having one's emotional developing blighted by fear or anxiety...

6. Practical reason. Being able to form a conception of the good and to engage in critical reflection about the planning of one's own life...

7. Affiliation... Being able to live for and in relation to others, to recognize and show concern for other human beings, to engage in various forms of social interaction; being able to imagine the situation of another and to have compassion for that situation; having the capability for both justice and friendship... being able to be treated as a dignified being whose worth is equal to that of others...

8. Other species. Being able to live with concern for and in relation to animals, plants, and the world of nature

9. Play. Being able to laugh, to play, to enjoy recreational activities

10. Control over one's environment... Political... Material... having the right to seek employment on an equal basis with others.[188]

Nussbaum further classifies these life-capabilities into three categories:

1. "*Basic capabilities*" constitute "the necessary basis for developing the more advanced capability."[189] Although glimmers of life-capability may be observable since people's earliest childhood, it is only through much parental care, social interaction, and prolonged schooling that children develop any of them into significant features of their life.
2. "*Internal capabilities*" are those "states of the person" that

establish "sufficient conditions for the exercise of the requisite functions."[190]

3. Finally, *"combined capabilities"* are the internal capabilities endowed with the institutions that allow for the expression of the internal capabilities of each as a genuine option in life.[191]

Since it is assumed that "all, just by being human, are of equal dignity and worth", Nussbaum believes governments and public bodies to be morally bound—not just legally or politically—to the universal fostering of combined capabilities.[192] Accordingly, governments and public bodies ought to pursue steadfastly the promotion of life-capabilities by establishing, maintaining and expanding societies' life support systems or, as McMurtry defines them, civil commons.

Reminiscent of analogous considerations by 18th-century British Reformers such as Thomas Spence or William Oglivie (1736–1819), Nussbaum's list of life-capabilities is nonetheless insightful and thought-provoking. To some extent, it points toward McMurtry's later WBI and the underlying three ontological modes of life that McMurtry identifies throughout his philosophical production, i.e. motility, felt being and thought. Still, Nussbaum's list appears somewhat rhapsodic compared to McMurtry's WBI, which is organised precisely and consistently around the fundamental criterion of human life need(s) and the corresponding good(s), without provision of which life capacity is always reduced.

To be exact, McMurtry's WBI is *grounded* in a universal onto-axiology of life-value that applies to all individuals and cultures. Contrastingly, Nussbaum's own list might possibly be shown *via* transcendental deduction to presuppose such a life ground, which is nowhere recognised in her work as an ontological or ethical ground. As a result, her selection is at risk of being subject to the endless relativisation of opinion on what is good for people with no underlying objective and self-evident foundation. Contrary to the life-grounded principle of universal vital needs and goods, Nussbaum's list is more likely to be reduced to the subjective notions of "desire", "preference", or "want" that constitute the psychological given of standard economic and psychological anthropology. At the same time, her focus on what the individual can do—indeed the capabilities approach itself—loses sight of what is required for the individual's doing to be possible in the first place. Although the capabilities approach does aim at promoting life-enhancing institutions as humanity's moral duty, it too can ironically contribute to today's widespread blindness to social and natural life support systems beneath the "separate individual" that she regards as the fundamental fact of ethics.[193]

Nussbaum's position points also towards the already-cited ICESCR, which pursues "the ideal of free human beings enjoying freedom from fear or want" and requires States "to take steps, individually and through international assistance and co-operation, especially economic and technical, to the maximum of its available resources, with a view to achieving progressively the full realization of the rights".[194] Life-considerations are at the heart of this covenant as much as they are at the heart of Nussbaum's work, for no "freedom, justice and peace" are said to be attainable if States fail in this task.[195] These rights are so important that individuals themselves are said to be morally bound by them: "The State Parties to the present Covenant… realiz[e] that the individual, having duties to other individuals and to the community to which he belongs, is under a responsibility to strive for the promotion and observance of the rights recognized in the present Covenant."[196]

Nussbaum's capabilities approach, her concern for people's substantive freedom, and her denunciation of the ongoing for-profit assault upon learning and humanity are no idle speculation by an elitist armchair philosopher. Quite the opposite, they reverberate, articulate and further substantiate the genuine aim of international law in its highest form as well as the observable failure in adequately securing this aim forty-four years after the ICESCR was opened for signature by the convened representatives of the world's nations.

Economic Wrongs and Human Rights

Often, within the de-humanised academic environment denounced by Nussbaum, the authors who have addressed the fundamental contradiction between life-requisites and for-profit activity have been neglected, marginalised, if not even derided as "nostalgic communists", "radicals", "leftists", or other "-ists", depending on which disqualifying predicate was in fashion at a given time in each given rhetorical setting. Clearly indifferent to the importance of dissent and "the Socratic ideal" commended by Nussbaum, entire disciplinary sectors would appear to have been cleansed of alternative conceptions, the lack of which has even been blamed by official State bodies *vis-à-vis* the current economic crisis.[197] Representative of this un-Socratic indifference, the Indian economist Jagdish Bhagwati (b. 1934) wrote sneeringly back in 2002: "The disappearance of alternative models of development provoked anguished reactions from the old anticapitalists of the postwar era... from socialists to revolutionaries... captive to a nostalgia for their vanished dreams... *in fields other than economics.* English, comparative literature, and sociology are all fertile breeding grounds for such dissent".[198]

From a life-grounded perspective, this rhetorical use of disparaging terms makes hardly any sense. For one, the particular economic model in place is not of crucial importance. What matters, instead, is that human needs be met and that life-capabilities be protected and promoted. If forcibly regulated in a life-grounded perspective, for-profit trade itself might actually be able to secure at least some of those results that Swedish defender of global capitalism Johan Norberg (b. 1973) connotes as "the important things in life—love, family, friendship, one's own way of life".[199] Profit, it should be noted, is not cited amongst them, for profit ought to be a means, not an end. In this sense, the plausible civil-commons function of intelligently steered for-profit trade had already been acknowledged long ago by Sang Hongyang (152–80 BC), who claimed that "crafts and commerce" have to be encouraged so that "people" be no longer "poorly fed".[200]

From a life-grounded reconsideration of economic activity, it follows that if public endowments are routinely privatised and the existing civil commons turned into money-making devices— e.g.

Nussbaum *vis-à-vis* public universities—then it is of the essence that such devices serve human needs *and* spur life-capability regularly and widely, in both space and time. If vital needs are not met and if life-capability is spurred in no such way, then alternatives must be sought and implemented, embracing economic pluralism, re-regulating life-detrimental de-regulated economies, and rejecting un-Socratic intolerant orthodoxy, including so-called "market fundamentalism".[201]

Under the perspective of the life ground, life alone can be paramount; nothing else should carry as much weight, or more. Consistently with this axiological axiom, a life-grounded reconsideration of economic activity is bound to discard stances that make life secondary. Stances of this kind are far from rare in theory or uninfluential in practice. As the former is concerned, neo-liberal guru Robert Nozick (1938–2002) wrote in his most famous book, *Anarchy, State, and Utopia*: "[A] right to life is not a right to whatever one needs to live; other people may have rights over these other things. At most, a right to life would be a right to have or strive for whatever one needs to live, provided that having it does not violate anyone else's rights."[202]

In its standard review of the 2001 report about Hong Kong, the UN's Economic, Social and Cultural Rights Committee stated that the region's "philosophy of 'positive non-interventionism'" was hampering the implementation of the ICESCR, to which they are party.[203] This business-centred philosophy "had a negative impact on the realization and enjoyment of the economic, social and cultural rights of Hong Kong's inhabitants, which has been exacerbated by globalization."[204] From a life-grounded perspective, the ends are the obligation; the means can vary. If life-capabilities-enabling substantive freedom is to occur, then it can reasonably happen that some degree of positive interventionism must be accepted, whether in the form of progressive taxation, public investment, or else. Political and economic doctrines can and should be reviewed, revised, and rejected, if they cause non-beneficial life-depletion. Fundamentally, from a life-grounded perspective, any "economy succeeds or fails to the extent to which it provides or does not provide its members with th[e] means of life severally and as a whole".[205]

In accordance with this statement, not any for-profit commodity counts towards the generation of genuine, life-consistent wealth: "Claimed 'economic goods' which disable or do not enable life abilities are not means of life; they are economic 'bads'."[206] Kalashnikovs, addictive cigarettes, actual toxic pesticides and virtual "toxic assets" are not good. They may engross a firm's or an individual's profits but, like slaves or DDT in the past, they are bad, for they harm life-capabilities. Puzzlingly, the jargon of standard economic theory and the practice of ongoing economic activity refer indiscriminately to all traded items as "goods". In fact, they all count towards wealth "creation", despite their destructive impact upon God's creation, the survival of which so deeply concerned Hans Jonas.

The economists' and economic agents' surprising yet ordinary inability to perceive and/or acknowledge the successful/failed civil-commons function of for-profit trade is due to the technical jargon's almost complete lack of effectively life-grounded criteria for the adequate conceptualisation of the living, and henceforth of what is actually good. Given the jargon of standard economic theory and the observable practice of ongoing economic activity, life support systems, life-capabilities, and living beings themselves are sheer economic "externalities" until, say, labour costs, carbon trade parameters, pharmaceutical research, and the purchase of land by climate-change-doomed archipelagos make them economically "visible", either *qua* business opportunities or *qua* possible costs.[207]

The social science of economics, which so much sway has enjoyed in late-modern policy-making, is quite simply unequipped to conceive of and tackle life *per se*. If economic activity is blind to life *de facto*, mainstream economic theory is so *de iure*. The life ground is presupposed throughout its conceptualisations and operations, but it cannot be grasped by its standard categories of thought. To such categories of thought, a biodiversity-rich virgin patch of boreal forest is uneconomic, whilst its transformation into a "coniferous monoculture" makes utmost sense.[208]

Unsurprisingly, the policies guided by these categories of thought have been often most harmful to life-capabilities. On this point, one of Argentina's leading experts in medical science remarked:

> *According to neoliberal dogma, the market is the perfect allocator of resources and the ideal arbiter of priorities and policies. Beginning in the unfortunate decade of the 80's, the market, in both general society and in health, weakened labor, increased unemployment, dismantled universal social coverage, lowered salaries, reduced public health expenditures, privatized services, mandated user fees, and decreased supervision of private health care providers and of the pharmaceutical industry. All these initiatives deteriorated the collective physical health. As to mental health, the replacement of more or less predictable individual lives with the uncertainties and unpredictability of unchecked market forces quite clearly deteriorated it.*[209]

On a contrary note, Lawrence Summers (b. 1954), former economic advisor to US President Barack Obama (b. 1961) and Chief Economist of the World Bank, crystallised the life-blindness of both mainstream economic theory and dominant economic praxes in a succinct and poignant statement: *"the economic logic behind dumping a load of toxic waste in the lowest wage country is impeccable, and we should face up to that"*.[210]

The conceptual vacuum acknowledged by Lawrence Summers is yet to be filled in any serious way within dissent-cleansed economic theory and economic activity.[211] Certainly, environmental economics, empirical studies in human happiness, and alternative views of development and growth have been emerging visibly over the past years. This growth notwithstanding, they remain marginal both within and, above all, outside academia. The dominant conceptual apparatus available to major advisers and major advisees is still so limited *vis-à-vis* vital issues that a bizarre though emblematic argument is commonly heard today amongst central bankers. According to it, the countries affected less dramatically by the "credit crunch" of 2008 were somehow shielded by "backward" tightly regulated banking systems and legal impediments to innovative financial activities.[212]

Instead of recognising such regulation and impediments as appropriate, these appear to the economic expert like some sort of defiant archaeological specimen from an arcane past. In a parallel fashion, despite the ongoing crisis and its blatant origin in de-regulated for-profit finance, life-enabling economic, social and cultural rights have been surrendered to its recovery, insofar as States have secured private pecuniary returns by reducing public investments, from decreased parental leave in crisis-hit Iceland[213] to cheaper, lower-quality meals in Italy's State-run primary schools.[214]

To a conceptual apparatus that cannot discriminate between universally needed sources of nourishing carbohydrates and the unnecessary means of financial speculation upon the same that make these sources less available and yet capable at the same time of "wealth creation", the prioritisation of private pecuniary returns over life-enabling economic, social and cultural rights is truly an impeccable logical option.[215]

Concluding Remarks

Given such an impeccable logic, Jonas' opening statement does not appear at all hyperbolic, but rather like the reasonable fear arising from a prolonged process of global life-destruction that has been perpetuated by a widely accepted life-blind conceptual apparatus that is incapable of comprehending anything that is not growth-directed, whether it is the 19th-century industrial workers' demand for free time or "the liberal arts model" of the American educational system that Nussbaum writes about in *Not for Profit*.[216]

If the life-capabilities praised by McMurtry and Nussbaum are ever to become the true goal for collective action, then the experts and the policies of those who seek their counsel must change dramatically. Unfortunately, in the wake of the current crisis and of most nations' responses to it, that which Finnish jurist Aulis Aarnio (b. 1937) laconically stated in 1991 stands still true today:

"Environmental values and economic values often clash, as in the protection of the forests and waterways. Almost without exception, the values that have prevailed have been economic."[217]

Apart from showing further the paradoxical understanding of the economy in today's received forms of consciousness—such that for-profit processes destroying their own ontological preconditions (i.e. "environmental values") are claimed to be "economic values"—this quote refuels Jonas' concern that an overly ingenious humankind may actually "die on this desolate Earth which used to be the Creation".

Chapter 4: Giulio Tremonti's Exit Strategy: Ending the Tyranny of Finance

A law professor at the University of Pavia, Italy, and a long-time charismatic member of that country's political right, Giulio Tremonti served in Silvio Berlusconi's conservative governments as Finance Minister in 1994–1995, 2001–2004, 2005–2006, and 2008–2011. An active participant in high-profile policy-making and trend-setting institutions (e.g. the Ecofin Council, the G7 and G8, the Aspen Institute, the Italy-USA Foundation), Tremonti has been the promoter of the Global Legal Standard, which the OECD adopted in 2009.[218]

A self-proclaimed "neo-mercantilist", Tremonti has been critical of the *laissez-faire* approach of the world's countries with regard to transnational finance, envisioning a pivotal role for State authorities *vis-à-vis* economic regulation and overall steering *via* apt fiscal policy.[219] Whilst defending classical liberal principles of free enterprise, trade and private property, Tremonti has been advocating more and more vocally a much stronger role for public institutions at all levels—local, national and international—as watchful regulators, along the lines of traditional ordoliberalism and as also purported by the Social Doctrine of the Church, both of which Tremonti acknowledges as key-influences in his worldview.[220] Also, Tremonti has never stopped acknowledging the importance of taking stock of the geopolitical interests of countries and associations thereof, such that market distortions created by such interests should never be underplayed or disregarded in the proper study of economic reality.[221]

The Crisis

In 2012, faced with the implosion of deregulated finance and the eventual massive intervention of State authorities worldwide in order to stem in at least some of the most dramatic consequences of the global economic crisis unfolded thereof, Tremonti published his most scathing attack against liberalised transnational finance, i.e. the book *Uscita di sicurezza*, translated into English as *Exist Strategy. Ending the Tyranny of Finance*. Its first chapter discusses the "three tragic errors" that led to the current international economic crisis, that is to say:[222]

(a) The blind faith in financial globalisation as a path to prosperity that caused Western political leaders not to acknowledge either the nature or the magnitude of the 2008 financial crisis, thus misinterpreting it as a sheer downswing of a normal business cycle;
(b) The same leaders' willingness to rescue the world's *de facto* bankrupt financial giants instead of liquidating them and substituting them with public banks; not doing so meant socialising private losses that have escalated into the alleged sovereign debt crisis (i.e. as though the crisis were public rather than private in essence);
(c) The same leaders' irresponsible and subservient decision to allow the *de facto* bankrupt financial giants to see to the much-needed task of writing new global rules on the products and modalities of virtual trade, which have translated since then into "finance dictating its own rules to the governments".[223]

The second chapter tackles the history of the latter half of the 20th century and the beginning of the 21st, so as to reveal the thorough shift in overall economic value and political influence from the real economy to the virtual one or, as Tremonti dubs it, from a "productive economy" to a "speculative" one.[224] The third chapter sketches an insightful and at times humorous picture of the utter disconnection between the aims of this speculative economy and those of the real economy, upon which rest the livelihoods and lives of billions of human beings. The fourth chapter denounces the complete failure of mainstream economics and leading economic institutions to foresee, forestall and address effectively the ongoing crisis.

Not only does Tremonti criticise the majority of professional economists, who have lost sight of the real world in lieu of the abstract realm of deductive models. Also, Tremonti criticises the private rating agencies and the Bank of International Settlements' (BIS) Basil Committee and Financial Stability Board. These emanations of the BIS have been characterised by a "hypertrophy" of official guidelines and recommendations that have been not solely egregiously ineffective, but also a proud display of obtuseness, given that they dare suggest, for one, that banks and financial institutions should follow the "best practices... of the hedge funds" involved in the "speculative economy" of the planet.[225] The fifth chapter flags out the European Union's (EU) structural deficiencies in managing and protecting its rather young new currency, the Euro, which the "American will to power" has possibly targeted as a threatening rival to the US dollar *qua* "reserve currency of the world".[226]

While assessing such deficiencies, Tremonti highlights the profound political character of the EU's economic policies, which are regularly depicted as sheer technical issues. Thus, the sixth chapter dwells further on Europe's systemic weaknesses and so does the seventh, which offers a masterfully concise yet insightful overview of European economic history. The overall picture that the author offers to his readers is one in which all European countries are inextricably interconnected and bound to succeed or fail together. According to Tremonti, the age of national self-interest and isolationism belongs to the past. Consistently, he argues that Europe would be better off, and certainly more likely to cope with crises like the current one, by seeking a higher degree of integration than a lesser one.

The eighth chapter recalls Tremonti's first-hand experiences at a number of highest-level 2010 gatherings of EU State officials, who were not able to buttress the Euro with adequate defence policies and financial instruments. The ninth chapter deepens the analysis of the EU's inadequacies *vis-à-vis* its own currency. The tenth chapter adds to the previous one a number of considerations on the positive and negative aspects of the policies promoted as well as opposed by the EU's leading member, i.e. Germany, whose national self-interest runs sometimes counter the EU's, while some others does coincide with, yet without ever moving past its narrowly national centredness.

Having talked amply about the past and the present of the world's economies, and of the EU's in particular, the eleventh chapter discusses four hypotheses on what is likely to lie ahead for the EU, depending on the decisions that its member States will take or fail to take in the near future:

(a) Waiting passively for its demise;
(b) Separating weaker and stronger areas within it;
(c) Reorganising the EU and providing it with new and better instruments, such as a more flexible Central Bank and the Eurobond;
(d) Advancing a "New Alliance" between Europe's nations, along the lines of Roosevelt's New Deal.[227]

The twelfth chapter articulates and explores the implications of the fourth hypothesis, which Tremonti favours. Although he opposes an inflationary way out of the sovereign debt crisis, which resulted from a suicidal subservience of the world's government to the banking industry, Tremonti does believe that co-ordinated action by the same governments could lead to a positive solution. The thirteenth and final chapter explains in finer detail Tremonti's "exit strategy", which builds upon three pillars:

(i) "placing the State above finance and finance under the State";[228]
(ii) "letting rules prevail over the anarchy" of finance, as done in the past with the Bretton Woods agreements;[229] and
(iii) "launching great public investment projects for the sake of the common good", thus following in this case the example and the wisdom of the age of Keynesianism or, to find cases that are closer to us in time, the unorthodox economic policies of Malaysia in 1998 and, to a lesser extent, Iceland after 2008.[230]

The book comprises a closing appendix containing several intriguing reflections and original documents, including a 2008 letter written by Tremonti to the then French Minister of the Economy, Industry and Labour, Christine Lagarde (b. 1956), i.e. today's director of the International Monetary Fund (IMF). Excerpts from his previous book, *La paura e la speranza* are also published in the closing appendix, in order to acknowledge the progression of Tremonti's criticism of financial globalisation. Over the years, in fact, Tremonti moved away from an overall positive acceptance of the new economic world order, and towards a less serene reading of its implications for Europe at first and, eventually, for the world at large.

Financial Fascism

It is highly unusual and equally significant that Tremonti's book be so open and so forceful in denouncing how a global "financial élite has been left to hold power's reins" on the international stage.[231] Normally, this sort of language is associated with internet-based conspiracy theorists, alt-right populists and nostalgic communists, not mainstream high-profile European politicians and statesmen. Nonetheless, combined with the severity of the ongoing economic crisis, Tremonti claims this global power shift to be morphing into nothing less than "financial fascism, white fascism".[232]

This new form of fascism is said to be the consequential, most undemocratic expression of the dangerous "monster" unleashed by globalisation, as Tremonti characterises it, that is to say, a "financial market, based upon a powerful and dominating ideology, which tends towards the annihilation of the best part of human nature, reducing life to the economic sphere, and the economic sphere to finance... devouring us and eventually devouring itself."[233]

For Tremonti, behind the threatening power structure bringing forth "white fascism" lurks a life-blind, economistic reductionism that prevents the most valuable dimensions of human existence from being considered, respected or promoted. Grave conceptual inabilities thus reflect onto the real world, causing havoc and suffering. Under this respect, Tremonti's 2012 book highlights how the paramount guiding principle in the economic order that has been built under the banner of "globalisation" is whatever profit the accountant may jot down in the books of a corporate firm.

Everything else, if perceived in any measure, does not seem to matter much, whether it is the environment, the welfare of families and children, well-established industrial networks, centuries-old cultures, or even Western democracy itself. This chilling axiology is commonly revealed each and every time political leaders do not describe their paramount task as fulfilling their constitutionally mandated duties to the citizenry, but rather as "reassuring the markets", "reducing the spread" levels, making or keeping a country "competitive", or "attractive to business" and to "foreign investors".

The analyses offered in Tremonti's book spell out in their complexity the profoundly un- and anti-democratic implications of such business-oriented interpretations of political life. This interpretation has been embodied by a long series of either myopic or conniving political leaders that opened the door, over the past "twenty years", to the actual marginalisation of representative institutions.[234] Even the German philosopher Jürgen Habermas, usually quite cautious and rather indirect in his public statements, described in 2011 the EU's "embedded capitalism" as "post-democracy".[235]

Oligarchy, not democracy, is the name of the game, exactly like post-communist Russia, where the businessmen who made a killing from the mass privatisations and liberalisations of the 1990s are still known as "oligarchs". In other words, the representative institutions of many nations have been overtaken by a technostructure emanating *in primis* from the world's largest financial holdings. As Tremonti remarks, for instance, just nine such holdings have come to dominate today's US financial market and exercise an enormous influence over US politics and policies.[236]

And if "oligarchy" is too mild a descriptor for this sort of reality, the English-language translation of Tremonti's book include a subtitle that makes use of an even stronger one, "tyranny", which occurs in the Italian original, but not in the title.[237] What is more, this tyrannical oligarchy has proved even more myopic than the national governments permitting its affirmation over the past two decades, since the world's largest financial holdings have been patently unable to operate sound business models and caused their own collapse in 2008.

Still, as their gravy train came to a sudden halt, these incompetent financial holdings have nevertheless succeeded in compelling the world's governments and central banks to operate as their pork-barrel and rescue them from themselves. This rescue operation has been conducted whilst withdrawing much-needed resources from the domains of real-economy credit and public services. No clearer instance of their overwhelming power could be given.

That Tremonti may call this power as the path leading to "fascism" should not be entirely surprising: this is the sort of private power over public institutions that none less than Roosevelt decried in 1938 as quintessential to "fascism".[238] After many years spent preaching about market discipline *via* their associated think-tanks, opportunistic academics, affiliated journalists or privately funded university chairs; as well as after lobbying successfully for de-regulation and reduced State intervention in the economy, the State was called in by the largest financial holdings in order to fix their own failures and let them continue to operate as recklessly as before.

There can be no underestimation of the massive post-2008 State-led interventions that rescued the deregulated and liberalised international financial system from self-inflicted implosion and, slowly, re-established a modicum of trust in it. All the mantra-like principles of "competition", "survival of the fittest", "toughness", "merit", "efficiency" and the "invisible hand" proclaimed since at least the age of Reagonomics and Thatcherism were forgotten overnight in favour of the very visible hand of State aid and State protection.

Such readiness and generosity by State authorities were reserved for such financial 'giants' only, however. Schools, hospitals, scientific research, public housing and poverty relief programmes, national opera companies and local cultural centres had already been starved of funds for decades, under the banner of "free markets", "business-friendliness" and "liberalisation". After the 2008 global collapse, they kept being starved as perplexingly unaffordable public expenditures. In 2008, as Tremonti's book candidly observes, the world witnessed a glaring contradiction between the words and the deeds of the so-called "masters of the universe"; a contradiction that shows the sort of impunity that truly powerful hypocrites can enjoy.

An Institutionalist Interlude

It should be noted that these hypocrites are in great part the same managerial class that regularly pay themselves stellar salaries and huge bonuses irrespective of performance, whilst opposing better salaries to the average employee for the microeconomic sake of remaining competitive and the macroeconomic imperative of price stability. Somehow, as John Kenneth Galbraith stated long ago while distinguishing between actual economic behaviour and the fictional one presumed by orthodox economics, market discipline is always expected of others, never of oneself.[239]

Galbraith kept recording proofs of this fundamental distinction over the years, and glaring contradictions emerge at every level of the actual business world.[240] Thus, one can still see how MBA students are taught to praise the pioneering entrepreneurial individual above and against any corrupting State interference. Once employed, the same students are required to lobby State representatives of all kinds, under the banner of public-private partnerships. This way, public money is to be spent on hefty commissions for their corporate masters, which have been known to profit enormously and, in the case of Galbraith's US, especially from the most evident form of State interference into the lives of private individuals: warfare.

The same MBA students are taught to respect consumer sovereignty and admire the way in which it determines production and prices. Later on, these students are employed alongside the most ingenious minds that society can offer in order to survey, predict, condition, programme and brand, like slaves of old, actual consumers. Similarly, any MBA student can soon distinguish between the private sector and the public sector, typically equating the former with eulogistic notions (e.g. efficiency, discipline) and the latter with dyslogistic notions (e.g. inefficiency, corruption). Later on, nearly all of them serve in corporate bureaucracies, whose heads command crucial State institutions through a system of campaign funding, advertising strategies, media ownership, legal advice, scientific lobbying, capital strikes, kickbacks and revolving doors.

"Competition" and "merit" may be said to be the Polar Star of the market system, hence of progress and well-being. Still, even if progress and well-being were its actual by-product, in the real market economies: wealthy shareholders care not about their businesses as long as they get their dividends; managers pay themselves stellar salaries and bonuses irrespective of performance; entrepreneurs seek and obtain by hook or crook any special legislation that they may wish in order to be sheltered from more efficient competitors; and workers try to follow their bosses' example by unionising enough as to enjoy stable and well-paying jobs whether adequately productive or not.

Some of the contradictions highlighted by Galbraith throughout much of his career and here merely hinted at do surface in the new volume by Tremonti. Nevertheless, Tremonti's focus remains fixed upon the one between former claims about the financial markets' beneficial freedom from so-called "State interference" and the subsequent involvement of the State to save the financial markets from their own incompetence. Within this area of analysis, Tremonti's book reveals another glaring and important contradiction, that is to say, the one concerning the actual liquidity available on the global market and the recurrent notion—aired by politicians, pundits and media outlets alike—according to which *there is no money*.[241]

On this point, Tremonti remarks that, due to many years of low interest rates by the world's main central banks, liquid capital was already far from scarce before the 2008 crisis. After 2008, the world has become awash with money. Specifically, an ocean of cheap *fiat* money has been created *via* special subsidies and credit lines, quantitative easing programmes and further various liquidity injections by the most important central banks, whose coffers could become so generous thanks only to the States' unprecedented and promptest emission of novel waves of public debt.

These central banks, sanctioned by governments and visibly forgetful of their *public* functions, have therefore assisted the world's over-indebted gargantuan *private* banks to stay afloat in spite of their own recklessness (following Tremonti, I am using here the term "bank" quite loosely, for it applies also to institutional investors, very high net value individuals, and the most important financial managers.) Indeed, their recklessness has been allowed to go unpunished as well as to grow further through ensuing and enduring waves of speculation, which have included speculation upon the very debt issued by those States that saved such inept private banks from themselves.

No significant drop of this flood of cheap *fiat* money has reached either the productive structures of the world, i.e. most firms and households, or the States' own budgets, upon which depend vital programmes for the poor, the elderly, the infirm and the youth. The former received no credit from private banks that were too afraid of one another and of the mess that they had created to lend anything to anyone. The latter have long self-emasculated by granting boundless freedom of movement to private capital—including from and to tax havens—and by setting up finance-friendly fiscal systems. Thus, firms, households and States were hit by a deadly drought during a Biblical flood.

Tremonti does not say much of the well-paid sycophants of the dominating banks that have resisted any alternative course of action, for such a course could create inflation, which is taken to be the worst of all evils under any circumstance. Inflation, though potentially eating away the accumulated debt that strangles today's "productive" economy, would also reduce the value of the assets listed on the books of the banks entangled within the "speculative" economy—and the banks wouldn't like that.

Rather, Tremonti remarks that, given the nature of the response to the crisis, enterprises have been forced into extinction, jobs destroyed, social programmes slashed, poverty and destitution increased, while those chiefly responsible for the ongoing crisis have often avoided bankruptcy, returned to profit and further concentrated their control over the world's capitals, both financial and political. In short, national sovereignty, genuine economic prosperity, human wellbeing and actual lives have been sacrificed to the whims of a handful of ruthless gamblers playing a dangerous game in what Tremonti terms a "financial casino", in a direct reference to John Maynard Keynes' famous indictment of reckless speculators in his 1947 *General Theory*.[242]

Financial Autocracy

That such a high-profile member of the world's political élite, indeed one associated with Italy's liberal and conservative parties, may use so strong a language should lead us all to ponder.

First of all, Tremonti's choice of words reveals deepest preoccupations about the composition and the reliability of the international power structure. Not only is it clear for Tremonti that democracy has been side-stepped, if not suspended altogether. Also, it has not been replaced by an alternative system that can deliver any concrete wellbeing to the world's populations. Despotism is back and it is not an enlightened one.

Secondly, such a choice of words reveals that major political leaders of the world, with whom Tremonti himself co-operated throughout the 1990s and 2000s, did accomplish to a significant extent the demise of forms of democratic self-government that Tremonti hails as the mark of distinction and honour of the Western nations. Rather than defending or promoting them, these political leaders, whom Tremonti does not name individually and describes as feigning knowledge of the financial universe, allowed a silent take-over by the planet's banking giants. This is no small incident or institutional *faux pas*. Indeed, Tremonti writes of a present "financial autocracy"[243] begetting a future "white fascism" headed by the same financiers.[244]

Tremonti is certainly not the first one to have done so. The bankers' tacit *coup d'état* had already been denounced in the 1990s and the 2000s by a few scholars and fewer dissenting politicians, whom mainstream academia and mass media had however either neglected or accused of "radicalism" and "incompetence". Whilst reading Tremonti's account, the reader can realise how intellectuals like Cornelius Castoriadis, Eduardo Galeano (1940–2015) and John McMurtry, or political 'eccentrics' like Oskar Lafontaine (b. 1943) and Mahathir Mohamad (b. 1925), had long been right on at least *some* crucial issues, such as the establishment of a finance-centred worldwide oligarchy, the life-threatening effects of financial globalisation, and the mainstream economists' trained incapacity to address either of them as major factors of actual economic life as well as of economic instability.

Tremonti, who started expressing some degree of concern over these phenomena in the early 2000s, has eventually come to agree with such long-time neglected and/or loathed "incompetents" and "radicals" who had been, despite their frequent rhetorical dismissal, right and on the ball long before him. History's lessons notwithstanding, and despite the ongoing economic crisis and its aetiology, most countries are still resorting to the alleged wisdom and leadership of the same agents that were in power while the maelstrom was in the making.

For example, institutions like the IMF and the BIS had been promoting international financialisation for decades and yet they enjoy today even more clout upon the world's governments than they did before the 2008 crisis. Treasury secretaries and national central bankers that sponsored massive waves of speculation for twenty years, or that reassured the world about the international financial system's ability to self-manage without State interference, have been promoted to more prestigious positions. Revealingly, as a member of Italy's governing cabinet, Tremonti conflicted on several occasions with the president of the Bank of Italy, former Goldman Sachs vice chairman Mario Draghi (b. 1947), who serves today as president of the European Central Bank. Re-regulation of the banking industry, which had successfully lobbied for de-regulation in the decades preceding the 2008 collapse, has been mostly postponed and generally left in the hands of the very same industry that should be bound by it. Can we expect anything good from this perplexing decision of the world's leaders?

Tremonti does not, and laments: "Five years after the explosion of the crisis, if we consider and add together the little and often damaging actions that have been taken, as well as all the inaction that has occurred, it is clear that its causal factors have not only persisted, but increased".[245] To make things worse, mainstream newspapers and media outlets seem to have forgotten Lehman Brothers, the deadly bubble of "toxic assets" and, in general, where exactly the crisis comes from. Rather than addressing the fountainhead of all problems, public debates have veered away from the "financial casino" deplored by Tremonti.

Instead, when dealing with financial matters, the mainstream media have been focussing selectively upon particular effects of the casino itself, such as the outstanding public debt resulting from the recession and the rescue operations that have saved the private banks from themselves, whereby private debts became public debts. There have been media campaigns on individual private frauds, which have involved rich financiers preying upon rich people, e.g. Bernie Madoff (b. 1938). Not to mention poverty-fuelled increased international migration fluxes, i.e. a hot and divisive topic that can help to shift popular anger from the culpable yet powerful banking industry to the largely innocent and weak scapegoats trying to cross the US-Mexico border or the Mediterranean Sea.

Even when dealing with economic matters *sensu stricto*, mainstream journalists and pundits have been attacking what little is left of the welfare State as "unsustainable", or particular criminals in the financial sector as dangerous black sheep, rather than denouncing the lethal and criminogenic character of the economic system established, according to Tremonti, by the financial oligarchy and their obedient political servants. Whether this shift of the media's spotlight is the direct result of the pervasive power of the "financial autocracy" denounced by Tremonti, or yet another sign of a bourgeoning "financial fascism", is something that his book does not address, but that is worth reflecting upon.

Concluding Remarks

These unanswered questions notwithstanding, it must be acknowledged that Tremonti's book, alongside a growing number of publications on global economic trends, does highlight how much need there is on the planet for an "emergency exit" like the one that he announces in the title. Whether this exit will be taken or not is not yet clear. The grip of the financial oligarchy upon the nations' governments and many super-national institutions is still very tight, as exemplified by the recessive austerity and deflationary anti-labour policies implemented after the 2008 crisis all over the EU. Banks on the verge of bankruptcy were granted lifelines. Citizens were told to tighten their belts. Autocracy, not to mention fascism, was never a paper tiger; why should it be so in the 21st century?

That an emergency exit may eventually be taken, however, is possible. Signs of forthcoming change abound. Many of them are far from reassuring. Growing unemployment, popular protests, the resurgence of terrorism, looming wars in the middle East as politically viable spending programmes, diplomatic tensions within the EU, BRIC's complaints about currency wars initiated by Western countries, and the electoral success of xenophobic parties in civil Finland and France cast dark shadows upon the future of Europe and of the world at large. The emergency exit awaiting us may be a truly dramatic one. Though terrifying, this is no surprising possibility. World War I followed the first prolonged global experiment in free capital trade (i.e. 1870s–1914),[246] whilst World War II (WWII) concluded the Great Depression that was begotten by Wall Street's "roaring twenties" crashing down in 1929.

On his part, Tremonti offers an exit that is *civilised,* not only because it does not rely on State violence for its accomplishment, but also because it calls upon the world's governments to be "leaders" once again, rather than "followers" of the "financial economy", and therefore regain the awareness of the *civic* function that is expected of them by constitutional mandate.[247] No longer must power be left to "ventriloquists of finance, lobbyists, replicants according to the liturgy of the mercantile word and financial orthodoxy".[248] States can and actually ought to play a much more significant role, also with regard to the economic sphere, as indicated by the third pillar of his exit strategy. Tremonti believes that today's political class must learn to resemble "the old political leaders [of the post-WWII era], forged in social struggles, ideological conflicts, human adventures, even incarceration and wars; but capable, because of this, of deciding for better or worse upon the destiny, the future, the fate of their peoples."[249]

Politicians of formally democratic nations can be corruptible and even loathsome at times, yet they must respond, in the end, to their peoples. International financiers must not; at best, they may have to respond to their largest shareholders, who are anyway a tiny proportion of the world's population and are frequently deprived of any genuine instrument to restrain the managers' self-serving control of the actual firms.[250] Despite its imperfections, Tremonti does believe "democracy" to be the best political system available.[251] Therefore, if democracy is going to have any meaning in the 21st century, power must be wrested away from the financial oligarchs and restored to constitutionally elected politicians, who themselves are to regain their forgotten ability and duty to lead. If this is not done, then we are likely to experience the full force of "financial fascism, white fascism". The 2010s may be the new 1930s.

As dramatic as it may sound, this is Tremonti's warning and call to arms. Will anyone listen to him, however, or will he be discarded into the bin of those semantically side-lined "radicals" and "incompetents" that were, however, right all along? History alone will tell.

Chapter 5: Arthur Fridolin Utz's Economic Ethics

The present chapter offers a detailed, reasoned synopsis of the 1994 book *Economic Ethics*,[252] written by the German-Swiss[253] social philosopher Arthur Fridolin Utz, OP.[254] Utz is known chiefly in German-speaking[255] theological circles and in Catholic ones in particular. He is also known in those of southern Europe where, to date, only a handful of his many books have been translated into Spanish, French and Italian.[256] Utz's research deserves attention, both for its inherent value and in connection with Peter Koslowski's (1952–2012) reflections on economic ethics, which have been growingly influential outside German-speaking academia.[257]

For almost thirty years, Utz taught social and moral philosophy, economic ethics and legal theory at the University of Fribourg in Switzerland, where he also directed the International Institute for Social and Political Sciences of the Union of Fribourg.[258] Together with Austria's Johannes Messner (1891–1984),[259] Utz was a key-member of the German-speaking Catholic school of thought that, in post-war Europe, exercised considerable influence in the development of both the Social Doctrine of the Church[260] (SDC; also known as Catholic Social Teaching) and the social market economy, which was promoted by Christian-democratic parties both at a national level (especially in former Western Germany[261], Austria[262] and Switzerland) and at a continental one (i.e. in what we call today the European Union).[263] Among Utz's interlocutors on economic matters were the world-famous Canadian-born liberal economist John Kenneth Galbraith and the Czech socialist economist Ota Šik (1919–2004), who is best remembered as the architect of the economic section of Alexander Dubček's (1921–1992) Action Programme in the Prague Spring of 1968.

A Thomist Ethics of, and for, Society

The book is the fourth instalment in the author's monumental *Social Ethics*, which comprises five volumes in total: (1) *Principles of the Social Doctrine* (1958; 2nd ed.1964); (2); *Philosophy of Law*

(1963); (3) *The Social Order* (1986); (4) *Economic Ethics* (1994); and (5) *Political Ethics* (2000).[264] None of these volumes has been translated into English yet. I myself, being far from fluent in German, owe my initial acquaintance with Utz to the Italian translations of volumes 4 (1999) and 5 (2008) of his *Social Ethics*, both published by San Paolo, and to the 1997 French translation of his 1975 book *Zwischen Neoliberalismus und Neomarxismus: die Philosophie des dritten Weges* (Köln: P. Hanstein).[265] Before engaging in the detailed, reasoned synopsis of the book, I summarise here its main elements.

In his *Economic Ethics*, Utz applies a Thomist ethics to the domain of economics. Economic life is thus seen as a sub-domain of human and, as such, of social life—for we are essentially social animals. Henceforth, economic life can be deemed good or bad on the basis of whether it assists coherently in the realisation of the inherent ends of the human person, who is essentially social. The Thomist epistemology of our inherent aims is articulate.[266] Firstly, there are tokens of rational insight (*intellectus*) requiring no articulate inference on our part, i.e. Aquinas' *lex naturalis*, which is the rational creature's partial participation in God's *lex aeterna* (e.g. the pursuit of happiness as good). Secondly, there are general principles inferred from the person's rational nature, i.e. Aquinas' primary *ius naturale* (e.g. the common good being prior to the private good, human liberty being paramount). Thirdly, there are general principles born out of rational reflection (*synderesis*) beyond the person's rational nature alone and aimed at fulfilling the previous two levels, i.e. Aquinas' secondary *ius naturale* or *ius gentium* (e.g. private property being justified). Finally, such principles must be applied to mutable circumstances *via* practical reason, which can be more or less successful in this task.[267]

Thomist ethics is a teleological ethics: human actions have a defining material object—for example, eating has the acquisition of nourishment as its proper object—and also a defining human end—for example, eating aims at sustaining the person towards her achievement of happiness. Aquinas combined Aristotle's (384–322 BC) eudemonism, whereby human beings seek by nature a fundamental end i.e. happiness (aka perfection, completion, well-being), and Christian belief, whereby final happiness lies in *post mortem* beatitude. Human reason, albeit imperfect, is considered capable of abstracting from experience the fundamental principles of organisation of reality, including the aims that are natural and therefore truly positive for creatures, their societies and creation itself to have.

Consistently with this approach, Utz himself does not reduce "the common good" to the sheer aggregate of individual goods. Seeking personal perfection is paramount for human happiness, but it must take place within, and in coherent connection with, the good of larger units, e.g. the Earth's ecology and the communities to which each person belongs and is duty-bound [268] Articulate, logical reasoning upon experience can produce knowledge of the deepest layers of reality, while empirical science stays closer to the surface of observable, quantifiable facts. Utz derives from Aquinas the idea that all norms are identified by means of reasoned reflection (i.e. metaphysical abstraction) on the individual's inner experiences of moral duty and responsibility, which, however, can only be given, understood, formulated and acted upon in a socially established system of interpersonal existence, thought, language and mores situated beyond each individual. No man is an island; not even "Robinson Crusoe" himself.[269] As Utz writes: "The philosopher moves at the level of inherently immutable essences", provided that she starts her "abstraction" from concrete "empirical-ontological data".[270]

According to Utz, our natural faculties, albeit imperfect, are still capable of identifying what "*natura humana*" consists in, especially if they make use of the body of intelligent reflection on human experience provided by centuries of philosophical and theological study, rather than rejecting it as archaic or unscientific.[271] *Pace* today's ordinalist, post-modernist, relativistic and variously consensus-based worldviews, Helen Alford praises Utz's Thomist position in light of the on-going environmental collapse of our planet: "the possibility of seeing nature, including human nature, as a guide for human action in general could be more widely recognized" because of "the current recognition of the 'nature' of the environment, that is, that we cannot treat our planet only according to our supposed 'consensus' (many would say 'what consensus?'), but that we need to treat it according to its own nature." Building on tradition, intuition, observation (including the scientific one) and reflection, human intelligence can dig deep.[272]

Whether then the will follows reason's discovery and assessment of natural inclinations is a different issue. Given our imperfect condition, there is no guarantee. The Christian revelation, under this perspective, comes to our assistance, e.g. God's grace, Christian rites and sacraments, character education in religious schools, etc. Philosophy itself, in its Thomist understanding, can make an important contribution in this perspective, and specifically by contributing to human knowledge at its highest or deepest degree of clarity and existential significance. This is at least what, according to Utz, metaphysicians and ethicists can do that is unique to their profession.

In the field of economics too, the philosopher can ascertain deeper and more essential aims of economic agency, which the economist would not consider, for she would limit her investigation to the "technical questions" of economics.[273] As Helen Alford observes in her study of Utz's work, ethics explores paths that scientists trod upon inevitably but blindly: "Technical disciplines that do not recognize that they are based on more profound assumptions or premises that they take as self-evident (unexamined) and on which they are built do in fact have such assumptions, but their experts are not aware that this is the case, and… [it] is not a question on which they reflect."[274] Then, a philosopher can assess as negative a booming national or international economy, which grants unprecedented wealth to the members of today's society and yet imperils the wellbeing of tomorrow's society because of the overexploitation of natural resources. Empirical data are the beginning of reflective wisdom, not its end.

Utz discusses the deeper and more essential aims of personal and social life, of which economic life is but a part, in the first instalment of his five-volume-strong *Social Ethics*. In the fourth volume,

Wirtschaftsethik, he merely hints at some of them. In addition to expressing general agreement *vis-à-vis* Ota Šik's list of universal human needs,[275] Utz speaks recurrently of bodily sustenance,[276] meaningful and dignified self-direction,[277] family life,[278] acculturation[279] and religious life.[280] These natural or rational aims correspond almost point-by-point to the "supreme principles" of Aquinas' "natural law", i.e. "self-preservation, self-perfection, mating, generation and education of the offspring, acquisition of knowledge, (natural) knowledge of God."[281]

In typical Thomist fashion, "God" is defined by Utz as "the ultimate and integral end of the human being", i.e. the true attainment of "happiness" or "perfection".[282] Having such an "ultimate end" in the next life means that, in this life, we ought to pursue the penultimate ends of virtuous behaviour (i.e. prudence, temperance, justice, etc.), all of which can be sought only by way of consistent, responsible, personal agency under particular social circumstances.[283] The good life, i.e. the road to human fulfilment, consists in the harmony of coherent natural aims that self-instantiate in each person's actions within society.[284]

Plurality of aims is generally the case and is often good, i.e. consonant with *natura humana*. Sometimes, however, the opposite is good too. First of all, not any aim is equally good: some can be better; some can be bad. Secondly, some aims can be good for everyone. Examples of coherent aims that are valuable and common to all humankind are "universal human rights", which Utz mentions as the most obvious and glaring negation of individualistic and cultural relativism.[285] Though differences among individuals and cultures do exist and may contribute to the proper functioning of human societies, there exists a fundamental shared ground, which the Thomist tradition would dub rational or natural. It is, in essence, the life-enabling ground identified by the Thomist "natural law" tradition, upon which human rights jurisprudence was developed over the centuries.[286]

As such, Utz's worldview and understanding stand opposed to traditions that separate sharply human beings into casts (e.g. Friedrich Nietzsche (1844–1900)), races (e.g. Joseph Arthur de

Gobineau (1816–1882)), orders (e.g. Adam Smith), makers/takers (e.g. Ayn Rand (1905–1982)), proletarians/bourgeois (e.g. Stalinism), and grant them accordingly different rights (e.g. classical liberals' opposition to universal suffrage), if any at all.

A Thomist Ethics of, and for, the Global Economy

Similarly, according to Utz, there may be differences among national economies, their laws, business environments and specific arrangements, but only economic organisations consistent with the nature of the human person can be good, as they succeed in establishing the specifically economic conditions facilitating each person's pursuit of happiness, or "perfection".[287]

Thus, after examining the various natural needs of humankind and the main varieties of economic order experimented with during the 20th century, the book concludes that "the only real" definition of an ethical economy, i.e. one "correspond[ing] to the integral economic ends of man", is the following: "*the competition economy, founded on the universal right to private property, both for production and consumption, with the greatest possible diffusion of productive property, with stability of price levels and full employment.*"[288] This definition is the only "real" one, even if it may not describe any concrete imperfect economy: "in anatomy, the physician does not define the sick man, but the healthy one."[289]

Utz's *Economic Ethics* comprises twelve chapters, which are conceptually ordered like a Gothic arch. After the preface, the first chapter articulates a lengthy introduction to possible definitions and studies of the economy, including an ethical study of it. The ensuing five chapters address, in light of Thomist ethics, seven fundamental categories that apply to any economy: (i) "order" or "system"; (ii) "rationality"; (iii) "need"; (iv–vi) "factors of production" (i.e. land, labour and capital); and (vii) "property".

Other basic economic categories—such as efficiency, growth, want and gain—are also addressed, but as corollaries of these seven. The seventh chapter, which constitutes a sort of apex within the volume, evaluates the main modern economic systems and significant varieties thereof. The successive short five chapters apply the critical wisdom produced in the previous ones to specific issues of modern market economies, e.g. inflation, currency speculation, structural unemployment.

A vast, thematically structured bibliography and two alphabetically organised critical indexes of, respectively, cited persons and cited topics, conclude the 379-page-long book. Helen Alford argues that mainstream economists are likely to find peculiar the thematic order and the areas of emphasis of Utz's book (e.g. a mere handful of pages on profit "in a book of 300 odd pages").[290] Yet both reflect the fact that the book is "about the *ethics*" of economics, not economics as such, as well as its intention to erect "a Thomist economic system" of great "breadth and coherence", which she claims Utz to succeed in, thanks to his "encyclopaedic knowledge".[291]

The book's preface, unlike most, contains some very important statements. Utz—he too unlike most thinkers—shows his philosophical cards from the very start. Instead of feigning neutrality or assuming uncritically theoretical presuppositions that may be shared by his audience and therefore taken as obvious, he states that the "ethics" to be applied in his book is a specific one, namely "the teleological ethics of Thomas Aquinas".[292] The reason for this choice is that, after "sixty-five years" of keen philosophical scholarship, "no other ethics" has proven to be nearly as "adequate in order to find the logical path leading from universally valid human norms to the correct solution of concrete practical problems".[293]

According to Utz, Aquinas' "natural law", which lies at the heart of the "universal human rights" cherished by most political and legal thinkers, is also the best theoretical framework to understand and defend them, leaving aside the "superficiality" and "dreadful ignorance" of many intellectuals, who discarded Aquinas' wealth of knowledge without truly studying it, e.g. "Hans Kelsen" (1881–1973).[294] If Utz's audience will listen to what he has to say, then it is good and well. If they will not, then Utz states that he is bound to sound like "the doctor of a patient suffering from addiction": correct, but unheeded.[295]

What does it mean to apply the teleological ethics of Thomas Aquinas to the field of economic phenomena? It means "to investigate more deeply than those who have a merely empirical viewpoint".[296]

First of all, insofar as we, by studying economics, study cases of voluntary human agency, then we must acknowledge that economics has always and inescapably "a moral background, even when the immediate object [of economic agency] is not of a moral nature".[297] All voluntary human agency, whether directly or indirectly, has origins (e.g. intentions) and repercussions (e.g. social effects) that are ethically laden.[298]

Secondly, following Aristotle's and Aquinas' understanding of human agency, there exist universal ends inscribed in nature, including human nature, which ethical reflection can identify. Knowing what these ends are, i.e. grasping "the meaning of creation and of the human being" and how economic agency can help us fulfil these ends, means that "the integral good of the human being" can be served, instead of a partial or a false one.[299] For instance, economists and businesspeople would be likely to welcome "the pure material success of capitalisation", as this is shown by a national economy's conspicuous growth, even if "one third of the persons seeking employment is left out of the labour process."[300] A Thomist assessment of the same "material success" would not, for capitalisation of this ilk harms both materially and spiritually the unemployed, their families and their communities, and therefore works against integral human goodness by causing, *inter alia*, "moral degradation… crime [and] addiction to narcotics".[301]

The Scientific Study of the Economy

In the first chapter, Utz defines the economy as "the activity whereby the human being" *qua* "corporeal being… meets the need for material goods in view of her own perfection", which, following Aristotle, is understood as the realisation of "her many potentialities".[302] Albeit each individual is free, "in general she is already inclined by nature towards her final end" i.e. "perfection" or "happiness".³⁰³ Were a person to "seek perfection outside her own nature", she would find none.³⁰⁴ Error is possible, in other words, for our nature is not perfect to begin with, nor is freedom a guarantee of its own good use.

For instance, were a healthy person to choose freely to seek perfection without consideration of the interpersonal fellowship or of the rational mind characterising our species, she would find none, as both loneliness and irrationality are pernicious to wellbeing, survival and, *a fortiori*, happiness. Happiness is the end towards which we are naturally inclined, but from which many men and women distance themselves in real life because of a plethora of deficiencies (e.g. lack of self-control, mistaken conceptions of the good, obtuse selfishness).

Natural inclination is not natural determination. Health, knowledge and understanding are needed, among other things, in order to increase the chances of recognising, accepting and pursuing genuine, natural happiness as our key existential goal. Utz's initial definition of the economy is then refined as follows: "the totality of those actions whereby the human being utilises the material goods in order to meet her vital and cultural needs".³⁰⁵

Given our social nature and the fact that we share "one and only one World", any real economy is bound to be "a social economy", i.e. "the cooperative utilisation of the material goods to meet the vital and cultural needs of *all*", as implied by commonplace phrases such as "common good, national wellbeing or shared interest".³⁰⁶

Whether this end is better served by a "communist or capitalist… form of organisation of the social economy" is yet to be seen at this stage of Utz's argument, but one important substantial conclusion is already reached. "Since humankind" is *de facto* "without temporal limits" and the "World" that we share is one and limited, "every economic community is duty-bound to use it with parsimony".³⁰⁷ The textbook distinction between "scarce" and "non-scarce" goods is merely contingent.³⁰⁸ In absolute terms: "All goods are limited as concerns the needs of the entire humankind".³⁰⁹ Most "economic science" is myopic in this respect, for it focuses upon limited time-frames, despite being traditionally keen on the notion of "scarcity" (e.g. textbook definitions of economics such as "Paul A. Samuelson['s]" (1915–2009)).[310]

The more an "economic good" does in fact "contribute to the fully human wellbeing of all", the higher is its "value", which must not be confused with its "price".[311] By "all" Utz means all: not only those who are presently "economically active", but also the inactive members of society (e.g. the infants, the elderly, the ill) and the "generations" to come.[312] Their "vital and cultural needs" must be computed too, which implies that a "rational" economy would not imperil the chances for a healthy and "socially ordered" existence of the human beings that will come after us.[313] Their future cooperative efforts to attain "human perfection, i.e. the common good" must be served too, even when this service may involve restrictions over present "liberty".[314]

Within any well-ordered society, norms that qualify and, at times, restrict freedom are necessary in order to pursue the common good. Liberty is a pivotal human aim, but Utz does not prioritise it uncritically above all others, unlike many liberals. After all, responsible acceptance of good restraints to freedom is a standard feature of Christian thought. Even from John Milton's (1608–1674) aggressively Protestant and anti-Catholic perspective, to seek freedom above all was Satan's misguided aim: "...*Here at least / We shall be free... Better to reign in hell, than serve in heaven.*"[315]

Another point of contention with liberalism is the claim whereby the "classic theory of the national economy" is allegedly "value-neutral".[316] According to Utz, this liberal theory does in fact "posit surreptitiously determined axiological premises", as these are captured in Alfred Marshall's iconic definition of *"homo economicus... who is under no ethical influences and who pursues pecuniary gain warily and energetically, but mechanically and selfishly"* whilst enjoying "formal liberty".[317] Albeit "unreal" and unpalatable, this free yet "morally perverted human being" helps us understand "socio-economic processes" in a "market economy", which is one of several possible economic orders that aim at serving the material needs of humankind.[318]

It suffices to say that, given such premises, classic economic theory can and does reveal important aspects of human agency in market economies, but misses out far too much to be able "to offer universally valid advice for concrete political economy" (i.e. policy-making), including significant aims of market agents that go beyond "the desire for profit", such as the "entrepreneurial drive" studied by "Joseph A. Schumpeter" (1883–1950).[319] Not to mention some of the major "contradictions" of unfettered market economies that Marx himself had correctly identified in the 19th century, such as "social misery", "paralysis of labour", "moral[,]… social[,]… [and] economic collapse", "corruption" and, as Utz adds on his part, the devastation of "the ecological pre-conditions for life".[320]

Political economy too, whether "philosophical" (e.g. Marx) or "empirical" (i.e. the study and "computation of costs and benefits resulting from different alternatives" open to political decision-makers under specific "social and political circumstances"), claims to be "value-neutral".[321] However, as Utz argues, political economy does in fact "take stock of the many possible aims and therefore also of the values" at issue in any and every "economic computation".[322] An axiology is present, then.

This axiology is even more visible as the economic computations are performed in the name of "efficiency", i.e. the actual chief aim of political economists, who prioritise it above all other aims, passing *ipso facto* an implicit "value judgment".[323] Besides, this implicit value judgment is ethically "debatable", not least because of its consequences for "distributive justice".[324] For example, wider wealth disparity is deemed acceptable for the sake of increased efficiency, despite its negative moral and social impact.[325] Such a debatable ethical character explains why, according to Utz, John Rawls (1921–2002) developed a novel criterion for the justification of wealth disparity, alternative to the "optimality" criterion devised by Vilfredo Pareto (1848–1923) and commonly endorsed by liberals. Even though implicitly biased in its axiological presuppositions, political economy remains primarily a descriptive science and, *per se*, "empirical data cannot produce ethical norms".[326] The determination of a "hierarchy" of "aims" within society is the province of philosophy, and ethics in particular, for such a hierarchy "can be known only *via* a[n explicit] moral judgment".³²⁷

"Ontological reflection" on economic phenomena can limit itself to studying "human behaviour *vis-à-vis* goods serving their survival and development", as many branches in the social sciences have been doing for generations.³²⁸ "Philosophical" ontological reflection, i.e. "economic ethics",³²⁹ must dig deeper, however, so as to unearth "which behaviour[s] can be defined 'according to nature'... in the sense of classic natural law theory".³³⁰ It is at this level of reflection, for instance, that we can grasp the socio-economic implications of "the catalogue of human rights emanated by the United Nations", which is not a mere list of "individual rights", but rather an articulate expression "of the collective duty to create the preconditions for the realisation of everyone's fundamental rights".³³¹

Understanding the quintessentially "social nature" of the human being can also lead us to appreciate as natural, for example, the human "desire to self-realise and develop by one's own agency and initiative, the search for a global juridical order... [and] solidarity".³³² More generally, the same understanding can help us realise how any ethics, including an economic ethics, cannot but be a social ethics too. Abstracting towards broader generality is not a move away from reality, but one into a more profound layer of the same—beneath, beyond and above data gathering, from which one must start, though, to avoid empty speculation.

Utz distinguishes three logical levels of reflection in economic ethics. The first one, "value theory", deals with "the supreme, most general and still very abstract norms of any economic activity".³³³ It is an Aristotelian "metaphysics of economics" focused upon the most fundamental personal and social aspects of *natura humana*.³³⁴ It is at this level, for example, that we can retrieve "the imperative commanding that the common good be higher than the private" good, which is in fact ordinarily justified on the basis of its beneficial social outcomes (e.g. eminent domain/compulsory purchase/resumption legislation; Adam Smith's assumption of a socially beneficial invisible hand).³³⁵ The second level deals with the "actual inclinations and modalities of human behaviour in its relationship with economic goods".³³⁶

Characteristically economic implications of *natura humana* are considered at this level, e.g. the paramount "organisational principle of economic planning" known as "private property", the "socially just economic order (or system)",[337] and the inability of centralised "State authority to capture the productive potential and willingness [to contribute] of the members of society".[338] The third level deals with "problems" affecting specific economic orders, such as "contractual autonomy[,]… just price formation[,]… credit, etc.", i.e. the typical issues of "business ethics" in Anglo-American academia.[339] Utz underlines how crucial it is to set in place a rational economic order, which prevents problems from arising (e.g. the conflict between the common good and "the desire for profit of the individual manager"), and *a fortiori* how it is up to "the politician… not… [t]he entrepreneur" to establish constructively rational "social conditions for the competitive economy".[340]

The first chapter continues and concludes with an overview and discussion of significant 19th- and 20th-century theological views on economics, both Catholic (Taparelli (1816–1890), Messner, John Paul II (1920–2005), liberation theology) and Protestant (Gerhard Weisser (1896–1989), Arthur Rich (1910–1992), Sigfried Katterle, Helmut Thielicke (1908–1986), Ellert Herms (b. 1940), the German Lutheran Church). In a positively Thomist perspective, Utz explains how "the harmony of reason and faith" can be established, arguing that the conclusions on economic ethics to be reached by a philosophical ontological investigation are bound to be consistent with those reached by a theological one, as long as the latter is conducted under the guidance of the Revelation in all of its forms.[341] Citing Saint Augustine (354–430), Utz states: "*anima humana naturaliter christiana*".[342]

Thanks to the wealth of wisdom offered by a Christian social ethics, Utz derives further normative elements conditioning the proper functioning of a sensibly designed market economy, i.e. one that works for and not against *natura humana* (e.g. Sunday rest, human dignity). According to Utz, a religious inquirer can grasp aspects that a purely technical approach to economic affairs would miss: "The pure market mechanism, which liberals invoke under the guise of a complete deregulation, is a failure with regard to social problems, especially unemployment. The person that is inspired by faith and oriented towards the afterlife has naturally, because of her conception of life, a different attitude *vis-à-vis* development and productivity than the one who thinks in purely economic terms."[343]

On this point, Giovanni Bertuzzi argues that Utz's book shows how Christians should not rely upon the Gospels alone for the understanding of socio-historical phenomena. The Thomist tradition offers "an objective abstraction-based knowledge[,]... natural law[,]... and the teleological interpretation of human ethics", all of which, albeit eventually consistent with revealed doctrine, spring out of reason, not faith.[344]

The Ethical Study of the Economy

In general, the existing literature about economic ethics assumes the existence and motivated "rational" agency of "individual[s]", who pursue their "self-interest" by way of cooperative behaviour, or "solidarity", in the economic sphere.[345] Liberals would like to reduce all relevant economic considerations to this level, i.e. "contractual" interactions among assumedly free individuals (e.g. "Friedrich A. Hayek" (1899–1992)).[346] All the justice they seek is commutative.

Socialists, on the contrary, typically subsume the existence and motivated rational agency of individuals under the higher level of social processes and collective values, which individuals are meant to serve in a more or less self-less manner. All the justice they seek is social (aka general or legal). Utz, in a consistent Thomist fashion, stands between these two poles, for he assumes, in addition to "individualism", the notion of "a common good to be realised through economic actions" undertaken willingly and responsibly by the individuals.[347]

Justice, as Aristotle and Aquinas had already argued, is both general and particular, and as the latter is concerned, it is not only commutative, but also distributive. Utz's book addresses repeatedly the notions of commutative and distributive justice, which are respectively fairness in the exchanges between individuals, and fairness in the distribution of goods and responsibilities among the same individuals. Aquinas described both forms of justice as the two species of *particular* justice, i.e. virtuous behaviour directed to the good of *individual* members of the community (e.g. specific customers, employers, spouses, etc.). Above them both stands *general* justice, i.e. virtuous behaviour directed to the *common* good i.e. the good of the *community* in which the individual members operate (e.g. being law-abiding citizens).

Following Aquinas' 19th-century scholar Taparelli, who mentored Pope Leo XIII (1810–1903) as Thomist specialist, Utz refers to general (aka legal) justice as "social justice" and claims it to have priority over particular justice: a dysfunctional society will inevitably fail the well-being of its individual members.[348] *Pace* today's dominant liberalism, before contracts among assumedly free individuals are considered, one must determine whether the "economic order" allowing for such contracts is morally justified.[349]

Whilst current business ethics presupposes "as obvious… the capitalist system" or "market economy", Utz's economic ethics does not.[350] According to him, if we wish to pursue a genuine ethical investigation of economic phenomena, rather than engage in mere "apologetics", we cannot presuppose the legitimacy of any existing economic order, but rather consider "the philosophical-anthropological premises determining the supreme norms of every systematic construction".[351]

The structure of the analysis to follow in the rest of the book is thus announced clearly under such premises: "I shall focus upon the problem of the economic order, starting with the issue of the common good, e.g. by wondering whether the [centrally] planned economy or the market economy correspond to the *a priori* principle of the common good, then which institutions may be essential in a market economy as demanded by the principle of the common good, and under which ethical conditions they must operate."[352]

Specifically, Utz speaks of "two stages" of analysis: "the general principles and the application to the concrete situation."[353] First of all, one must determine which abstract rules pertain to "human nature, in view of the universal common good"; then it will be possible to proceed to their application to specific national and international contexts, with due consideration for the "empirical data" that can be gathered.³⁵⁴ If insufficient caution is exercised with regard to national and international specificities, then "unrealistic and excessive expectations" can be forced upon "a nation", as exemplified by the one-size-fits-all approach of international financial organisations operating in the developing world.³⁵⁵

In this connection, Giovanni Pallanti highlights the importance of Utz's critique with regard to major negative side-effects of "globalisation", such as the increased job insecurity caused by the "pulverisation of productive systems" into a plethora of "flexible" contractual forms, the widespread varieties of denial of "labour rights" in the name of "competition", and the return of outright "exploitation" in "Asia, North Africa, Eastern Europe".³⁵⁶

Economic Rationality

Given the glaring and multifarious social failures of 18th- and 19th-century classical liberalism, constructive reforms have been sought repeatedly, including Walter Eucken's (1891–1950) "market social economy", which proved very influential in 20th-century German-speaking Europe.³⁵⁷ According to this conception of the economic order, next to the "purely economic rationality" *à la* Alfred Marshall (1842–1924) that liberal "economists far too easily overestimate", "the life norms of a society" are also to be considered, for they are bound to qualify, condition and even conflict with rational economic activities, hence co-determining their fate.³⁵⁸

Utz suggests that these "life norms", often exquisitely ethical in character (e.g. fairness, dignity, trust and duty in all domains of social life, business included), should be studied from a Thomist "rational-teleological" perspective, which would then allow to "harmonise" socio-ethical rationality and "economic rationality" in view of "a single definition of well-being".³⁵⁹ Thus, and thus only do we attain a rich, deep and true understanding of economic categories *qua* essentially "socio-economic"—indeed socio-ethico-economic— categories.³⁶⁰

For example, "productivity" should not be merely the entrepreneur's or planner's efficient use of available resources to meet existing demand, but also and above all the economy's ability to meet "the integral needs of all members of society... for example health[,]... culture[,]... future ecological needs[,]... labour rights[,] ... Sunday rest".[361] Similarly, a sound socio-economic "market order" would not simply tolerate and accept "just social requirements" because of their inevitability, but actually "stimulate... personal initiative and responsibility *via-à-vis* the establishment of [good/rational/natural] values".[362]

On an analogous note, proper economic "gain" should not be the satisfaction of whatever selfish pursuit the individual market actor may opt for, including "sheer speculation", but rather the deserved "remuneration for a rendered service contributing to the common good".[363] It is on the basis of, and in proportion to, the ability of an economy to be productive—just as *per* the examples above—that the legitimacy of any actual economic order can be gauged. Thus, Paolo Carlotti argues that Utz's Thomist interpretation of "financial ethics" leaves the concrete field of business agency open to many profitable operations, as long as "they allow and favour the adequate development of necessary economic functions" and, *a fortiori*, its "social aims".[364]

Failures, in this connection, abound, for allegedly rational economic behaviour can actually be nothing short of insanity. On the one hand, an unfettered "market economy" can lead to "the danger of the economisation of society", as witnessed already in the early days of liberalism.[365] Human beings are then attributed value solely as means to a profit, and their exploitation is positively sanctioned. However, according to Utz's Thomist analysis, the good economy is "a means for the realisation of life values", not of sheer pecuniary profit.[366]

On the other hand, a "planned economy", even if well-meaning and explicitly built upon ethically sound social aims, is bound to end in "bankruptcy because of its neglect of self-interest", which is a powerful natural drive to be taken most seriously in view of a rational organisation of society.[367] Productivity, meaningful self-direction and human dignity depend on it. The right path is somewhere in the middle. This middle ground is what Utz's "teleological rationality" aims for: individual self-interest is to be acknowledged, harnessed and steered towards the common good; it is not to be given into (e.g. the liberals' justification of callous selfishness), denied or underplayed (e.g. the socialists' rejection of private property).[368]

The intellectual "determination" of the natural "socio-ethical aims" of human life is paramount, for no economic system can transgress repeatedly and consistently "human nature" without leading to "undesirable and inadmissible results", as best exemplified by the Earth's "ecology", which both liberal economists and socialist economic planners neglected for generations.[369] Fundamental social equilibria must be paid heed as well. Thus Utz identifies additional, normatively relevant socio-ethical aims: "the free development... of every human being[,]... humane [and] dignified employment[,]... assistance to persons that are unable to work".[370]

These socio-ethical aims too must qualify and, if needed, limit the scope and the typology of allowed economic undertakings. Good norms are imperative. Given our imperfect nature, some stumbling along the logic of "trial and error" is bound to persist in the domain of socio-economic organisation.[371] Nonetheless, to possess a clearer notion of "the objectively founded aims of the economy" is going to reduce the number of trials and the degree of the errors to be encountered.[372]

Human Need and Economic Need

If the standard, textbook liberal notion of economic rationality is deemed inadequate to capture the social as well as the diverse natural aims of human life, equally inadequate is deemed the standard, textbook liberal conception of "human needs".[373] In this respect, according to Utz, the empirical research of "anthropologists, ethologists and psychologists" should be used in order to integrate, refine and correct that of "economist[s]", who seem prone to oversimplification because of factually unwarranted *a priori* thinking.[374] Furthermore, well beyond sheer empirical research, any serious "economic ethics" should reach back to "the essential determination, i.e. the abstract yet real nature of the human being".[375]

By doing so, it becomes possible, on the one hand, to discriminate between the natural and "unnatural" needs that comprehensive empirical research may come across (cf. Gerhard Merk's (b. 1931) distinction between "goods" and "non-goods";[376] and Utz's own distinction between "factual needs" and "latent" ones "activated" by ethically "disturbing" advertising).[377] In a later sub-section, Utz goes as far as to argue that market economies cultivate and exploit immature consumers that are very far from the rational self-interested individuals assumed by liberal textbooks: "Competition among producers degenerates into the advertising market, where the one who wins is the one that can afford the most expensive advertising", even if the sold "goods" are "harmful to the environment, the health, or the morality of society" (the influence of John Kenneth Galbraith on Utz's analysis of modern consumer societies is most evident here.)[378]

On the other hand, it also becomes possible to "assess their relative importance", e.g. "environmental needs" are "primary" under whatever economic order one may wish to establish,[379] and a starving man's need for bread has clear priority over the bread's well-fed owner's claim of private property (*ergo*, as Aquinas argued, its furtive acquisition is *not* "theft").[380] Granted such a richer, deeper and truer understanding of human needs, political decision-makers can produce, if willing, rational regulations, i.e. consistent with *natura humana*.

Utz agrees with the socialist economist Ota Šik on what constitutes *in abstracto* "universal human needs", that is, "fundamental material needs, needs of safety and health, needs of spiritual development, environmental needs, needs of psycho-physical self-realisation, social needs, needs of rest, needs of self-affirmation, needs of social activity".[381] However, he disagrees with Šik on whether even a reformed socialist economic order would be capable of being so efficient as to grant their satisfaction for all "members of society", whether they are able to participate in "the economic process" or not (e.g. minors, the unemployed, the gravely sick, the elderly, the severely handicapped, future generations).[382]

Socialist economies, like monastic orders, presuppose the members' agreement on "the common end as the end of their own lives".[383] Yet, the citizens of a socialist or, for that matter, of any other State have not made a free, thought-through and responsible decision to pursue such an end as their own. In fact, within any State, there can be considerable disagreement on, and diversity of, "worldviews".[384] This plurality of "worldviews", i.e. individual preferences and value-attitudes, is what the market order, unlike the socialist or "communist" one, can acknowledge and deal with, at least to a significant extent, through its polycentric productive and allocative processes.[385] That is why, according to Utz, market economies are better candidates than socialist ones *vis-à-vis* the universal satisfaction of genuine human needs.

Still, Utz does not praise market growth for growth's sake. Citing Aristotle, Augustine and Marx, Utz emphasises how humankind would be better off by needing less and better, rather than seeking endless increases of "productive force" to match insatiable wants, especially if these wants result from the marketing experts' "manipulat[ion]" of "demand".[386] Pursuing endless growth is blatantly unnatural, indeed irrational, as the World's ecology keep telling us. Rules and regulations of the market order are, then, *de rigueur*. Without them, "liberalism" can only face a "shipwreck" akin to the one suffered by communism in the 20th century.[387]

The Factors of Production

The application of a Thomist rational-teleological ethics to the economy means that, as done with the categories of rationality and need, also the standard understanding of "the factors of production" must change.[388]

To begin with, "land", i.e. "natural resources" in the broadest possible sense ("utilisable nature"), must be considered in light of the "super-temporal" needs of the human race, and not merely in light of the commonplace and yet myopic "economic interest limited in time" commanding its allegedly efficient and yet destructive exploitation.[389] Once again, Utz highlights the issue of long-term ecological sustainability.

Major emphasis is then placed by Utz on rethinking the second factor of production, i.e. "labour" (to which "management" can be reduced).[390] "Labour", whether "intellectual" or "bodily", must not be treated like "investments", which can be "cut or regulated" at will in order to generate higher returns.[391] Labour is "part of human activities" and, as such, it is ethically obligatory to "pay heed to the conditions under which human agency preserves its own human dignity".[392]

Starting with Aristotle's distinction between "*actio immanens*" (i.e. "an action that serves uniquely the perfecting of the agent" e.g. "play or sport") and "*actio transiens*" (i.e. "an action that produces an object that lies outside the agent" e.g. the "toiling and damaging" labour of "slaves"), Utz seeks a mediating conception of human labour.[393] His mediation reads as follows: "the human being, in her economic agency, creates a product that serves the ends of her own nature and that, for this reason, is valued by the members of society because of its utility (use value)".[394]

"Manchester liberalism", which Marx rightly rejected, was culpable of lacking "respect for the inseparability of labour *qua* factor of production" and "the moral essence of the human being", thus causing "workers' uprisings" and, eventually, harm to "the economy itself".[395] There exists therefore a "right to labour", which is not the right to having jobs created *ad hoc* for the unemployed by the State (as many socialists have argued), but the tangible expression of each person's rights "to sustenance[,]… self-affirmation within social cooperation… [and social] integration".[396] The fulfilment of this right is to be attained by means of a rational, comprehensive regulatory framework that facilitates job creation and, therefore, sets proper incentives and disincentives to all economic agents, such as "invest[ors], entrepreneurs and… even employed workers".[397]

It follows in practice from Utz's theoretical analysis that, within a well-regulated market economy, employment must be as broadly available as possible. It is only in this manner that most suitable individuals will take responsibility for their own self-perfection and participate constructively in the social generation of well-being *via* the economic sphere. Not any line of employment will do, though. This ideally full employment must be in activities that are ecologically (cf. what said about "land" above), socially (e.g. not leading to "uprisings") and economically sustainable in the long term (e.g. "humanised" working conditions allowing for the "reproduction" of the workforce).[398] It must be personally meaningful, since "pay alone" is not enough; there is a "spiritual root to all labour" (e.g. "the worker expects to achieve her own social integration" or "social status" through her labour).[399] It must be consistent with the fundamental human needs (e.g. "family life… [and] culture"), aims (e.g. "self-realisation") and dignity of each human person.[400] That is why, in practice, there exist "labour legislation or workers' protection", e.g. binding norms on "free time[,]… safety[,]… hygiene[,]… prevention of accidents[,]… unemployment benefits[,]… [and] special protections for women and children".[401]

That is also why there exist internationally codified universal social, economic and cultural rights to be respected, protected and fulfilled. Though costly in the short- and medium term from the perspective of a firm's bookkeeping, to do away with such binding norms and internationally codified universal rights would mean doing away with workers' human dignity. No society and, *a fortiori*, no economic order could operate for long under such inhumane and undignified conditions, which would also destroy the humanity and hence the dignity of the workers' exploiters and their academic legitimisers.

The reader should recall, for example, the classical liberal Drummond professor of political economy William Nassau Senior (1790–1864) who, when told that a million Irishmen had already died in the potato famine (1845–1849), famously replied: "It is not enough!"—the iron law of supply and demand had not yet run its full course.[402] Or consider Adam Smith, who had argued in his 1776 *Wealth of Nations*: "in civilized society it is only among the inferior ranks of people that the scantiness of subsistence can set limits to the further multiplication of the human species; and it can do so in no other way than by destroying a great part of the children which their fruitful marriages produce."[403] Not to mention Larry Summers' infamous 1991 memo, which the reader has already encountered in this book (cf. notes 210 & 211 in particular).

Contra all such individualistic and literally homicidal understanding of rational economic agency, Utz states: "the individual good must be integrated within the collective good", that is, whatever businesses and jobs are in place, they must serve the natural aims of human life.[404] It is only under such a rational, comprehensive regulatory framework, i.e. "a juridically ordered economic society", that there can be "freely stipulated... labour contract[s]" as those advocated by the liberal tradition and, more broadly, an ethically justified market order.[405]

Much progress has been made since the callous 'iron laws' of classical liberalism and the industrial horrors of "Manchester liberalism", but much remains to be done, according to Utz. For one, "international competition leads often to violations of humane labour policies".[406] For another, "abrupt technological revolution[s]" cause frequently "the social misery of workers".[407] The respect of the workers' "teleological" claim over "production", in addition to the commonly recognised "causal" one, finds still little acknowledgment in legal and business practice (e.g. workers' "co-management" of enterprises being rare).[408]

On top of this, "growing capitalisation creates over time a mass of unemployed", and although socially responsible "unemployment benefits" may soften the blow, "the problem is not at all resolved" at its root.[409] Indeed, according to Utz, "given the international economic network" emerged with globalisation, "the imperative of the complete respect of the personal-individual character of labour cannot be fulfilled" today.[410]

Utz reiterates his critique of "sudden" and "complete opening of the markets" in the seventh chapter: "each individual national economy was born out of particular social conditions, which cannot be changed abruptly without social and political shocks".[411] Also, delocalisation into Third-World countries, the US pressures over the EU to establish a common agricultural market despite the US' less healthily regulated agricultural sector, and the corporation-friendly processes of "GATT and European unification" are all criticised in light of their nefarious "social consequences".[412]

In particular, Utz singles out "unemployment", "the exploitation of poor populations", necessity-driven "immigration", and "identity loss" in the socio-cultural and political spheres,[413] which is reinforced in his *Political Ethics*, as he expresses preoccupation *vis-à-vis* migration from Muslim countries and doubts on its effective integration within Europe.[414]

As regards "capital" (to which "technology" can be reduced),[415] Utz argues that any "economic ethics" trying to be "general" must start with "a definition" that does not "presuppose a given economic or social system".[416] At this level of abstraction, "capital" cannot be "productive investments" and even less "money", both of which presuppose socio-historically specific institutions.[417] Therefore, the definitions offered by Smith, Weber, Schumpeter and Eucken are rejected by Utz because too system-specific. Only Eugen Böhm-Bawerk's (1851–1914) definition is praised, since it would apply "even to Robinson Crusoe".[418]

Following Böhm-Bawerk's lead, capital's "original concept" is defined by Utz as "a reserve of useful services withdrawn from immediate use",[419] or "useful service detracted from immediate consumption".[420] *Qua* "factor of production... capital is not a 'thing', but rather the function of a thing".[421] In this perspective, even a Robinson Crusoe must put aside resources (e.g. food, seeds, timber, time and labour) that, later on, will enable him to produce further means of survival. "Savings" are then the heart of "capital", i.e. "the presupposition for the possibility of operating on the means of production".[422] *Contra* Keynes, Utz claims that "savings come before investment, not vice versa".[423]

From an Aristotelian perspective, "productive investments" are "capital only 'potentially'", for they must find adequate "demand", which can be absent, as Keynes rightly argued this time.[424] "[T]he actualisation of means of production" constitutes "capital", in an Aristotelian perspective.[425] Commenting on this point of Utz's *Economic Ethics*, Ferruccio Marzano argues that Keynes' actual ethico-economic stance was close to Utz's, especially as regards the social functions of "money and credit", the disruptive nature of unfettered financial speculation, and the economic key-role of "savings" and individual "responsibility".[426]

In a broader, more complex society, this abstract notion of "capital" implies that a rational regulatory framework must be set up so as to save adequate resources to be employed in later forms of production meeting actual demand and "leading to a useful growth that benefits the whole population", present as well as future.[427] "[E]nvironmental needs" are once more highlighted most forcefully in this context, for both so-called "capitalist" and socialist economies (or "State capitalism") have been culpable of pursuing alleged efficiency whilst sacrificing the "nourishing basis for the production of the means of production", i.e. they have "failed to save".[428]

Similarly, large-scale debts and expenditures, both public and private, are criticised by Utz, for they erode the "capital formation" needed for future useful production.[429] In a rational market economy, all economic agents, i.e. "investors", "entrepreneurs", "State authorities" and "workers" (especially through their "trade unions"), must be free to operate in a self-interested manner, i.e. with their own particular good in mind.[430] However, they must do so truly *within reason*, that is, within a regulatory system that prevents excessive debt and expenditures and that aims at the "real utility for the economic society" in the long term, i.e. with the common good in mind.[431]

It is only under such premises of sound "political economy" that one can justify "interest" on borrowed credit—a historically thorny matter for Christian scholars.[432] In order not to be usury or speculation, interest on borrowed credit must be the just remuneration for a rendered service, namely the provision of "real capital", i.e. "a nourishing basis" for the "production of [further] means of production" benefitting the common good.[433] It may be olfactorily true that, as the Romans said, *pecunia non olet*, but it does not mean that "capital formation" is devoid of "an ethical role".[434] According to Utz, it too must serve eventually "the perfection perceived in human nature", for its use to be ethically justified.[435]

Private Property

Utz's principled revision of basic economic categories tackles property too. Given the importance of this notion, and rather unusually for this book, Utz offers in the sixth chapter an ample historical overview of the main conceptions and justifications for different property regimes. The list of thinkers cited and discussed is extensive, somewhat uneven, and certainly stimulating. It goes from Plato (ca.425–347 BC), Aristotle and the Stoics in classical antiquity to Marx, Taparelli and Rawls in times closer to us, whilst also dealing with philosophers as diverse as Francisco Suárez (1548–1617), Hugo Grotius (1583–1645), Samuel Pufendorf (1632–1694), Christian Wolff (1679–1754) and Christian Thomasius (1655–1728) —among others.

Conceptual differences, but also continuities, are retrieved across the centuries. Some are pleasantly surprising, such as the early Church Fathers' "paradisiac state" and "the original position" in Thomas Hobbes (1588–1679), John Locke, Jean-Jacques Rousseau (1712–1778) and John Rawls, or Karl Marx's primeval communist societies.[436] Others are intriguingly insightful, e.g. modern contractualists' abstraction from actual individual peculiarities in their thought experiments about "the original position" as "masked natural-law reasoning" i.e. closet metaphysics.[437]

The centrepiece is, however, Thomas Aquinas' conception and justification of private property, to which Utz devotes four subsections.[438] The emphasis placed on Aquinas' understanding is due primarily to Utz's belief in its ability to offer a point of equilibrium between the ancient approach, which focuses on the needs of society at large or "the common good", and the modern one, which focuses instead on the "property rights" of individuals endowed with private ownership, especially but not exclusively in the liberal tradition of Locke, Smith, Hayek, Buchanan (1909–2013) and Friedman.[439]

The former approach lacks specificity on individual rights and cannot guide "the praxis" of concrete social organisations *vis-à-vis* "easily controllable property relationships removed from any arbitrary authority, whether the legislator's or the administrator's".[440] Too much emphasis on general justice jeopardises particular justice. In the name of socially valuable aims, the former approach can allow, "one piece at the time[,]… the destruction of the order of private property, without a definite criterion delimiting the justification of State intervention".[441]

The latter approach, on its part, concentrates too much upon the claims of individuals who already own property and neglects "those who wish to become property owners[,]… the workers[,]… those who seek employment" and, more broadly, "the utility of all human beings", present and future, who may not have any "capital" at their disposal, or whose fundamental needs may not be served by owning any.[442] Too much emphasis on commutative justice jeopardises general justice.

Utz's present fears about global dehumanisation by way of societies' "economisation" and the past horrors of "Manchester liberalism" loom largely in the background.[443] For one, even if a competitive market economy can produce and allocate resources efficiently across much of society, it does not secure *per se* genuine "universal wellbeing, in a humanistic and not only material sense".[444] Good rules and regulations are needed to secure this kind of wellbeing. For another, as Utz writes, persons "are not machine[s] that can be thrown away" once they no longer bring in profits: "rebellion" and its attendant "social costs" are the likeliest outcomes of short-term profit-maximisation by way of economic exploitation, exclusion and insecurity.[445] A more balanced position is required, which is what, according to Utz, Aquinas can help us find.

By no means individualistic and contractualistic in the modern fashion, Aquinas' metaphysical approach makes use of the classical notion of "common good", but it also includes a line of argument whereby "the absolute necessity to administer rationally the goods in view of economic productivity" leads to the justification of private property *qua* "individual… right".[446] On a general, "metaphysical" hence fundamental or "real" level, Aquinas acknowledges the "duty to consider material goods as a gift from God for the advantage of the whole humankind and to behave accordingly."[447] Given her "rational nature", the human being was "chosen" by God as "master of the World… so that she uses it in view of the ends proper to her nature."[448] Rational creatures ought to make a rational use of the existing resources, i.e. in view of rational ends, which reflect the rational order of the universe created by God's supreme rationality.

Accumulation of wealth for its own sake, or callous and undignified disparities in ownership and derived life-capacity, are irrational, i.e. contrary to human nature, which too ought to express the divine order of the universe. As Utz observes, liberals themselves acknowledge this fact implicitly, indirectly, yet frequently, whenever they admit of the citizens' duty to perform military service "in case of war" or as they seek, as they always do, the justification of their own policies as beneficial to "the common good".[449]

On a specific, historical and pragmatic level, the best system that can secure the goal of using rationally the existing resources for the sake of the common good is, according to Aquinas, one based upon private property. Here, Aquinas no longer thinks of humankind in general, metaphysically, or 'really'. Rather, he thinks of concrete individuals under contingent socio-historical circumstances, such as those of the "fallen natural state" of humankind, whereby the "deplorable… inclination… to accord preference to one's own good over the common good" has become almost as "natural" as our inherent rationality,[450] a "quasi-nature".[451] Taking stock of this situation, hence thinking 'realistically' rather than just 'really', how can anyone "procure" the material goods needed for "bodily sustenance"?[452] And how should she "use" them, once they have been procured?[453]

As regards the first question, Aquinas argues that a system of private property is preferable to one of "communal property", e.g. those of ancient "Sparta and Taranto", about which Aristotle had written in his *Politics*.[454] Private property "spurs [individual] industry, hence... productivity"; it identifies clearly who is "the responsible person" for given goods and services, and therefore "allows for a better administration devoid of confusion"; and it secures "social peace" by avoidance of "disagreements" thanks to clear "legal bounds" on who owns what.[455]

As regards the second question, the answer ties back into the metaphysical level and the rational aims fulfilling *natura humana*. Even if "held in private hands... all existing goods maintain their original destination, i.e. they must serve all human beings."[456] Therefore, even if "the owner may dispose of her possessions as she wishes", she is under "the grave obligation of helping those in need".[457] As already recognised by the Church Fathers and, later, by Pope Leo XIII, the founder of the SDC, "in the use of their property, the wealthy must be considered administrators, not owners"[458]—and a just administration of their wealth implies "the sustenance of the poor".[459]

Similarly, existing pecuniary reserves, once their owners' "own use and production" have been satisfied, should be made available to "social productivity" as an ethical imperative.[460] This moral duty has hefty legal repercussions. For example, a person that, "fallen in a state of need", stealthily alienates some of an unhelping wealthy person's goods, is no criminal.[461] By failing to meet her "moral duty", the wealthy person "loses her right over those goods".[462]

Costly legal, judiciary and administrative institutions must be established too, in order to ensure that "social justice" is actually served, for "social justice" has "priority over market law" i.e. "commutative justice", as exemplified by: unemployment benefits funded by a money pool in which "all enterprises" participate;[463] a tax-based "common fund" aimed at integrating the income of low-paid workers so that they are able to provide for "a family";[464] and a centrally administered monitoring and steering authority that, by means of "fiscal" dis/incentives, leads to "the productive use of the land" (cf. Summers's 1991 memo as a reasoning based on commutative justice alone, devoid of social justice).[465]

Fundamentally, as Utz states later in the book, "the order of private property" is justified because it serves "social ends".[466]

Economic Systems

No "economic order" or "system" can exist "without plans", according to Utz.[467] Individuals, businesses and societies, unless pathologically lazy or mad, plan ahead all the time. Which forms of planning, however, are the most likely to "overcome or, at least, lessen the burden of the scarcity of goods, in order to meet the needs"?[468]

In order to find an answer to this interrogative, Utz outlines and discusses the main known paradigms of economic order, i.e. the liberal and the socialist, and some varieties thereof, assessing their strengths and weaknesses. The result is the longest and possibly most complex chapter in the whole book.

Four economic aims are particularly important in Utz's ethical analysis of economic systems, i.e.:

(i) "price stability" *qua* "duty of justice towards the saver";
(ii) "full employment" *qua* "human right to labour";
(iii) a "well-ordered balance of payments" *qua* "justice… [towards] partner States"; and
(iv) "continuous growth" *qua* "duty of the human being to pursue self-perfection".[469]

In light of the revised economic categories tackled in the previous chapters, Utz's understanding of these four aims is different from the one found in mainstream economics' textbooks. For one, "saving" applies to the "correct use" of "ecological goods" rather than to mere money with which a consumer could buy "environmentally harmful… luxury comforts".[470] "Growth", on its part, cannot be "merely economic", i.e. measured by the sheer volume of produced and/or traded goods and services, but must also include our "human perfection[,]… a growing knowledge of the universe[,]… spiritual values… [and] social costs",[471] "the axiological ends of the human being[,]… the environment[,]… access to labour… [and] the living standards of the whole society."[472]

As regards the market economic order of the liberal tradition, Utz tackles first classical and neoclassical economics, the latter with reference primarily to Hayek. Utz praises "the liberal vision... of the pure market economy" for "constructing logically" a "theoretically valid... argumentative scheme of the market economy" based upon "self-interest".[473] Utz stresses the theoretical coherence leading from the 18th- and 19th-century philosophical roots of "sensualism" and "individualism" to the political and economic doctrine of "liberalism".[474] On the basis of such roots, "altruism" was deemed inadequate to form the basis for a well-functioning "ramified network of interactions, particularly in the field of economic agency", and the "self-interest" of "private" economic agents was therefore taken to be the prime "motive of human commitment" in society.[475]

An alternative system of "commutative justice alone" emerged then, demanding "perfect competition" and "rational price formation", so that it is possible for "the goods required for the universal satisfaction of needs to be produced in the most economic manner", i.e. for the "parsimoniously" generated "supply" to meet most "efficiently" its corresponding "purchasing demand".[476]

Within this system, "value", hence "social value" too, means the "price" of goods and services supplied, as their price is determined by the demand of "purchasers or consumers".[477] This determination applies to all forms of "goods", including "labour", "land" and "capital",[478] and must operate free from price-distorting State interference on both "national" and "international" levels.[479] Under this perspective, "private" agency is paramount and preferable to that of public authorities at all levels, including "social security", "unemployment" remedies, "pensions" and "expecting mothers' protection on the workplace".[480]

Albeit a mere abstract "image" or "idea", many liberals have believed this system to be "ethically justified, because of its economic efficiency" and therefore worthy of being pursued in reality in a "total", if not totalitarian, implementation.[481] Were their abstract idea a real one, in the Thomist sense of reality, then it could be a valuable operation. However, according to Utz, the liberal idea is deficient.

Liberals may believe that they are depicting an image akin to the anatomist's perfect abstraction of a healthy body, but in actuality their depicted body is a mutilated one. Undoubtedly, self-interested "individualism" has firm roots in reality, as also shown by the widespread "loss of honesty" characterising "the modern age".[482] As such, it cannot be excluded from view, like the Marxists would like to do. However, it is equally true that "individualism" misses out many other aspects of human nature that, *pace* Hayek,[483] allow for the notion of "common good" to be intelligible and reasonable, our natural sociability *in primis*.[484] It is not possible to reduce "society" to the "individualistic... market only", lest we wish to face unbearable contradictions.[485]

For example, liberals miss out the participation of human beings in a greater ecological order, which cannot and must not be sacrificed to "unlimited growth" as "the supreme end of political economy".[486] Unless we intend to face worldwide environmental, social and, *a fortiori*, economic collapse, standard economic criteria for "growth" must be revised radically.[487]

As Utz observes, thus defusing *ab initio* any controversy on climate change, no major novel scientific discovery is needed to understand this point: "That cars pollute was known since the beginning... The same goes for oil-powered heating".[488] Nothing less than "the moral renewal of society is necessary to save the market economy" from sheer short-term self-interest, which has led to profitable venues being sought relentlessly without consideration for long-term ecological effects.[489] For one, industrial "research" in market economies has been geared towards "the most powerful engines... the most comfortable heating systems", not towards "renewable energy sources".[490] In actual market economies, "industry" keeps resisting "change... because of the previous investments that have been made" and for "fear of unemployment".[491]

As Utz concludes, a viable "compromise" between standard self-interested economic behaviour and an enlightened notion of the common good should be pursued, which makes an ecologically sound use of "taxes[,]... interest rates" and "subsidies (*contra* the theory of the pure market economy)" in order to attain an "ethically correct growth" aiming "at the global human ends."[492] *Pace* the liberal idea of *homo economicus*, "the individual must be able to think beyond her own self-interest in order to save the market economy."[493]

Utz argues that liberals self-contradict when dealing with the issues of "unemployment" and "poverty".[494] If it is true, as liberals assume, that "the individual with her desires must be the norm for common behaviour", why should the unemployed or the poor be prevented from taking over the existing institutions, notably the State, and using them to improve their lot?[495] Liberals claim that these individuals should not seek market-distorting means of coercive wealth "distribution" and wait until "growth" will deliver improvements.[496] Why should they wait, however, if individual self-interest is the fundamental norm? And for how long should they wait exactly, if they are willing to pay some heed to the liberals?

There are countries in the world where poverty has been the legacy of several successive generations, despite liberal institutions being the norm in the economic sphere (Utz is thinking here of the US).[497] At this point, "the individualistic principle placed at the beginning of the argument in favour of economic efficiency... is abandoned".[498] Utz reveals how the key-criterion at work here is not concrete individual self-interest, but the "highest possible growth" of the "economy as a totality".[499]

As long as economic growth is attained in accordance with the liberals' criteria, flesh-and-blood individuals can endure prolonged "martyrdom" by way of, *inter alia*, "unemployment" and ruthless exploitation on the workplace.[500] The self-interested "individual" about whom liberals speak so much is no concrete human being, but the abstract "*homo economicus*" of their aprioristic textbooks and theoretical models.[501]

This liberal fiction, according to Utz, will not do. In order to function on a vast scale and over the long period, the "market economy" requires "human beings with a certain ethical and cultural level" of competence and performance.⁵⁰² It is only in this way that they will pursue "a common rational exploitation of the resources" available to them and "advance" beyond the present condition, guided by a "high degree of responsibility[,]... enthusiasm in personal initiative and the willingness to offer personal performances" of the highest standard.⁵⁰³ *Homo economicus* does not possess all these attributes and inclinations. A far richer and more complex socio-cultural milieu generates the kind of individuals that a well-functioning market economy requires to come about, function and endure.⁵⁰⁴

Again, on top of being self-contradictory, the image of the self-interested individual lying at the heart of the liberal paradigm is shown to be severely incomplete. According to Utz, "the stability of the market economy depends on the moral behaviour of the members of society: honesty and responsibility" *in primis*: "The more wanting the respect of the moral conditions becomes, the more necessary prohibitions become and the more expensive the economic process turns out to be."⁵⁰⁵

Former US president Barack Obama claimed an "ethic of greed" as the prime cause of the 2008 international financial meltdown.⁵⁰⁶ In this perspective, Utz's stance resembles Michael Polanyi's idea that "public liberties" are prior to "private liberties", insofar as a freedom-loving citizen must be committed to a certain set of social values (e.g. beauty, justice, knowledge) in order to enjoy room for personal idiosyncrasy, eccentricity, obsession and isolation, which are justifiable only if they eventually benefit society.⁵⁰⁷

After exploring and exploding the contradictions of liberalism in its classical and neoclassical versions, Utz tackles one variety of liberal thinking and economic policy that has tried to deal with the many elements of human nature forgotten by the classical and neoclassical versions, i.e. the social market economy (hereafter SME) of Walter Eucken, Alexander Rüstow (1885–1963) and, "above all", Alfred Müller-Armack (1901–1978).⁵⁰⁸

Unlike classical and neoclassical liberalism, SME conceives of a market system that takes place within a set of well-specified legal, social, political and economic conditions that State authorities establish, monitor and enforce throughout, such as "an austere monetary order[,]… competitive credit[,]… State policy for competition[,]… labour and social rights[,]… environmental protection[,]… land planning[,]… consumer protection[,]… direct assistance to individual enterprises on a regional or typological basis, etc."[509]

In particular, SME allows and aims for a "first distribution" of income that "occurs within the economic process as wages and profits", as well as for a "second distribution" reaching all those members of society that cannot participate in the first one, e.g. "the ill, the elderly, families, etc."[510] Within any society, there are individuals whose particular preferences are efficiently reflected in market transactions, but also "those who have no purchasing power… the unemployed" and economically dependent persons whose "needs" too must be "met".[511] If only a privileged section of society benefits from the liberal economic system, then it is arduous to see the "ethical justification of the commutative justice underpinning the market."[512]

Albeit appreciated by Utz for its holistic socio-ethical understanding, SME fails to tackle two major flaws of the liberal approach, with which SME has historically sided (SME is also known as ordo*liberalism*).[513]

On the one hand, by accepting international competition and "flexible labour contracts" as positive givens of a well-functioning market economy, SME fails to notice how the global competitive system brings wreckage upon "national economies", to the point of causing dramatic "sociological" and "political" consequences.[514] According to Utz, a worldwide market economy puts such a "pressure" on the "level of wages" that these can "drop to the minimum needed for subsistence, if not below", which is a recipe for massive social and political instability.[515] Moreover, whilst legally weak countries are selected by transnational businesses for their competitive low costs of production, stronger ones suffer waves of "unemployment" by way of delocalisation, loss of investments and inability to compete.[516] These horrors being absent from view or neglected, SME's emphasis is set squarely on the fear of "inflation" instead, thus reflecting the chief preoccupation of moneyed individuals rather than, say, the working poor or the unemployed.[517]

On the other hand, SME accepts the trade unions' "taboo" institutions of "universally binding labour contracts" and labour disputes by way of "strike and closedown" *qua* normal features of the market order, even if they are disruptive (e.g. harmful to production), ethically dubious (e.g. akin to extortion) and, above all, conceivably replaceable with sounder alternatives (e.g. Ota Šik's socialism).[518] The combined result of international competition and the trade unions' power of blackmail is structural "unemployment" which, in the end, cannot be paid for by social provisions, since international competition reduces the resources available to State authorities, such as taxation and inflationary monetary largesse.[519]

Keynesianism is treated briefly by Utz as a variation on the liberal theme. It is stated that, in its original formulation, it correctly individuated the "significance of demand", hence seeking a solution to a glaring and recurring market failure, to be contrasted by "increasing the money supply" for some time; doing it indefinitely would lead to skyrocketing "inflation", however.[520] As such, Keynesianism was primarily a temporary solution to one specific problem of the liberal order, not a new overall conception. In its "post-Keynesian" developments, it is praised by Utz as much more realistic than either classical or neoclassical liberalism, for it is capable of considering "the effective constellations of power within society and the economy[,]... the family[,]... regional, social and cultural units and institutions".[521]

Still, no distinction is drawn by post-Keynesians between "mutable" and "immutable" socio-economic institutions in the way "natural law" would do (e.g. "matrimony and family"); nor have they developed a critique of "the classic liberal conception of growth", which is "economic" only in a most short-sighted sense (e.g. growth leading to greater human fulfilment *versus* growth that is life-destructive; cf. once more Summers' 1991 memo on international trade of toxic waste or McMurtry's distinction between economic goods and bads).[522]

Utz introduces then the "socialist market economy" (hereafter

OS) of Ota Šik as a better, albeit little known, combination of purely economic goals and socio-ethical concerns. Even if Šik does not use the term, OS can be deemed "socialist" because it does not entail "private property in the sense and forms of [standard] market economies" and it is critical of "capitalist... systems" in general.[523] OS takes seriously the liberals' "self-interest" *qua* chief human motive, but also SME's acknowledgment of the "major importance" of the "State... for macro-level equilibrium", plus the traditional socialist emphasis on "planning".[524]

According to OS, minor "micro-level disequilibria" are part of normal business life and generally acceptable, but major "macro-level" ones require substantial State monitoring and careful planning by the public authorities.[525] Without such monitoring and planning, "income distribution" goes astray.[526] Specifically, OS observes a systematic "disequilibrium" at the macro level between "supply" and "demand" in the capitalist economic order.[527] This disequilibrium is caused by the capitalists having the upper hand in market economies, where entrepreneurs and stockholders enjoy too large a portion of the pie produced therein, hence leaving the workers with too small a portion of it.

As a result of this disequilibrium, the historical experience of capitalist economies has shown repeatedly how the wealthy seek further profits by means of destabilising speculative manoeuvers and/or industrial "overinvestments".[528] (OS does not tackle "the oppressive debt" induced by "the abuse of consumer credit", which Utz also acknowledges as a sign of disequilibrium between supply and demand.)[529] The latter are investments aimed at production and pecuniary gain that are unmatched by the workers' actual "wages", which inexorably "lag behind" and therefore lead into crises of "overproduction", i.e. a macro-level mismatch between supply and demand, as also signalled waves of dramatic "unemployment".[530]

As a first, fundamental solution to these problems, OS advises "income distribution" not to be left to the market, but rather carefully "regulated" by the democratically elected authorities, e.g. by means of equal "retributions" for all workers performing the same job, wherever that may be.[531] This way, private demand would be increased by better wages, to which OS adds also better pensions and targeted investments coordinated by State authorities.[532]

Additionally, the democratically controlled State authorities should make sure that environmental and workplace regulations are enforced too, as well as shorter working hours for the sake of "full employment".[533] This democratic macro-level regulation applies also to the "profits of the enterprise", of which workers should become co-owners.[534] This is OS' second fundamental solution to the problems of capitalist economies. Property must not be 'aristocratically' concentrated in a few hands, but 'democratically' distributed as widely as possible. In this way, the opposition between employers and employees can be abolished, so that the paralysing industrial conflicts arising from such an opposition are abolished too, whilst at the same time allowing the citizens to acquire more balanced, less sectarian "motivations" in politics.[535]

"Democracy" must then apply in the economic sphere, not just in the political one, according to OS.[536] This is possibly OS' most 'radical' point. According to OS, a new, well-functioning economic system is not going to arise by the mere mixing of elements from the liberal and socialist camps, but from deeper changes in the "political order" and the "mentality" of economic actors.[537]

As 'radical' as it may be, Utz himself recommends letting workers "participate" in the "formation" and "ownership" of "capital" in a "market economy", so that they too be personally "co-responsible" for its proper, productive use.[538] This is in fact a tenet of the SDC that has had a small impact on business life (e.g. cooperatives), which mostly takes employers and employees as two tribes at war with each other. Utz claims this bellic conception of industrial relations to be the "original sin" of historical market economies, where "capitalists, for the sheer sake of profit, refused capital formation in the workers' hands."[539] The opposition between "capitalist-entrepreneurs" and "workers" ensued, which continues today with its chaotic legacy of uncooperative and conflictual "class spirit".[540]

Utz claims OS to be an innovative and intelligent proposal, which is not immune to critique, however. As Utz argues, the State is granted by Šik considerable power to exercise "pressure" on the private sector, as well as to decide "retribution levels and investment quotas".[541] This would be all good and well, if and only if democracy's chief pitfall did not exist, i.e. the voters' diverse "motivations" and, above all, their diverse short-term self-interests, which could be in mutual agreement only under the unrealistic condition of equal distribution of property among them.[542]

According to Utz, economic systems where the State possesses the undemocratic power to enjoy the "central planning of the economy" are even less likely to succeed.[543] First of all, such systems fail to recognise the just and productive institution of "private property" and the self-interested "motivation of the persons involved in the economy" as fundamental to any economic order.[544] Secondly, by doing so, these systems' pursuit of "efficiency" and human "happiness" has always ended in failure: "until now, no centrally planned economy has ever succeeded in fulfilling its own proposed plans."[545]

Upon the basis of the previous six chapters and of his extensive analyses and critical assessments in the seventh chapter, Utz concludes by offering the "only real… healthy… ethico-economic definition of the economic order: *"the competition economy, founded on the universal right to private property, both for production and consumption, with the greatest possible diffusion of productive property, with stability of price levels and full employment."*[546]

Supply and Demand

The "justification" for the "existence" of the "market economy" pivots around the issue of whether it can also address "those who, for whatever reason, have no purchasing power".[547] "[C]lassical theory" focussed on "supply" so much that it became incapable of understanding and dealing with the problems proper to "demand", including noticing those who may not exercise any (cf. Jean-Baptiste Say (1767–1832) and John Stuart Mill (1806–1873)).[548]

John Maynard Keynes, studying in depth the issue of "unemployment", offered a significant and substantial integration of the liberal paradigm.[549] Still, not even the State's injections and withdrawals of "investments" and "credit" for the sake of "full employment" and, with it, the balance between market "supply and demand" can address clearly and fully the issues of a "socially" and environmentally "sustainable economic growth", i.e. a growth that is truly consistent with *natura humana*.[550]

Quite the opposite, by lack of adequate axiological criteria, Keynesianism remains trapped within a logic of indiscriminate "consumption" that, especially *via* the powerful means of modern "advertising", leads to life-disabling consequences on both individual and collective levels.[551] Its "ethics of demand" is flawed.[552] And so is its "ethics of supply", for no genuine commitment is present therein to "the integral human good", but only a competitive scramble for "profits" that, inherently, "knows no morals".[553] Buoyant and balanced buying and selling of goods is all that liberals can perceive as good, including Keynesians. Utz helps us gauge instead the distinction between natural and unnatural goods, i.e. good and bad goods.[554]

No intrinsic logic of the market economy, or consequence thereof, serves specifically or primarily the good of *natura humana*, as amply shown by past (e.g. Manchester liberalism) as well as present forms (e.g. car-related pollution) of capitalism. Pressured by morally enlightened persons, the State alone can introduce, monitor and enforce rational "laws... directing supply towards the common good".[555] International competition works against State regulations, however. Entrepreneurs, seeking profits in a larger and increasingly competitive business environment, and managers, pressured by the imperative of maximising stockholder value, will resist, bend, circumvent and break the law, or move to countries where none or more "permissive" laws can be found.[556]

As Utz concludes, a "socially" and "ecological[ly]... just" economic order requires the enforcement of rational "regulation" at the "global level".[557]

Money and Credit

"Money" *qua* "universal and atemporal means of exchange" is understood by Utz as both a "claim over goods of the same value" and "a legal right to participate in the fruits of socio-economic cooperation", present as well as future.[558] With their money, the economic agents of market economies do not only buy goods and services, but stake claims over contemporary and later portions of the economic system's productivity (e.g. *qua* interest payments and dividends).

Besides, the value of money is not a mere matter of alloy, as it was in Aquinas' Middle Ages, or of equivalent purchasable goods, as it is still applicable today, but also of the overall "economic prosperity" to which money contributes (e.g. *qua* productive investment).[559] In modern "dynamic economies", money is much more than just a useful instrument to operate fair exchanges according to "commutative justice", for its value ties directly into the "social justice" that "economic prosperity" is meant to serve.[560]

Keynes had already observed that "the value of money is not determined by its quantity, but its circulation" (e.g. in periods of "stagnation", the monetary mass may increase, yet the value of money remains unchanged).[561] Monetary and fiscal policies are therefore tools that State authorities can use in times of crisis. Yet, too much money poured into circulation may also lead to disruptive "inflation", which is a "scourge" to be avoided, for it is "unjust" to the people whose rightfully earned money can no longer purchase as many or as valuable goods and services as when they earned that money.[562]

Above all, however, stand the social purposes which the circulation of money serves or facilitates. Not any circulation will do, even if conducive to short-term equilibrium between market "supply and demand".[563] For one, Utz deplores the increased economic roles and ownership levels attributed to State or other public authorities in the name of "manipulating at will" the monetary mass, for they reduce the room for private initiative, responsibility and ownership.[564] For another, Utz deplores the historical applications of Keynesianism, which were far too one-sided, i.e. keen on injecting money in times of crisis, but timid in withdrawing it in times of economic boom. The resulting conspicuous "inflation" experienced in many countries caused enduring harm to "the elderly", whose pensions lost value, and the youth, whose employment was made more unlikely, "the entrepreneurs" preferring their "substitution by technological innovations" to which the higher "retributions extorted by the trade unions" were not to be corresponded.[565]

Concerning "credit", Utz begins by recalling its Latin etymology (i.e. *"creditum"*, that is, "believed", "trusted"), for it implies a bond of "trust" between borrower and lender.[566] *Ipso dicto*, a viable credit system cannot do without the moral substratum of inter-personal trust underpinning human cooperation in the economic order. Also, Utz recalls how medieval "scholastics, in connection with [the philosophy of] Aristotle", did firmly condemn "usury", but also distinguished it from rightfully earned "interest", which applied whenever the loan involved:

(i) "a loss for the lender" (i.e. *"damnum emergens"*, e.g. "the owner of a [lent] hammer… for the duration of the loan, had to use a more rudimentary tool");
(ii) "missed profits" (i.e. *"lucrum cessans"*, e.g. "the lender… [cannot make] an investment");
(iii) the "risk" of loss of part or all of the loan (i.e. *"periculum sortis"*); and/or
(iv) its late "restitution" (i.e. *"poena conventionalis"*).[567]

Important is also for Utz the scholastics' acceptance of gains derived from "investments" in "somebody else's enterprise", which are earned "participation in profits", not unearned "rent".[568] Medieval scholastics allowed money to be lent and hence interest to be rightfully gained for the sake of "productive aims" (e.g. lending money to merchants launching a new trading fleet).[569] Their condemnation of "usury" applied to "loans for the aim of consumption" (e.g. giving money to a person to let her buy bread to eat; in this case, the restitution of the borrowed sum was all that should be allowed).[570]

In this connection, Utz criticises Weber's superficial knowledge of medieval economics, which Werner Sombart (1863–1941) is said to have studied much more closely. The latter identified the "root" of "capitalism" already in Aquinas' thought and age.[571] Following Sombart, Utz highlights the teachings of Antonin of Florence (1389–1459) and Bernardine of Siena (1380–1440), who took as "capital" the money serving for "productive investment", hence setting it aside and above "loans", some of which could be unjust "usury" (Antonin of Florence studied even the ratio between the "velocity of capital movement" and "profit increase").[572]

Not any profitable economic endeavour is a genuine "productive investment", however.[573] A good "growth" is not "quantitative", but "qualitative", e.g. it avoids "waste and environmental damages" even if doing so reduces consumer "comforts" that we take for granted in today's societies.[574] Seemingly old virtues need recovered and revaluated for their deep ethico-economic implications, e.g. "parsimony, abstinence and patience" constitute "objective presuppositions" for capital formation.[575]

From Utz's perspective, serving the common good is the "more profound" criterion that separates an unhealthy market economy from a "healthy" one.[576] In the latter, "the owners of pecuniary patrimonies participate" responsibly and freely with their "productive investments" in a well-regulated market system, which is based upon "profits" and "private property" (*contra* "communism"),[577] and yet avoids a number of crucial evils that still plague market economies worldwide: "high taxes on enterprises' profits[,]... the enterprises' own exiguous dividends[,]... the stock-market oscillations caused by socio-economically unjustified speculations",[578] excessive "inflation" (*contra* "the Keynesians"),[579] and "the oppressive debt" induced by "the abuse of consumer credit".[580]

Rational regulation, i.e. laws and rules that have *natura humana* as their axiological axis, is particularly paramount *vis-à-vis* "banks and the stock exchange", for failure to do so leads to major crises "disturbing the whole economic process" both in the short term (e.g. financial losses, unemployment spikes) and in the long one (e.g. post-crisis "recession" brings about "mergers of banks" that "weaken competition" and exercise unjustifiable "influence over the entire credit market, economic policy and State politics").[581]

It may be true that "money has got its own market", but it cannot be treated like any other commodity: "the real economy" depends on it in far too many and too crucial ways (e.g. price stability, investment decisions, wages).[582] For example, transnational "currency speculation" is sternly condemned as disruptive of both national and global economic orders.[583] As Utz argues, "individual self-interest", which market economies harness to the fullest extent, "must remain inscribed within the general interest" by way of powerful "legal instruments" applying at all levels, so that "the common good" is served by the economic process.[584]

Price Formation and Just Price

Rational regulation of the economic order is also at the basis of ethically justified contractual transactions. Without rational regulation, "prices" and "contracts" can far too easily be formed devoid of "good faith", e.g. unbalanced transactions occurring because of another person's state of urgent need ("hunger").[585] In this case, speaking of free contracts, free trade and individual responsibility is either naïve or hypocritical; it is like accepting as valid "sport performances" by athletes taking forbidden drugs, or the "legal order" established by "dictators" who violate "human rights".[586] For the system of "commutative justice" known as the market economy to be justified, the conditions for "social justice" must be in place first.[587] These conditions may require some degree of State interference in economic activities, but they are not primarily and certainly not exclusively about that. "Social justice" means that a just economic order presupposes a just social order, within which the former is contained and sustained.[588]

Following Augustine and Aquinas, Utz accepts the notion according to which an individual's assessment of the "usefulness" of certain goods is at the basis of price-formation in all commercial exchanges, rather than some abstract "ontological value".[589] However, as Aquinas had already highlighted, such assessments and exchanges take place within a "social space" that is not "empty", but filled instead with "social aims" that ultimately justify the lawfulness and desirability of precisely such price-forming assessments and exchanges.[590] For any "ethically just price" to be, then, two fundamental conditions must be met, one *ex ante* and another *ex post*: "the given economic order [must be] ethically justified"; and "the price-formation occurring within it makes it possible for the needs of the members of society to be met completely."[591]

Hypothetically, under the ideal textbook conditions of "perfect competition", the liberals' market economy might be able to meet both conditions; however, in the real world, "there exists only an imperfect market."[592] Imperfection in the real world is what calls for and justifies State "intromissions" in "market price-formation", including some that are often "qualified with the disparaging term 'protectionism'" and yet are ethically imperative, especially when "basic food staples are at stake".[593]

As to the exact type and specifications of such intromissions, they vary with country, goods, services and time in history. Universal abstract principles, even the most just and most consistent with *natura humana*, must be applied to particular, concrete contexts. In his *Political Ethics*, Utz argues that consideration for local conditions means that caution must be exercised not only with regard to the opening of national economies to liberal standards of international trade, but also to their reorganisation around liberal standards of government (e.g. 'exported' democracy). The traditional virtue of prudence leads to gradualism, not to revolution, whether the latter is sought in the name of equality or of liberty.[594]

Income Distribution

Analogous considerations apply to the domain of "income" and workers' "retributions" in particular.[595] It is not the exploitative desire for profits of the entrepreneur,[596] nor the ability for extortion developed by modern trade unions[597] that should determine the income of employers and employees in a rational market order. If anything, the inability to consider lucidly the other party's legitimate interests and their relevance for the long-term well-being of society are the chief source of frequent, deplorable and disruptive forms of "warfare" within market economies,[598] where the economic party enjoying "superior power" wins the day.[599]

In earlier phases of capitalist history, workers had no other way to make their voice heard and their rights respected. Today, in conditions of widespread prosperity, that justification no longer applies. Utz is vehemently critical of the legally accepted and judicially defended rights to workers' "strike" and employers' "lockdown" in the private sector,[600] as well as of the unfair "double vote" of personnel in "the public sector", whose "right to... political strike" blackmails "elected politicians" while harming "the public" that is supposedly to be served.[601]

In *lieu* of such "civil wars",[602] "the supreme norm of justice" *vis-à-vis* "retributions" should be "the overall economic productivity" of whatever "economic system" is in place.[603]

Once again, this is no mere economic determination in standard liberal terms. Utz's understanding of "overall economic productivity" requires taking into full account "the global social issues" that justify ethically the economic order, which *a fortiori* may not:

(i) "seek... productivity... by increasing unemployment";
(ii) do without "full employment" *qua* cardinal "principle of justice"; and
(iii) imperil or ignore the imperative "to ensure the future of the whole society", both in the short- or medium-term (e.g. the "second distribution of income" to "the sick, the elderly, families") and in the long one (e.g. "population growth... and... cultural needs (schooling, formation, etc.).)"[604]

In order to facilitate the respect of "justice" in employer-employee relations and the consequent determination of due income, workers' "unions" and entrepreneurs' "cartels" must stop thinking of themselves as enemies.[605] Therefore, "joint responsibility", cooperative behaviour and "trust" within "the enterprise" must be maximised by any available channel,[606] e.g. novel forms of "contractual autonomy", Johannes Messner's plan for a "global economic organisation" independent of political pressures,[607] or "collaboration in the formation of profit and capital, hence also in the entrepreneurial risk."[608]

Profit

In the concluding chapter, the notion of "profit" is also tackled "in connection with the global aims (social and cultural) corresponding to human nature", i.e. with *natura humana* according to the Thomist understanding of it.[609] Ethically, there is nothing inherently wrong with the "desire for profit" *qua* "adequately remunerated performance", this performance being measured according to the "objective" standards of the existing economic order.[610] If "the aim pursued through the desire for gain" of an individual is:

(i) "honest",
(ii) contributes to "growth in living standards", and
(iii) sustains "the family[,]… the poor… [and] the State community", then it is possible to interpret the "profit… sought… [and] need[ed]" by "the entrepreneur" in a capitalist system as the ethically legitimate reward for "individual performance and responsibility".[611]

Contra liberalism, which often conflates "self-interest" and "selfishness", Aquinas' understanding of "profit" emphasises its "justification" on the basis of "the service rendered to the global economy" by "the entrepreneur", her "enterprise" and, within it, "the workers too", whose crucial "participation" must be acknowledged not only by means of decent "wages", but also by "longer paid holidays[,]… a reduction of the working hours[,]… social contributions… [and,] in particular, …invested retributions" that increase the workers' stakes in the enterprise.⁶¹²

Arthur Fridolin Utz's Political Ethics

Utz's Thomist roots and socio-economic preoccupation find patent echoes in the other instalments of his monumental *Social Ethics*. To exemplify this point, I summarise succinctly in this section Utz's *Political Ethics*, which is also organised in numbered chapters, paragraphs and subparagraphs, along the same systematic lines as his *Economic Ethics*. The resulting echoes should cast further light on the nature and aims of Utz's Thomist project.

According to Utz, human actions are never purely economic, purely political, or purely legal; but all are moral.⁶¹³ On the one hand, the agent's intentions typically combine multiple ends, such as serving one's own family's or closest associates' well-being (i.e. a political end) by conducting intelligently one's own for-profit business (i.e. an economic end), whilst keeping to the existing laws (i.e. a legal end). Depending on the family's notion of well-being, the sort of for-profit business and the spirit of the laws at issue, the agent's actions may be good, better, worse, or bad. For example, the family or associates at issue could be a mafia clan, the business an ecologically devastating one, and the laws to comply with the most permissive that persistent lobbying and generous bribing have bought.

On the other hand, the agent's actions have consequences, which affect individuals, communities, societies, States, animals, natural environments, and the meaningful unity of the whole Creation. Depending on the consequences, the agent's actions may be good, better, worse, or bad. Maximising shareholder value by ecologically harmful licit business activities, whose legislation is the result of well-meaning business-friendly advice by liberal-minded international experts, is still going to cause negative consequences for present and future persons, even if no wicked intention is at play.⁶¹⁴ Indeed, if the eventual goodness of the market order is assumed *a priori* (e.g. the invisible hand's necessary beneficial spill-overs), such negative consequences may be easily overlooked.

It is logically possible and practically useful to separate different domains of investigation in the social sciences, which began their long path towards disciplinary specialisation in early modernity, thanks primarily to Niccolò Machiavelli[615] (1469–1527) and Francis Bacon[616] (1561–1626). Excessive separation, if not outright isolation, leads to monstrosities, though. Pure law, devoid of anchoring in metaphysics or ethics, accepts as valid the most unjust legal system, as long as it is formally and procedurally correct (e.g. Kelsen).[617]

Pure politics reduces the political arena to an unprincipled struggle for power (e.g. Max Weber),[618] if not to preparation for or execution of war against an enemy (e.g. Carl Schmitt (1888–1985)).[619] Unrestrained political struggle can lead to civil strife and/or loss of legitimacy of the political system.[620] War can be just, but it can be so by fulfilling very strict ethical criteria.[621] Both must be seen holistically in order to be healthy, i.e. in connection with *natura humana*.

Even in its democratic manifestation, as long as no deeper principled ground is retrieved, politics is reduced to the competition among different aggregates of subjective preferences, which may be as largely and as voluntarily adhered to as possible, and yet remain thoroughly unjust,[622] hence illegitimate.[623] States cannot be utterly neutral on matters of fundamental value.[624]

Not even the broadest shared interest of the democratic polity is necessarily the common good.[625] For instance, popular votes and elections may bear witness to the widespread support for a leader, party or political programme that exclude, expel or even exterminate an undesired minority. Under such circumstances, we can easily perceive that there is something is amiss. In today's legal jargon, we would claim that someone's fundamental rights—human rights—are being violated.[626] But what justifies and secures these rights against a large democratic consensus set squarely against them? And what justifies and sanctions, positively, open resistance to their negation?[627]

Universal human rights are not to be understood as mere individual rights bestowed upon individuals under a democratically run constitutional setting. They are not to be thought of as a matter of sheer agreement among individual citizens, which can change with changing circumstances. Universal human rights are the result of reflective abstractions from prolonged moral experiences, individual as well as collective. They are the fruit of centuries of socio-cultural and politico-legal consideration. They encapsulate our knowledge of the most important dimensions of what it means to be human. Universal human rights express what makes it possible for us to be human beings, i.e. both in terms of our being (e.g. "the right of everyone to be free from hunger" and "to the enjoyment of the highest attainable standard of physical and mental health");[628] and in terms of our humanity (e.g. "the widest possible protection and assistance... to the family", "the right of everyone to education... cultural activities... periodic holidays with pay... just and favourable conditions of work").[629]

Following the Aristotelian and Thomist traditions, Utz welcomes metaphysics and ethics as pivotal abstractive ontological reflections (i.e. reflections about facts of being) and includes them among the disciplines at our disposal in order to make sense of the world in which we live. Indeed, Utz includes also faith *qua* knowledge based on good testimony[630] and the Christian religion *qua* repository of axiological wisdom.[631]

Utz's gaze is set primarily on Thomist philosophy and the philosophical components of the doctrine of the Catholic Church, however, for they are not a matter of faith, but of rational reflection.[632] *Pace* Immanuel Kant (1724–1804), metaphysical abstraction is claimed not to lead necessarily and uniquely to empty forms of the intellect, but, if properly conducted (e.g. Aquinas' *recta ratio*), it can also grasp the fundamental principles of reality, including the aims that are natural to the human being and therefore good for us to pursue.[633]

The natural-law tradition emerged upon the basis of such forms of abstraction is what provides the epistemic and moral foundation of human rights legislation and it explains why, even if all citizens of a democratic human community but one agreed upon the denial of that one person's fundamental rights, an intolerable injustice would have occurred.[634]

Injustices have occurred in the past and keep occurring in the present, sometimes on a massive scale. Utz claims that these injustices, in the long run, cause major socio-political catastrophes, for consistent and prolonged violation of the nature of things—i.e. attacks on the integrity of their being—is the dark fountainhead of the worst human tragedies (e.g. war, genocide, ethnic cleansing). Ontological error breeds practical horror. It may be true, as Hobbes argued, that *"auctoritas, non veritas facit legem"*, but bad laws are not going to make such an authority enjoy prolonged legitimacy and success, for they contradict essential characters and aims.[635]

The starkest example that Utz discusses in this connection is that of the ecology of the planet, which cannot be treated as we wish, no matter the degree of authority enjoyed, and no matter what extensive democratic agreement there may be.[636] The nature of the Earth's ecosystems has to be seen for what it is, taken on its own terms, and allowed the ontological means required for its actual continuation, even if that may signify a considerable change in everybody's life-style. Though undesired and perhaps even painful for most, if not even for all the members of the present generation, such a considerable change of life-style ought to be accepted and pursued, so that life too, including human life, may continue in the future.

The good of Earth is a splendid example of common good i.e. that which is good to human societies, but that cannot be reduced to the individuals therein comprised. Doing what is good for the planet is not the same thing, especially in the short- and medium-term, as what the individuals acknowledge as good and therefore want for themselves. Doing what is good for the planet cannot even be reduced to a matter of agreement, at least in theory. If all citizens of Earth preferred to continue with the current life-destructive life-style and waste away the planet's ecology, that would be still evil.

The human being has its own nature, which involves ends that are intrinsic to our being (i.e. the analogical final causes of the Aristotelian tradition).[637] Pursuing happiness (aka perfection or well-being) is one of them, which can be delineated in many ways, depending on the specific circumstances that apply to each person, as well as derailed in many ways, given our freedom and capacity to err.[638]

Politics is one of the instruments at our disposal in the pursuit of happiness. Indeed, politics is, in concrete historical experience, one of the essential ends of the human being, for we are inherently social beings and we cannot seek perfection, individual selfishness notwithstanding, but in broader associations, which in large and complex cases take the form of political communities.[639] States, or better, the societies that they serve, have therefore their own order of perfection, i.e. the common good.

Again, Utz emphasises how the common good is not an aggregate, but that which is good for society (e.g. the rule of law), even if it may not be obviously or immediately good for the individuals inside it (e.g. some individuals would be better off, most certainly in the short or medium term, by having chaos, civil strife, corrupt judges or inept policemen, rather than the rule of law).[640]

Utz believes it necessary to stress this point repeatedly, because modern civilisation, unlike the ancient and medieval ones, has broken the unity between intellect and reality (cf. René Descartes (1596–1650)).[641] This break has left our mind uncertain *vis-à-vis* the validity of the claims of knowledge that we can make, and replaced the strong objectivity of older metaphysics with a weaker intersubjective one (cf. Kant),[642] which shifts the focus of our attention and admiration away from the world (and its Creator) and onto the individual instead. These are the philosophical roots of modern individualism, with which any contemporary political entity has to deal.

Concluding Remarks

To express concisely Utz's stance, I adopt and adapt hereby the characterisation of the sort of economic transactions that truly life-enabling market economies should have, as these are described by Canada's leading value theorist John McMurtry in his famous *Cancer Stage of Capitalism*. In symbolic formalisation, these ideal economic transactions read as follows:

$$L \to \$ \to MoL \to \$^1 \to L^1$$

Which means in extended formulation that:

- Textbook for-profit market economic exchanges occur (i.e. input capital "$\$$" generating output capital "$\$^1$", e.g. profits, interests, dividends, etc.);
- but in such a way (i.e. within such a strictly enforced binding legal framework) that the commodities (i.e. goods and services) therein produced, transported, traded, consumed and/or disposed of are always and exclusively beneficial to life (i.e. "MoL", means of life, e.g. zero-mile organic bread);
- that is, they are neither destructive (e.g. weapons, carcinogenic pesticides, junk food) nor blind to life-aims and life-requirements (e.g. financial derivatives);
- and they are conducive to broader and deeper levels of life-capacity (i.e. the initial input "L" engenders "L^1", e.g. healthier, happier and/or more cultured individuals).

This is as succinct and clear a theoretical template as I can provide of a rational, well-designed and well-conducted capitalist economic order that, at global and local levels, aims at securing life-fulfilment for present as well as future generations to the widest imaginable extent. It is the schematic depiction of a capitalist economic order that, *via* the countless transactions that it engenders and the many institutions that it establishes, takes the world as it is right now and makes it into a better one—a world where the conditions for continued human flourishing are secured.

McMurtry's life-value onto-axiology offers an articulate set of criteria to understand and direct such a flourishing, as I have amply discussed in my previous volume for Northwest Passage Books. On his part, Utz characterises life-fulfilment in relation to the fundamental aims of *natura humana*, i.e. the "supreme principles" of Aquinas' "natural law": "self-preservation, self-perfection, mating, generation and education of the offspring, acquisition of knowledge, (natural) knowledge of God".[643]

Under this perspective, a good economic order is one that facilitates throughout, say: longer and healthier human lives (cf. self-preservation), peaceful and happy personal existences (cf. self-perfection), a healthy demographic balance (cf. mating), universal schooling and free university education (cf. education of the offspring, acquisition of knowledge), freedom of conscience (cf. natural knowledge of God).

The implications for economies and, in particular, for policy-making (Utz's "economic policy"), are obvious: a good market economy is one that secures the conditions above (and many others); a bad market economy is one that does the opposite (e.g. by facilitating the destruction of the Earth's life-support systems).

Utz's own list is simple, generic and possibly incomplete, if compared to McMurtry's comprehensive study for UNESCO. Also, the interpretation of Aquinas' supreme principles may also vary, e.g. what may constitute a suitable family capable of raising children: a standard Catholic stance would contrast with a standard secular one (Utz's *Political Ethics* contains a strong condemnation of abortion as a violation of the unborn child's rights, for instance).[644] I do not intend to pursue here a detailed analysis of the points of disagreement between Utz's traditional Thomist account and life-value onto-axiology. Quite the opposite, I wish to highlight the points of agreement, or overlap. In particular, Utz's account is akin to McMurtry's in denouncing back in the 1990s:

(i) the life-destructive consequences of globalisation;
(ii) the primacy of environmental concerns;
(iii) the asymmetric focus of liberal economists and policy-makers over the risk of inflation rather than unemployment; and
(iv) the degeneration of finance into a speculative cradle of instability, which the 2008 collapse of Lehman Brothers and the ensuing international economic crisis have made visible to all today.

There are implications for the study of economic phenomena too. Once Utz, true to Aquinas' legacy, has established that the human being possesses a certain nature, which determines *de facto* and justifies *de iure* certain socio-ethical and personal goals and not others, it follows logically that no economy we may choose to study can be isolated from its socio-cultural milieu, for it is therein that human agency unfolds, economic agency included. No economic category can be treated as though such a milieu did not exist or were irrelevant to such categories' conception, selection and/or application.

All forms of economic agency *qua* human agency are, inherently, morally connoted, for they imply personal motives and social consequences that can be deemed ethically good or bad, whether economists realise it or not. Standard economics grasps and operates upon *some* important features of human social existence; but equally do other social and natural sciences (Utz mentions anthropology, ethology and psychology), as well as much older disciplines, whose task is to delve deeper than the empirical sciences themselves (Utz speaks in this respect of philosophy, ethics, theology and natural-law jurisprudence).

An intelligent economics capable of addressing the human condition holistically— its fundamental needs, rights, duties and aims— will have to be integrated, qualified and sometimes guided by these other disciplines. No discipline is an island, and most certainly not the discipline of economics. Above all, an intelligent economics will have to acknowledge how any legitimate and possibly good economy must serve what is good to the human person, now and in the future, universally.

It is unclear whether the 2008 global meltdown and the ongoing economic crisis resulted thereof have changed the way in which mainstream economics is pursued, not to mention the world's economic policy-making by State officials. As far as I have been able to ascertain, mainstream textbooks in economics have not been revised yet and it is far from clear whether State officials have stopped prioritising the corporate interests that they had been catering to before 2008 under the banner of globalisation, of which Utz is vocally critical. Perhaps, the powerful economists and the economic powers are as obtuse and as obstinate as the addicted patient who, as Utz mused, keeps harming herself by refusing to be cured. Utz-the-physician may yet be unheeded.

Utz's work does not come across as pessimistic. On the contrary, it is infused with Scholastic optimism in our natural faculties. The book assumes that human reason, albeit imperfect, can identify the essential aims of human existence and conceive of the institutions that are capable of maximising our likelihood to attain such aims. For a book written by the member of a religious order, *Economic Ethics* contains no mysticism, no appeal to faith, and very little theological commentary.

It is in the paucity of scriptural sources that I observe the most striking difference between Utz's book and the founding documents of the SDC, namely the Popes' encyclicals on socio-political, economic and environmental matters.[645] Conceptually, the similarity, indeed the identity of views, is patent to anyone familiar with SDC. Utz's stance in these matters is the one characterising the so-called "third way" of much European Christian Democracy, which strikes a balance between liberal principles and socialist ones, whilst also endorsing others that are either neglected or opposed by both liberalism and socialism, at least in their historical manifestations.[646] Thus, Utz's book can serve as an eminent example of SDC to anyone willing to explore this "third way" and understand its philosophical foundations.

Chapter 6: Hans Jonas *qua* Political Thinker

"An emergency ethics of the endangered future must translate into collective action the 'Yes to Being' demanded of man by the totality of things."[647]

Hans Jonas read theology and philosophy in Freiburg, Berlin, Heidelberg, and Marburg. He studied under the direction of three of the most influential Continental academics of the inter-war period: Edmund Husserl, Martin Heidegger and Rudolf Bultmann. As a German citizen of Jewish descent, he despised the astounding success of National Socialism in his native country and abandoned it for England in 1934. He then moved to Palestine and returned to Europe in 1940, as a volunteer in the Jewish Brigade of the British Army. He took part in the Allies' invasion of Italy and celebrated the end of the Second World War in Udine. After the conflict, he moved back to Palestine and fought in the 1948 Arab-Israeli War. He then taught philosophy at the Hebrew University of Jerusalem, which he left for McGill University and Carleton University in Canada. Eventually he settled in the United States of America, working chiefly at the New School for Social Research in New York.

Jonas' early scholarly publications were devoted to the history and theology of Gnosticism. Later, though never abandoning altogether religious and theological issues, he started to write about philosophy of science and became a true pioneer in bioethics.[648] In the process, Jonas developed an articulate ethical theory centred upon the notion of human responsibility *vis-à-vis* the threat to life on Earth posed by late-modern socio-economic development. In 1993, not long before his death, he was awarded the Nonino Prize in Percoto, near Udine.

Gnosticism

Whether wisdom can be taught is a thorny issue that has been discussed in philosophy since Plato's time. What rests assured, however, is that wisdom can be defective or absent in the soul of the ignorant person as well as in the soul of the knowledgeable one. Scholarship and professional competence, in other words, do not translate mechanically into wise conduct. Thus, it was possible for the highly learned Martin Heidegger, leading philosophical mind of the fragile *Weimarer Republik*, to side with the most brutal regime that Europe had the misfortune to witness during the 20th century. Certainly, Heidegger's indescribable political allegiance allowed him to gain even more power within the German academic world, at least for the duration of Hitler's ruthless rule, but also to betray the quasi-filial trust of his pupils, especially left-wing and Jewish ones.

Hans Jonas, then a young middle-class German Jew, was amongst Heidegger's most devoted pupils in both Freiburg and Marburg. He was one of his "children", as Richard Wolin (b. 1961) calls four of the most successful disciples of Heidegger's: Hannah Arendt (1906–1975), Karl Löwith (1897–1973), Herbert Marcuse (1896–1979) and Hans Jonas himself.[649] Like the others, he too was forced to escape from Nazi Germany and seek refuge abroad. Yet, he did not hide hopeless on foreign soil, nor did he forget the plea of those who had been left behind, crushed and brutalised by fascist thugs because of their belief in an international liberation from wage slavery or because of their religious and ethnic origin. On the contrary, Jonas soon returned to Europe as a soldier, fighting his way north from Apulia to Friuli, where he was stationed when the war ended in 1945.

Wounded and inspired by the extreme challenges faced in his personal existence—the primary and ultimate ground of any worthy intellectual endeavour—Jonas matured both as a human being and as a scholar. Working in England, Israel, Canada and the US, where he will eventually spend 40 years of his long earthly existence, he made himself known amongst theologians and historians of religion with an extensive study of Gnosticism, which is still regarded today as a pivotal contribution, i.e. *Gnosis und spätantiker Geist* (1934–1966).[650]

Gnosticism is probably the most complex and enigmatic expression of early Christianity, for it amalgamates elements of Jesus' new understanding of Judaism with countless others coming from Persia, Asia Minor, Greece and Egypt, particularly from Neo-Platonic schools.

Gnostic currents were present in the Eastern provinces of the Roman Empire before Jesus' predication, yet Gnosticism flourished remarkably in the new socio-cultural *milieu* created by the diffusion of Christianity around the Mediterranean area forcibly pacified by the Romans. Its English name transliterates the Greek for "knowledge", insofar as the Gnostics believed that the true path to salvation did not require uncritical adherence to God's will, often mysterious and arbitrary, but careful intellectual study, theoretical analysis and deeper understanding. In this manner, the perceived irrationality of Judaism—centred upon Abraham's obedience—and of Christianity—centred upon Jesus' love—was rectified along intellectualist lines, which are still influential among the Free Masons, for example.

As regards the ethnocentrism of the Jewish faith and the universalism of the Christian one, Gnosticism replaced them both with the elitism of the enlightened few *contra* the multitudes wandering aimlessly in the dark. Contrary to the former, the latter group were foolish victims of ignorance, superstition, and of the tyranny of their bodily cravings. In point of fact, Gnosticism posited a stark contraposition between the corporeal realm and the spiritual realm, the latter being regarded as axiologically superior to the former to an infinite degree. Humankind, connected with both realms by virtue of our being ensouled bodily creatures, were expected to privilege the spiritual realm above all else.

As a result, on the other end of the Gnostic value spectrum laid the corporeal realm, condemned not merely as contingent and imperfect, but also as the fountainhead of all evils, insofar as the body, with its countless needs, desires and forms of decay, distracted and curbed the full realisation of the human soul. The axiological condemnation of the corporeal realm was so thorough, that several Gnostic texts speak of two separate divinities, one responsible for the creation of spirit, the other for the creation of matter. In other words, the corporeal realm was so utterly despised that even the fundamental postulation of monotheism, i.e. the singularity of the

Supreme Being, could be sacrificed to the goal of its rejection. Ironically, all this was conceived of and taught notwithstanding the presupposition of corporeal entities throughout each and every stage of philosophical and theological activity by the Gnostics themselves.

Hans Jonas had commenced his study of Gnosticism during the 1920s, under the joint supervision of Martin Heidegger and Rudolf Bultmann. He published part of its results before the war, along with few other works in theology, most notably *Augustin und das paulinische Freiheitsproblem. Ein philosophischer Beitrag zur Genesis der christlich-abendländischen Freiheitsidee* (1930).[651] However, Jonas' conclusive assessment of Gnosticism was to see the light only after the war, enjoying wide circulation amongst the experts and translation into several languages.

From a strictly technical point of view, Bultmann was a less decisive influence than Heidegger, as Jonas utilised mainly the latter's existentialist phenomenology to interpret Gnosticism. Still, it was Bultmann's existence that Jonas cherished and emulated as an example of courage and integrity, not Heidegger's. While the raising National-socialist tide was flooding the German nation and the European continent, Bultmann put his life on the line and, as an outspoken minister of religion, opposed Hitler's regime openly and firmly. Against all odds, he survived, becoming one of the first persons that Jonas visited in Germany after the end of the conflict. Heidegger, on the opposite, became a cheerleader of National Socialism and benefitted from it by advancing quickly in the academe of Nazi Germany.

Bultmann's noteworthy example convinced Jonas of the opportunity to combine his theological investigations with ethical concerns regarding the social consequences of adopting certain religious and philosophical views. Scholarship was not to be an ivory tower or an excuse from challenging human affairs. In the following years, Jonas did not stop being active in theology,[652] nevertheless he increasingly devoted attention to metaphysics, particularly in connection with issues arising from modern science.[653] Eventually, Jonas started to write about ethics *tout court*, mostly, though not exclusively, in connection with medicine and biology.[654]

A calm but determined man, Jonas had come to realise that it was his duty to alert the intellectual community to the dangers contained within the forgotten, life-blind philosophical presuppositions of modern science and technology. Comparing himself to Socrates, Athens' buzzing gadfly, Jonas spoke out at conferences and meetings where inhospitable professionals from public administrations and university departments were typically too busy, too intelligent and too important to listen gladly to the worries of a philosopher and a war veteran that reminded them of the inherent value of life and of the potentially suicidal character of the modern faith in technology.

According to Jonas, whereas the Gnostics had neglected the corporeal in the name a purely spiritual God to be encountered *post mortem*, the dominant "Baconian" mindset of modern humankind was such that the utopian world to come (e.g. the socialist's classless society, the capitalist's ever-wealthier economy, the geneticist's experimenting on future human beings by embryonic bio-engineering) was being forced upon the present world by technological means that put unbearable pressures and costs onto the living (e.g. violent revolutions, wars for oil, callous trials on animals, prison inmates and the world's poor).[655] The modern age, developing its technological means on the basis of the most evolved science ever possessed by humankind, had attained the highest level of power over nature in the history of our species which, as Jonas admits, had never been very kind to nature: "The raping of nature and the civilizing of man go hand in hand".[656]

For Jonas, it was not unlikely that these modern utopias could bring about the *mortem* of the whole living planet, thus demonstrating the truth of the sarcastic complaint by the great Romanian essayist Ioan Culianu (1950–1991): "the Gnostics have taken hold of the whole world, and we were not aware of it. It is a mixed feeling of anxiety and admiration, since I cannot refrain myself from thinking that these alien body-snatchers have done a remarkable job indeed".[657]

Given that the dominant "Baconian" modern mindset informed most mainstream ethical and political doctrines and most intellectual attitudes, Jonas found critical elements in all of them. He therefore became an academic eccentric, with more foes than friends, self-condemned to being extraneous to the leading schools and factions, especially in the US (albeit based in that country, Jonas' work has received much more attention in non-Anglophone countries).

The leap from a fairly obscure area of early-Christian theology to moral philosophy and philosophy of science must have looked perplexing to many, but it was not so, at least if one considers the capital lesson that Jonas had learnt from his study of Gnosticism and from Bultmann's display of personal virtue: it is the precise responsibility of the honest intellectual to serve the purpose of preserving and enhancing life; in comparison to this imperative, career and reputation become secondary matters.[658]

Massive deforestation, energy crises, booming population, immense pollution, mass extinctions and depleted fishing stocks meant for Jonas, amongst other dramatic ecological phenomena to which we have become accustomed today, that the whole biosphere was facing the threat of destruction. He believed this threat to be the result of the derailment of the human spirit [*Geist*] which, arisen from nature's womb, was now forgetful of its birth and operated as the main cause of her destruction. The stakes were simply too high to be discouraged by the threat of unpopularity. As Jonas kept affirming around the end of his life: "To acknowledge our responsibility *vis-à-vis* the survival of all... problems must not be silenced, not even for a second, and consciences must be warned incessantly".[659]

Tenacious if not obstinate, Jonas continued to be a Socratic gadfly until his death.[660] In the end, the novelty, the scope and the courage of his radical questioning were recognised as innovative and praiseworthy even by Jonas' fiercest critics.[661]

Sustainable Development

Grounding his views around "the responsibility principle" or "imperative", Jonas developed a thorough critique of mainstream science, which pretended to have little to do with its destructive applications (e.g. nuclear bombs and oil-fuelled engines) and blamed them instead upon the politicians and industrialists funding that very same science. Secluded within laboratories like behind walls of deception, the members of the scientific community acted as though they did not bear any responsibility—perhaps their white gowns could protect hands and consciences from avoidable blood, pain or dirt. Yet, according to Jonas, things were neither so simple nor so benign.

Like his mentor Martin Heidegger, he too was conscious of the fact that science and technology formed a powerful, inextricable binomial both in practice and in theory. Like Heidegger, he too had noted how the modern world, after ages of agrarian docility, had mobilised both humankind and nature, transforming them into potential resources for productive use. Having no other end but perpetual growth for either private or State capital, this modern dynamism was self-referential and wanted more, more rapidly and more efficiently, oblivious to the costs paid by life itself. It therefore spiralled ominously around the axis of self-improving self-realisation: "Thus the danger of disaster attending the Baconian ideal of power over nature through scientific technology arises not so much from any shortcomings of its performance as from the magnitude of its success".[662]

Heidegger had spoken of the binomial science-technology as a destiny; Jonas began to call it a doom, which only a higher degree of self-awareness and moral commitment by the actual persons involved could counter. In other words, ends had to be rethought both individually and socially—by the allegedly value-neutral scientists themselves *in primis*—for fast-paced, perpetual growth was not only a self-referential end, but also a dangerous one.[663] Wisdom had to be regained, according to Jonas, by looking back at primitive communities as well as to nature herself, for she acts very differently from technological humankind: "The big enterprise of modern technology, neither patient nor slow, compresses… the many infinitesimal steps of natural evolution into a few colossal ones and forgoes by that procedure the vital advantages of nature's 'playing safe'."[664]

According to Jonas, the traditional animistic awe- and respect-inspiring sanctity of life had to be recovered somehow. Interestingly, he suggests that the roots of normativity may reside in our animal being, rather than in some abstract selfhood, as suggested most famously by Immanuel Kant. There is in fact a "timeless archetype of all responsibility, the parental for the child", which cuts across ages, communities and, one could add, all the most complex animal species.[665] It is experienced in instinct, rather than in deliberative reason, which explains perhaps why "responsibility" has been largely absent from the Western moral discourse compared to "duty" or "utility".[666] Cast in Heidegger's terminology, it is "an *ontic* paradigm in which the plain factual 'is' evidently coincides with an 'ought'—which does not, therefore, admit for itself the concept of a 'mere is' at all".[667]

One cannot separate the being of the parent-child relationship from the being of an imperative of responsibility, i.e. a normative command, an "ought". "Being" and "ought" coincide, in a formidable example of resurging Natural Law from a Jewish, rather than Christian, perspective:[668] "We can point at the most familiar sight: the newborn, whose mere breathing uncontradictably addresses an ought to the world around, namely to take care of him".[669] Jonas goes as far as to claim that "here the plain being of a *de facto* existent immanently and evidently contains an ought for others, and would so even if nature would not succour this ought with powerful instincts or assume its job alone".[670] Moreover, as the archetype of all responsibility, the parent's case should guide "the artist" *vis-à-vis* "his work" and "the statesman" *vis-à-vis* "the state".[671]

Whether Jonas' foundation of normativity is correct or naturalistically fallacious, it will not be assessed hereby. Rather, it is worth recalling how the Eastern philosophical tradition, and particularly Chinese Confucianism, has often regarded the parent-child relationship as the paradigm of moral behaviour. *De facto*, Confucianism has concentrated principally upon the bond of filial piety that the less powerful party has toward the more powerful one, analogously to Aristotle's and Saint Paul's (ca. 5–67 AD) allegedly natural master-slave relationship in the Western tradition. *De iure*, however, the recognition of the bond of humaneness that the latter party has toward the former has never been denied and it has been cast in the most mystical terms that Confucianism, an essentially secular doctrine, allows for, i.e. the "Mandate of Heaven".[672]

Jonas' writings reveal how a gulf between life and thought has characterised Western intellectual history.[673] This gulf could be rendered *via* a number of possible dichotomies: wisdom *versus* knowledge, sapience *versus* science, understanding *versus* explaining, intelligence *versus* shrewdness, *homo sapiens versus homo faber*, life-world *versus* idealisations. Standard intellectual distinctions could also be used to the same end: theory and practice, pure and applied, science and technology, means and ends, public and private, professional and personal. From an ethical perspective, they all share the ability to offer the self a potential escape route from the consequences of her actions; moral self-denial is always a tempting option for the human being. Then again, the best example of the same gulf comes probably from Jonas' own personal experience: the most eminent German philosopher of his day, i.e. Martin Heidegger, backing the most brutal dictator and his murderous plans, i.e. Adolf Hitler.

In this manner, Jonas' work reminds us also of how the scientist's professional virtues of intellectual honesty, cooperative team-work and candid acceptance of criticism do not transfer necessarily onto the private level, as though the professional training of the scientist could have no wisdom to teach to the actual person undergoing it. In other words, not only can phoney racial theories support the planning and implementation of mass extermination. Nor simply can the fiduciary duty to maximising stockholders' returns lead a financier to mastermind a speculative assault onto a nation's currency and the millions that depend on it for their livelihood. Also, the acquisition of academic titles and professional prestige is no guarantee against being a conceited, obnoxious, untrustworthy person. Similarly, the prolonged, methodical study of bullies and alcohol-related violence as societal malaises can teach no humaneness to a social scientist.

Whether self-deluding, paranoid or merely hypocritical, scientists have always been human—hence moral—beings. The same is true of politicians, businessmen, lawyers and anyone else that may be tempted to tell herself that what she does as a professional has nothing to do with her moral integrity. Jonas, like Michael Polanyi, Paul K. Feyerabend (1924–1994) and very few other 20th-century thinkers, could never disregard the philosophical relevance of the fact that scientists, no matter what they do, remain nonetheless and above all "persons", i.e. persons who do science, hence persons who have moral rights as well as moral obligations, whether they like it or not.[674]

As a theologian, Hans Jonas had observed how the defining element of Gnosticism was the rebuttal of the body in favour of the soul, and the related juxtaposition of knowledge and life with the latter alone. This dualistic view had already emerged in the philosophy of Plato, reaching vertiginous heights with Gnosticism. From there, it had persisted and affected much Christian thought of the Middle Ages. Subsequently, in a subtler yet more virulent manner, it had moved forward, pervading modern thought too. From Descartes to Heidegger, *via* Newton and B.F. Skinner (1904–1990), our civilisation produced a disembodied philosophy unable to answer the question "Am I hungry?", and a science of the corporeal modelled around quantifiable, inorganic physics, deaf to life as much as to death's sting, to the point of backing the fast-paced technological advances employed for the eco-social devastations of the 20th century.[675]

Though not always cast in the dramatic eschatological terms of Gnosticism, Jonas believed that modern Western thought had embarked in a journey that either ignored the corporeal realm in its organic dimension—devoting its attention to issues like mental associations of ideas and linguistic expressions—or attempted to reduce it to its inorganic aspects—i.e. those Galilean particular *affezioni* that abstract, de-spirited physics and chemistry were progressively learning to describe and predict *qua* regular uniformities by means of advanced mathematical equations.

However, according to Jonas, God is not a "pure intellect" that conceived of the universe like a perfect mathematician would do, for God's Creation is much more than that which can be understood through mathematical lenses: "That pure intellect could have, say, a minutely detailed inventory of the composition of the eye, the optical nerve, the cerebral centre for vision, and of the modifications taking place therein when visual stimulations occur, yet... it does not even know what 'to see' may actually mean".[676]

Swimming against the twin currents of intellectual history and economic power, Jonas shouted a loud "halt" to the so-called "development" of today's world. Anticipating—if not kick-starting—the discussions about "sustainable development" that have become mainstream in academe during the last two decades, he commented on how the simplest requirements of life and patent biological phenomena like individuation through metabolism, lived experience and freedom seem to escape the grasp of the modern philosopher and, above all, of the scientist, despite the sophisticated subtlety of the former and the advanced technology of the latter.[677]

Jonas believed that the philosopher's subtlety had made the organic realm unreachable, lost behind a barrier of concepts, words, meanings and symbols to be explained in the first place. On its part, the scientist's technology had been contributing relentlessly to the devastation of the Earth's biosphere, lost within the arrogant and superstitious belief that whatever errors scientific technology may generate, there shall be newer scientific technologies to fix them. Indeed the marvels or miracles of technology, more than anything else, have contributed to the widespread success of this modern, secular religion of "permanent self-surpassing toward an infinite goal. Science, the life of theory, would be much better suited for the role of end-in-itself, but it can be this only for the small band of its devotees".[678]

As concerns the alleged progress of the so-called "life sciences", Jonas deemed it to be dubious, for in most cases it served the same interests guiding the public and private institutions responsible for the planetary ecological meltdown.[679] The mechanistic presuppositions of modern science make it difficult not to fall into reductionism (e.g. a patient is not a person but the collection of data in her medical file) and appreciate the peculiarities of organic reality, which sets it apart from the inorganic one (e.g. growth, reproduction, goal-directedness, self-definition, identification *via* metabolism). Finally, both modern medicine and biology approach life as possessing merely instrumental value. For example, the widely accepted experimentation on live animals and the *ad hoc* redefinition of death in the age of organ transplants are as much instances of utilitarian thinking as the hotly debated patenting of genetic information, whereby the alphabet of life itself is subsumed to the higher value of profit for private investors.[680]

Jonas' relentless denunciation of the human-made dangers to human and non-human life stands as an impressive example of political activity. Also, important political considerations can be derived from Jonas' ethics of responsibility, e.g. the desirability of green taxes, the rejection of economic growth at all costs, the legal enforcement of bioethical standards, the State's duty to care for its citizens like a parent for its children.[681]

Nevertheless, Jonas is hardly ever described as a political thinker.[682] In part this is due to the topics to which he devoted most time and attention, from the rather obscure theology of Gnosticism to specific bioethical conundrums. In part this is due to his conviction that all major changes are fundamentally the result of individual persons making moral and/or immoral choices, rather than to political or economic systems *per se*. In part this is due to the technical languages that he uses, i.e. the theologian's and the ethicist's. In truth, the ethicist's language is predominant also in DPV, which is supposed to lead the reader to "see that *responsibility* with a never known burden and range has moved into the center of *political* morality".[683]

Although the environmental crisis of our planet is recognised as an economic and political issue, Jonas highlights predominantly its ethical dimension, for he believes that "the very same movement which put us in possession of the powers that have now to be regulated by norms—the movement of modern knowledge called science—has by a necessary complementarity eroded the foundations from which norms could be derived".[684] Humankind has gained unprecedented power over the awe- and respect-inspiring forces of nature which, across generations and cultures, had revealed the presence of divinity or "sacrosanctity", i.e. one of the deepest, founding expressions of morality.[685]

In the disenchanted modern age, neither nature nor divinity is feared any longer—nor is there any fear of taking perilous technological chances.[686] Bacon's dreams of mastery are a reality to modern humans, who have taken in their hands their own destiny and the entire world's. Yet, "mankind has no right to suicide".[687] As for the therapy recommended *vis-à-vis* the Baconian hubris of the modern age, Jonas highlights distinctive ethical points, i.e. "the pursuit of virtue… moderation and circumspection".[688]

The political philosopher and the political scientist are bound to encounter Jonas the ethicist even when he tackles the issue of which political order would better serve the end of preventing the environmental collapse of our planet; the socialist or the capitalist? In theory, according to Jonas, Marxism would be more likely to prevent ecological disaster than capitalism, which is bound instead to pursue growth at all costs. Frugality, altruistic sacrifice and a more articulate understanding of the human being *qua* sensuous organic creature are much easier to retrieve in Marx's writings than in the liberal-capitalist tradition.

Moreover, the top-down, authoritarian socialist State would probably attain the desired results much more rapidly and unfalteringly than the bottom-up, consumer- and voter-based liberal-capitalist State. After all, the latter involves a conspicuous amount of "waste attendant upon the mechanics of competition, and… the nonsense of a market production aimed at consumer titillation".[689] On the contrary, the former aims at meeting needs *via* a "centralized bureaucracy", hence it implies "the promise of a greater *rationality*".[690]

However, the practice of Marxism has been very disappointing. Not only has it flourished in a number of Baconian utopias (e.g. Ernst Bloch's (1885–1977) hope-fuelled Marxist philosophy), whereby the future is entitled to putting life-destructive pressures upon the present, since "the most colossal mass extinctions can appear as a necessary, alas painful, but beneficent surgical operation".[691]

Also, the practice of Marxism has shown how national interests take absolute priority over international concerns. This means that centrally planned countries such as Soviet Union and the People's Republic of China have been prone to pursue their own productive aggrandisement like big private conglomerates in capitalist countries, promoting industrialisation in agrarian realities and augmenting consumption. Their history has shown that Real Socialism meant State capitalism, and the disastrous environmental record of the European and Asian communist countries should be seen as a patent and well-known mark of failure.

Racism

On the 30th January 1993, at Percoto, near Udine, Hans Jonas, *qua* academic champion of the Earth's endangered environment, received the Nonino International Prize for Literature, which aims at "highlighting the permanent topicality of rustic civilization".[692] Upon conferral of the prize, Jonas delivered a speech that encapsulates his long philosophical journey and key-concerns, yet approaching them from a primarily political angle.

As typical of Jonas, philosophy and life are closely tied together also in this speech, which opens by revealing the reasons why he had decided to travel to Percoto from the US, in spite of his old age and frail health. First of all, Percoto is near Udine, where the war had ended for him. Secondly, in Udine, Jonas had been told of an amazing example of solidarity, which he had "kept for his whole life like a sacred task".[693]

The amazing example of solidarity at issue tells that, soon after the fascist government of Italy began the forcible deportation of its Jewish nationals to German extermination camps, two Austrian-born bourgeois sisters from Trieste found shelter in Udine, thanks to the intercession of the Catholic Archbishop of that town. There, after a short time, the sisters had sold all their valuables in order to buy foodstuff on the black market. Then, the two sisters, who feared deportation already, feared hunger as well. What they did not know is that the Archbishop and the other local citizens who, having heard of their predicament, had decided to help them by keeping them hidden and fed, would keep doing so until the conflict was over, despite the economic difficulties that they all had to face because of the war. Evidently, the two sisters' unfortunate plight was enough to justify the stranger's prolonged benevolence.

From this concrete example of solidarity Jonas does not derive an optimistic philosophical anthropology. After all, in the same years, many more people were busy participating in the expulsion of the Italian Jews, or simply did not care enough about their plight to take any risk. During "the darkest night of Europe" shone only "some solitary lights".[694] As for racism, Jonas believes it to be practically inevitable, insofar as "racial differences" are part of the cultures and history of humankind at large.[695] Indeed, "their disappearance would impoverish humankind" by reducing the cultural variety of humankind.[696] Whether scientifically unsound or morally reproachable, "one cannot deny the reality of race" and may actually find ways to acknowledge its wealth of insights and life-enabling connotations.[697]

Certainly, "antagonisms and tensions, whether reciprocal or unilateral" do not justify the "unspeakable crime" of genocide.[698] Rather, Jonas wishes to acknowledge that "for some psychological strangeness, a racist automatic reaction will always be within us".[699] Not even the Enlightenment and the Industrial Revolution succeeded in eradicating it; why should the theoretically much weaker post-modernism succeed?

Quite the opposite, Jonas tells us that we should not expect to be able to build a world devoid of such antagonisms and tensions, but hope instead that we all, both as individuals and as communities, may be able to cope with such antagonisms and tensions "better than we did in the past", in a civilised manner.[700]

This is particularly important for the allegedly "developed and much-celebrated Euro-American white civilisation", which has prided itself of having found and enshrined in its constitutions the universal rights of man, citizen, woman and child.[701] The "scabrous heritage of slavery in contemporary America" and the "hell" of the Holocaust are recent testimonies of how little weight these rights have in the "recesses of the collective mind" of that "white civilisation".[702]

In order to make "tolerance" or, if we prefer, toleration possible, "all forces of moral education and a vigil political attention" must be employed, for we are set against an untamed and possibly untameable "beast hidden within our imperfect human condition", which should be acknowledged and steered in a civilised manner, rather than buried under the carpet of generalised disapproval.[703]

According to Jonas, an unexpected ally in this complex fight against racism comes from a phenomenon peculiar to "the second half" of the 20th century: the planet's ecological meltdown.[704] Race, in the face of this terrible new "challenge", becomes "anachronistic, irrelevant, almost farcical".[705] No theoretical earthquake has taken place, though. Rather, *ubi maior minor cessat*: "A shared guilt binds us, a shared destiny awaits us, a shared responsibility calls for us".[706] Either we react and act together as "one", for our survival is at stake racial differences notwithstanding, or we perish and, with us, the Earth as we know it.[707]

Jonas does not believe that racial divides will vanish because of a higher sense of human unity, but he does think that such an unprecedented threat to human life is likely to reduce the relevance of such divides in world's affairs. Significantly, in the face of this terrible new challenge, a new picture of "the human condition" is said to be emerging.[708] Whereas the lexicon of religion had connoted our condition for centuries, at least before the secularising forces of science-technology supplanted it, it is now the lexicon of "ecology" that serves the same goal, according to Jonas.[709]

In the religious past, the doctrine of the original sin taught to humankind that "we were all sinners".[710] Today, it is the crippled environment of our planet that passes the same accusation, for we have abused of our ingenuity. Analogously, religion used to frighten us with notions of infernal punishments and "the Last Judgment" to come.[711] It is now "our tortured planet" that tells us that the end is near, without the need for any "divine intervention", in which fewer and fewer people believe any longer.⁷¹² The "last revelation" is not going to come from a divine Messiah or a novel otherworldly inspiration, but from "the Creation" itself, lest "we will all die" by wilfully and culpably ignoring it.⁷¹³

Such a strong language might sound surprising. Jonas was known for his insightful scrutiny of Gnosticism and his finely crafted ethics of responsibility, not for a particularly forceful rhetoric. Yet, that problematic reality to which we refer today under the conceptual umbrella of global warming did elicit very dramatic words from Hans Jonas' mind and mouth. This detail alone should cause us to ponder very carefully.

In his long life, Jonas had witnessed enough drama, persecution, injustice, violence and death not to be easily upset by human problems. As seen, with regard to racism, he was even willing to accept it as a fact of life; racism being merely one of our many faults as human beings. Veritably, in his speech, he invites his audience to be more careful about this psychological aspect of ours, but at the same time Jonas avoids offering any utopian dream of total elimination of racism from public life.

When it comes to global warming, though, Jonas' tone is far less accommodating. The reason for this stylistic change is that the survival of planetary life itself—and of ours in particular—is at stake. Moreover, the threat is not a future one; it is a present one. It is therefore preferable to alarm the audience, inasmuch as a "heuristic of fear" can wisely recommend and spur "the pursuit of virtue... moderation and circumspection".⁷¹⁴

Concluding Remarks

As concerns global warming, there is actually hardly any dissent within the scientific community about it, as the conclusions of the UN Intergovernmental Panel on Climate Change have repeatedly highlighted over many years.⁷¹⁵ The little dissent that exists is typically amplified beyond proportion by the intellectual hypocrisy of governments and corporate think-tanks that frequently parade themselves as politically conservative. Jonas' strong language, coming from a calm, erudite, conservative thinker—indeed the mentor of US conservative icon Leon Kass (b. 1939)—should resound powerfully and, hopefully, stay with us long and deeply enough to counter such a short-term-based and blatant hypocrisy. If anything, it should lead us all, and especially the self-proclaimed climate-change-denying conservatives, to consider what we can do, individually as well as collectively, in order to rescue the planet and our species from destruction: "we are the only possible saviour of both".[716]

Jonas' strong language should also lead us to restrain and free us from politicising in a vulgar, strategic manner such a vital issue, for no significant political game can ever be played if the planet's life support systems are ever to collapse. Similarly, Jonas' strong language should lead us to avoid and condemn economic gambling as well, even though nations have already started squabbling about who owns what in the melting Polar Regions on behalf of powerful industrial lobbies, while at the same time monetising the current carbon-dioxide pollution within the European Union's Emissions Trading Scheme and yet promoting no substantial reduction of the undesired emissions. If only few "solitary lights" are going to shine today and in the near future, then the darkest night ever is bound to fall upon us all, white as well as black, rich as well as poor, wise as well as knowledgeable, progressive as well as conservative. Death, after all, has long been known as the great equaliser of all differences.

PART II – Contemporary legal and social issues

Chapter 7: The ICESCR *qua* Civil Commons

Law and philosophy have met each other happily on many occasions. Indeed, jurisprudence, legal theory and, to a relevant extent, constitutional law are nothing but a combination of legal and philosophical concerns, aims, conceptions, and methodologies. In this chapter, I bring together the 1966 International Covenant on Economic, Social and Cultural Rights (ICESCR), which has already been referred to repeatedly in this book, and life-value onto-axiology, which was very briefly summarised in chapter 3.

Such a coupling, as the following pages will show, does not constitute a futile academic exercise. Rather, the ICESCR can serve as a prime example of "civil commons", that is to say an original philosophical conception of McMurtry's that has since entered the mainstream of the technical nomenclature in today's Anglophone social, human and health sciences as well as, on occasion, institutional practice.[717] At the same time, life-value onto-axiology can provide the theoretical underpinning required for a more nuanced understanding of, and plausibly an interpretative theoretical framework for, the ICESCR. McMurtry's work enables us to unpack the legal principles of the ICESCR as the real content of social justice: guaranteed access to those goods and institutions needed by human beings to survive, develop, and live good lives.

McMurtry's work is well recognised within the UN network, having been adopted as a key philosophical perspective within UNESCO's EOLSS. In what follows l analyse the ICESCR from the standpoint of life-value onto-axiology, emphasising throughout how it gives legal substance to the core values of McMurtry's life-grounded understanding of social justice. Before proceeding to the coupling of the ICESCR and life-value onto-axiology, an introduction to each is provided. Subsequently, McMurtry's theory of value is utilised in order to reveal: (a) what alternative conception of value systemically operates today against the fulfilment of the rights enshrined in the ICESCR; (b) the increased relevance of the ICESCR with regard to the current global economic crisis; (c) the parameters to determine the degree to which the rights at issue have been realised, (a) notwithstanding. Reflections on the environmental implications of the ICESCR in light of life-value axiology conclude the chapter.

The ICESCR

A human rights chapter was not included within the 1945 UN Charter itself, but the Economic and Social Council established under the Charter was entrusted to set up "commissions in economic and social fields and for the promotion of human rights", as specified in article 68.[718] At its first meeting in 1946, it established the Commission on Human Rights (CHR), with which it entrusted the task of drafting a binding treaty on human rights law, as well as the Commission on the Status of Women. In 1948, the UN Commission on Human Rights agreed and submitted to the General Assembly the Universal Declaration of Human Rights (UDHR), where it was approved with no negative votes: there were 48 positive votes and 8 abstentions. However, the UDHR is not a treaty and therefore not in itself legally binding. Instead, the UDHR was expected to form the foundation for a treaty to which states could commit themselves. During a process that took nearly two decades, two, not one, treaties emerged: the ICESCR and the International Covenant on Civil and Political Rights (ICCPR). It was another ten years before they would come into force.[719]

Modern readings often interpret the division of the UDHR into two distinct treaties as Cold-War politics: the West was suspicious of economic, social, and cultural rights *qua* rights; the East considered them as more fundamental than civil and political rights.[720] The truth is, as usual, far more nuanced and the UDHR owes the breadth of its content in some measure to the US and in particular Roosevelt's "four freedoms".[721] Western states and traditional allies of the US, including Australia, Canada, Germany and the UK, were amongst the first state parties to the ICESCR. However, having signed the covenant during the presidency of James Earl "Jimmy" Carter (b. 1924), American resistance to the ICESCR was only consolidated during the administration of Ronald Reagan (1911–2004).[722]

The transformation of the UDHR into two legally binding treaties, rather than one, was intended to address not so much differences of opinion about the relative importance of different rights but more pragmatic concerns about implementation: in particular, State capability and institutional justiciability.[723] To the extent that fulfilment of economic, social, and cultural rights had significant budgetary implications, it was not self-evident that the courts were the proper *fora* for such fine assessments.[724] Yet, it was pointed out that economic, social and cultural rights were no different from civil and political rights in this regard in that both groups contain both positive and negative elements, or, in the common parlance of the UN Committee on Economic, Social and Cultural Rights (ESCR Committee), established to monitor State compliance with the ICESCR, "duties to respect, protect, and fulfil".[725] Civil and political rights likewise require state expenditures.[726] From the standpoint of a life-grounded understanding both are equally essential as what any just society must guarantee to each of its citizens.

At the time of drafting, it was obvious that a number of states were in no position to guarantee overnight all the economic, social, and cultural rights promised in the UDHR but they were better equipped to facilitate civil and political rights. In most states, in 1966, there was already in place a rudimentary framework that could ensure even those civil and political rights that require extensive State investment, such as the right to a fair trial or the right to vote. In other words, the overwhelming majority of states had operational courts, functioning judiciaries and could hold rudimentary elections. Yet, most were very far from guaranteeing adequate housing or health-care facilities for everyone, nor could any such infrastructure be built in the anticipated three months period between ratification and entry into force.[727] Thus, whilst states agreed under the ICCPR to guarantee civil and political rights to the full immediately, they agreed only to work towards full enjoyment of economic, social, and cultural rights, i.e. they undertook the obligation to "progressively realize" these rights.[728]

The progressive realisation standard solved the capability problem: states had to take all appropriate means—within their means—to realise the rights in the ICESCR. However, this formulation brought with it its own set of problems, in particular, the justiciability problem. How could courts adjudicate the satisfaction or violation of rights that lacked explicit benchmarks, that were effectively contextual and which depended on the relative means of each State party? If there is no absolute obligation on the State, how can it be determined if the State has breached its obligation?

In reply, it can be observed that numerous rights within the ICESCR are not vague at all, such as the right to join a trade union of one's choice and the right not to be discriminated against in respect of economic, social, and cultural rights (articles 8 and 2(2)). On the other hand, there are likewise rights within the ICCPR that are inherently vague and subject to contextual interpretation such as the right to privacy, which can be subject to "lawful" and "non-arbitrary" interference and must be balanced against freedom of expression.[729]

With regard to more complex rights, two decades of output from the ESCR Committee has provided ever greater clarity and precision as to what is required of State parties and adjudication by the Committee under the new communications process will further enrich understanding.[730] Economic, social, and cultural rights have been introduced into modern constitutions and are regularly adjudicated by judges all over the world, most famously in South Africa.[731] The justiciability horse needs no more flogging here, since the actual institutional issue has long ceased to be *whether* economic, social and economic rights are justiciable, and has been about *how* they can best be adjudicated.[732]

The ESCR Committee is not a creature of the ICESCR, in contrast to its counterpart, the Human Rights Committee, established under article 28 of the ICCPR. Instead, the ESCR Committee was established nearly ten years after the Covenant came into force, on the back of resolution no. 1985/17 by the UN Economic and Social Council (ECOSOC). Like the Human Rights Committee, it reviews State reports, discusses them with State parties and makes concluding observations, and it issues general comments addressed to all State parties.[733]

If the heart of the ICCPR is the "right to life", as *per* article 6, the heart of the ICESCR might be considered the 'right to live' i.e. the right to live a dignified life; the right to a quality of life; the right to a life free of fear of hunger and destitution; a life where the human spirit has space to flourish. This flourishing, which is contingent upon the comprehensive satisfaction of the needs recognised by the 'right to live' is the ultimate goal of life-grounded social justice. Genuine fulfilment of the covenant requires realisation of many of the values that are at the heart of modern conceptions of "social justice", such as access to fair employment, education, and healthcare provision.

The substantive provisions of the ICESCR include: the right to self-determination of peoples, including the right to control their own natural resources (article 1); the right to work (article 6); the right to just and favourable conditions of work, including remuneration (article 7); the right to trade union organisation and participation (article 8); the right to social security (article 9); the right to recognition and protection of marriage and paid leave for new mothers (article 10); the right to an adequate standard of living, including adequate food, clothing, and housing (article 11); the right to the highest attainable standard of health (article 12); the right to education (articles 13–4); and the right to take part in cultural life, to benefit from scientific progress and to benefit from one's own intellectual creations (article 15). Overlying these rights is the principle of non-discrimination (article 2(2)), with gender equality emphasised (article 3), the prohibition of abuse of rights (article 5), and the permission for states to set limits on the enunciated rights only "for the purposes of promoting the general welfare in a democratic society" (article 4).

As an international treaty, the ICESCR is unquestionably binding as a matter of international law, *per* article 26 of the Vienna convention on the law of treaties (VCLT).[734] Nevertheless, State practice does not always conform to states' obligations. Indeed, alternative or even incompatible normative frameworks can shape the discourse. To name just a few examples *vis-à-vis* articles 1, 6, 12 and 13 respectively:

(a) in 2009, the government of Peru responded by means of police and military crackdowns to protests by indigenous populations against the legislation that opened Peru's virgin forests to oil- and gas-drilling operations;[735]
(b) in 2010, unemployment in the Eurozone reached double figures, but the European Central Bank engaged in no quantitative easing to counteract this trend, comparable to the steps taken between 2007 and 2009 to rescue failing private banks;[736]
(c) during the US presidency of Barack Obama, the adoption of a universal healthcare coverage in the United States of America was vocally opposed by mobilised individuals dubbing themselves the "Tea Party" movement, whose number and influence have been "reshaping the Republican Party" into an arch-conservative institution;[737] and
(d) the British Parliament passed legislation aimed at slashing education funding at tertiary level at English and Welsh universities, causing them to take in fewer students, demand higher tuition fees, and lead to higher levels of student indebtedness.[738]

Apart from suggesting that governmental authorities neglect the covenants to which they are bound, the examples above signal that alternative conceptions of value exist and may even be predominant in politics and institutional life, to the point of rejecting the rights enshrined in international law. How are such views to be assessed? Do they imply that the values embodied by the ICESCR are incomplete? In pluralist societies such as ours, which values should be upheld and, above all, upon what grounds? In the following sections, I show how life-value onto-axiology can help to answer some of these deep and controversial questions.

Life-value Onto-axiology

Possibly terrified by the consequences of the uncompromising statements of value characterising totalitarian ideologies, all major Anglophone theorists of value of the second half of the 20th century have offered highly abstract and impractical interpretations.⁷³⁹ Whether intentionally or not, these interpretations have reflected the dominant liberal economic conception of value of their age, whereby the so-called "preference satisfaction" of the contract-stipulating individual determines value by the exercise of allegedly universal and neutral money-demand in the nominally assumed "free market". Thus understood, value is ultimately subjective (i.e. different individuals have different values), atomistic (i.e. societies' values are aggregates of individuals' values) and quintessentially human (i.e. human beings ascribe value to non-human beings, which would otherwise possess none).

McMurtry is aware of the perplexities that arise regularly with regard to any objective determination of value: "As the recent history of philosophy discloses, the multiplying particular bearings of language games, specific practices, incommensurable epistemic perspectives, anti-foundationalist conversations and poststructural principles of difference have overwhelmed the very idea of a unifying value system, good or ill, as inconceivable to acceptable meaning."⁷⁴⁰ On this matter, Michel Foucault had famously observed in the late 1970s that the prolonged experience of top-down determination of social values by the State, from "Bismark's state socialism" to "National Socialism", was a crucial factor in the development of German-speaking neo-liberalism, most notably in Hayek's work and its emphasis upon individual independence in value options by way of the principle of free choice in the free market.⁷⁴¹

Nevertheless, after pondering upon the recurrent meltdowns of the post-Bretton-Woods age and the social and ecological losses accompanying them, McMurtry claims that we must: "follow reason where it leads to recover step by step the missing life-ground of values and the ultimate meaning of how we are to live."⁷⁴² Since the formal and relativist options debated in mainstream axiology have proven tragically useless *vis-à-vis* both economic and ecological crises, McMurtry endeavours to provide a substantial and objective alternative. It is in this sense that McMurtry characterises his own theory of value as "onto-axiology", thus stressing the connection between value—as indicated by "axiology" i.e. the technical term for the study of that which is paramount—and being as such—as indicated by the prefix "onto-" i.e. pertaining to being.[743] Yet what exactly is the "life-ground" that has gone amiss and that, if recovered, can reveal how we should live?

The definition of this key-term is unusually simple to grasp: "Concretely, all that is required to take the next breath; axiologically, all the life support systems required for human life to reproduce or develop."[744] Without enough bread, clean water, breathable air, open spaces in which to move, regular sleep, acceptable education and meaningful socialisation, no value whatsoever that we cherish will ever be expressed in reality. Here the life-ground works beneath established ideological and philosophical disputes about the meaning of social justice to expose its material core in the satisfaction of human life-requirements.

All values with no exception, whether ethical, political, economic, epistemic or aesthetic, rely upon this vital platform—the life-ground—typically in a pre-reflexive manner. There can be no life, not to mention any good life, outside this ground. As McMurtry states, "Life support systems—any natural or human-made system without which human beings cannot live or live well—may or may not have value in themselves, but have *ultimate* value so far as they are that without which human or other life cannot exist or flourish."[745] Logically, it is possible to distinguish between life as possessing intrinsic value and the life-ground as being instrumentally valuable. Ontologically, this is impossible: "All that is of worth consists in and enables life value *to the extent* of its experienced fields of thought, felt being and action (intrinsic value), *and* what underlies and enables these fields of life themselves, life support systems."[746]

Even the civil and political rights enshrined in liberal democratic constitutions and in the ICCPR itself—be they justice, equality, liberty, or democracy—are formal fictions if the prerequisites for prolonged survival and adequate individual and social existence are not met. We saw in chapter 3 how eloquently liberal icon Isaiah Berlin made this point: "It is true that to offer political rights, or safeguards against intervention by the state, to men who are half-naked, illiterate, underfed, and diseased is to mock their condition… What is freedom to those who cannot make use of it? Without adequate conditions for the use of freedom, what is the value of freedom?"[747]

McMurtry calls "needs" all these prerequisites, the scrutiny of which serves then the end of clarifying the composition and the scope of the life-ground. Not anything that we may claim to "need" is, after closer scrutiny, a need. According to McMurtry "'n' is a need if and only if, and to the extent that, deprivation of n always leads to a reduction of organic capacity."[748] Only that without which organic capacity is harmed regularly and unequivocally counts as need. We can live, and even prosper, without motorbikes or memory pens, but we cannot live, not to mention prosper, without nourishing food, shelter and several hours of sleep each night. Upon such needs and their prolonged, secure satisfaction rests everything else that may be regarded as valuable: art, sport, conversation, commerce, scientific research, sexual experimentation, political activism, philosophical meditation, etc. And whenever any such derivative form of agency harms or hampers the prolonged, secure, universal satisfaction of needs, then disvalue ensues.[749]

Whilst the recognition of human needs by McMurtry is an important beginning, the satisfaction of human needs is not the same as the recognition of human rights to the satisfaction of the same. Needs should not be met by the State as a matter of welfare, a matter of charity, which the State enjoys discretion to withdraw. A citizen should not beg for the assistance necessary simply to stay alive; instead they should be able to demand that their needs be met and, moreover, have confidence that their needs will continue to be met. "To enjoy something only at the discretion of someone else, especially someone powerful enough to deprive you of it at will, is precisely *not* to enjoy a *right* to it".[750] Holding a right is a special sort of entitlement for which there is no shame attached to its claiming; and it is an entitlement that remains notwithstanding budgetary uncertainty or constraints on the duty bearer.

Considering that McMurtry regards life as unfolding along three modes of ontological manifestation—i.e. "thought", "experience" (also "feeling" or "felt being"), and "action" (also "biological movement" or "motility")[751]—the fundamental coordinates of value are as follows:

- *X is value if and only if, and to the extent that, X consists in or enables a more coherently inclusive range of thought/feeling/ action than without it*
- *X is disvalue if and only if, and to the extent that, X reduces/ disables any range of thought/experience/action*[752]

Given these coordinates, McMurtry's onto-axiology allows for the determination of good and evil, cutting across received dualisms (e.g. utilitarianism vs. deontology, free choice vs. paternalism, free trade vs. protectionism, individualism vs. collectivism, etc.). Life-enablement and disablement signal respectively positive progress and negative regress.

Devoid of a theoretical underpinning as comprehensively abstract as McMurtry's life-ground—the attainment of which is after all the philosopher's *raison d'être*—the world's nations have provided themselves with an array of concepts, traditions, collective praxes, facilities, charities, foundations, and disciplinary branches whose main task is enable to foster life capacity expression and enjoyment. Ethical principles, notions of the common good, human rights, life-expectancy rates, hygiene standards, methods for waste disposal, suicide rates, manic-depressive pathologies, crime rates, literacy levels and many other dimensions of individual, social and natural existence have been conceptualised, discussed, followed, scrutinised, addressed and managed daily by corresponding institutions, such as ethical committees, scholarly communities, human rights treaty bodies, municipal registrars, public hygiene offices, mental hygiene departments, police corps and other law-and-order enforcers, schools, research centres, etc. Whether conscious or not of their life-serving function, much of organised human existence, both material and immaterial, has been spent in view of conceiving, perceiving, preventing, denouncing, and countering any assault on life capacity, as this is revealed by the particular, standardised indicators that are specific to each institution.

It is on the basis of this long- and well-established concrete human praxes for life-enablement that McMurtry unearths and articulates life-value onto-axiology as an abstract philosophical conception. Consistently, as seen in chapter 3, he can list as embodiments of his axiology a vast and diverse array of conceptions, arrangements and artefacts that have been aimed at fulfilling the continued satisfaction of life-needs in most diverse socio-historical contexts:

> *[U]niversal health plans, the world wide web, common sewers, international outrage over Vietnam or Ogoniland, sidewalks and footpaths, the Chinese concept of jen, the Jubilee of Leviticus... water fountains, Robin Hood of Sherwood Forest, the air we breathe, effective pollution controls... music... old age pensions, universal education, Sweden's common forests... the second commandment of Yeshua... the rule of law, child and women shelters, parks, public broadcasting, clean water... the UN Declaration of Human Rights, occupational health and safety standards, village and city squares, the Brazilian rainforests, inoculation programmes, indigenous story-telling, the Ozone Protocol, the Tao, the peace movement, death rituals, animal rights agencies, community fish-habitats, food and drug legislation, garbage collection, the ancient village commons before enclosures.*[753]

All of these human creations are "civil commons" i.e. "[a] unifying concept to designate social constructs which enable universal access to life goods. Life support systems are civil commons so far as society protects and enables their reproduction and provision for all members."[754]

Economic Systems

From a life-grounded perspective, which system of ownership, management and trade ought to be predominant is not relevant *per se*, as an ideological, ethical or political *summum bonum*. Similarly, and in contrast to many international agreements of recent decades, the ICESCR is neither a trade agreement presupposing significant degrees of free-market activity, legal frameworks and economic policies; nor does it depend upon free-market activity or any particular legal framework or economic policies. The ESCR Committee has taken care to point out that the treaty does not exclude a libertarian model as long as everyone's rights are in fact fulfilled, noting in 1990 that:

> *[T]he undertaking "to take steps... by all appropriate means including particularly the adoption of legislative measures" neither requires nor precludes any particular form of government or economic system being used as the vehicle for the steps in question, provided only that it is democratic and that all human rights are thereby respected. Thus, in terms of political and economic systems, the Covenant is neutral and its principles cannot accurately be described as being predicated exclusively upon the need for, or the desirability of a socialist or a capitalist system, or a mixed, centrally planned, or laissez-faire economy, or upon any particular approach.*[755]

It is thus quite reasonable for the State to assume that individuals will be able to a large extent to satisfy their own rights, with a minimum of State intervention. For example, individuals should be likely to be able to satisfy their rights to work and to an adequate standard of living, with the State only stepping in for those who are unable to do so independently.[756] There is one notable exception in the treaty: the right to education, which, at least at primary level, must be compulsory and free.[757]

In practice, the ESCR Committee's ecumenical approach to market systems only goes so far; a State party is not simply empowered to intervene to guarantee the relevant rights for its inhabitants but is obliged so to do when a dogmatically anti-interventionist approach leaves some individuals unable to secure their own economic, social, and cultural rights. For example, concluding the review of the report on Hong Kong in 2001, the Committee considered that the region's reliance "on the philosophy of 'positive non-interventionism'" was a factor limiting the full implementation of the treaty and "had a negative impact on the realization and enjoyment of the economic, social, and cultural rights of Hong Kong's inhabitants, which has been exacerbated by globalization."[758] Similarly, the Committee has expressed the view that increasing privatisation of services has been accompanied by increasing challenges for certain groups of vulnerable individuals to satisfy their own basic rights; hence increasing responsibilities for State parties to intervene to ensure their rights are guaranteed *qua* rights.[759]

From a life-grounded perspective, if the appropriation of the commons for private ends is preferred and performed, as ceaselessly done worldwide in the past three decades, it is crucial that it be able to spur life-capability more widely in both space and time.[760] From such a perspective, an economy is truly successful if it can "secure provision of means of life otherwise in short supply (i.e. the production and distribution of goods and the protection of ecosystem services which are otherwise scarce or made scarce through time)".[761] Consistently, true civil commons are only those life-support systems that genuinely allow for such an economy to operate. Since life is the value-compass utilised by McMurtry, not any priced commodity contributing to the generation of profit or to augmented GDP figures should be counted as wealth-creation.

Once again, let us reiterate a fundamental insight of life-value onto-axiology: "Claimed 'economic goods' which disable or do not enable life abilities are not means of life; they are economic 'bads'".[762] Carcinogenic pesticides, cluster bombs, junk commodities, speculative financial products and hazardous mining are not good. They are bad. They may be extremely profitable, like slaves had been for many centuries, but inasmuch as they reduce life-capacity, they are "goods" if and only if we wish to indulge in oxymoron. Perplexingly, standard economics endorses unflinchingly such an oxymoronic language. All life-reducing items of trade mentioned above are called, in standard economic language and praxis, "goods", with no exception.

This glaring conceptual confusion, whereby nourishing bread is equated with golden toilets, can take place because in a value-system devoid of life-coordinates all that which does not compute as an item of trade in the free market is marginal or *de facto* invisible unless it is reconstructed as monetary loss or business opportunity. Non-moneyed people, cultural homogenisation, pollution, the loss of biodiversity, and the melting of the Arctic ice-shelf are conceived of as economic externalities until, say, reduced cost of labour, carbon trade mechanisms, medical research, and lawsuits by indigenous communities seeking compensation make them expressible in money-based terms. It is only whether and when the externalities can be internalised that economic calculus can actually compute them in its equations.

This externalisation of living beings and life support systems takes place regularly even if no economic calculus can actually exist without many of them and, in reality, presupposes several externalities throughout (e.g. the generation of children, human languages, Earth's breathable air and oceanic plankton). As soon as this internalisation occurs, any item may become a tradable "good", even if the former externality has not been reconstructed as life-serving civil commons, but rather as a non-universal and even life-damaging for-profit activity (e.g. unnecessary stress-inducing medical testing of paying pregnant women, disappearance of traditional birthday songs from films and plays due to copyright attribution, exclusive air stations in polluted Asian capitals).

Moreover, once the internalisation has occurred, these novel "goods" and "costs" can be attributed a value-expressing price by exercise of money-demand in a comparative market system of aggregate individual preferences. This seemingly simple and neutral fact implies that sight may be lost altogether of their *other* axiological dimensions, their economic value being now forcefully on the foreground and not, say, their religious sacredness, incomparable beauty, categorical moral normativity, vital ecological function, etc.

This conceptual blindness and the consequent axiological loss explain why life-enabling economic, social, and cultural rights, albeit enshrined in the ICESCR, have been repeatedly sacrificed to the pursuit of life-impairing economic efficiency. The examples are many and diverse: longer working hours (as *per* article 7(d) of the ICESCR); less-inclusive pension schemes (as *per* article 9); reduced parental leave (as *per* article 10); cheaper, lower-quality school meals (as *per* articles 11(1) and 12); reduced healthcare provision (as *per* article 12); increased market opportunities for performance-enhancing drug-dealing, whether legal or illegal (ditto); cuts to educational services (as *per* articles 13 and 14); and reductions in publicly funded cultural programs (as *per* article 15).

Similarly, since at least the late 1970s, when it comes to determining the course of monetary policy in free-market economies, their sovereign right to issue coin and credit, and the levels of taxation for capital gains, there seems to have been no other guideline but to make entire countries attractive to business. This attractiveness has been so interpreted as to be achieved by slashing protective regulation, thereby maximising returns for private shareholders, even if entire societies are harmed in the process and democratic self-rule is thwarted by oligarchic privilege, as Giulio Tremonti, among others, has lamented.

The Crisis

After sponsoring for decades vast programmes for the privatisation, liberalisation and deregulation of the world's financial industry, the IMF acknowledged in 2008 that "[t]he world economy is entering a major downturn in the biggest financial crisis since the 1930s".[763] On an analogous note, as seen in chapter 3, the UN's Secretary-General stated one year later that the "economic and financial turmoil sweeping the globe is a true wake-up call, sounding an alarm about the need to improve upon old patterns of growth and make a transition to a new era of greener, cleaner development."[764]

Under these momentous and dramatic circumstances, McMurtry's substantial and objective theory of value, which treats life as the paramount end of human agency and economic activity as a means, becomes a plausible conceptual tool for reconsidering the axiological hierarchies that have led the international community to the crisis denounced by the UN's Secretary-General. Indeed, if one considers that McMurtry's main works focussed already in the 1990s on the pernicious axiological confusion of de-regulated financial activity in the face of persistent socio-economic meltdowns and environmental losses, their relevance as the current crisis is concerned is manifest and Cassandra-like. As he writes: "[F]inancial crises always follow from money-value delinked from real value, which has many names but no understanding of the principle at its deepest levels."[765]

Under the same circumstances, the ICESCR becomes a major point of reference *vis-à-vis* the sort of value-choices that should be made so as to guide policy-making and international cooperation. First of all, the rights addressed by the ICESCR are precisely the sort of rights that today's crisis affects most critically. In times of crisis, it becomes more difficult for people to realise their own needs, fulfil their own rights, without State intervention; yet the State is simultaneously under pressure to cut such assistance, both domestically and internationally. Official surveys, scientific journals and mainstream media sources have been revealing amply and candidly the astounding social, economic, and cultural losses due to the economic crisis since 2008.[766]

Secondly, as discussed in this chapter, the ICESCR addresses economic, social, and cultural rights from a position that is ostensibly neutral as to a State party's economic system, at least up to a certain extent.[767] As such, the ICESCR endures as a set of binding goals for the international community regardless of the dominant market ideology within a State and irrespective of whether the crisis incites more or less intervention. In fact, the ESCR Committee has pointed out that in times of economic crisis, the treaty becomes more, not less important: "under such circumstances, endeavours to protect the most basic economic, social, and cultural rights become more, rather than less, urgent".[768] Let us not forget that the 2008 credit crunch was due to aptly named "toxic assets" created and traded for profit by the world's largest financial institutions, which were rescued from the brink of bankruptcy by massive State intervention and henceforth allowed to: (a) lend money for profit to taxpayers whose tax-money had saved them; (b) deny money to public bodies to the point of near-bankruptcy (e.g. the US State of California); (c) pay bonuses to executives responsible for the "crunch" due to "toxic assets"; and (d) speculate against and/or force states to cut public spending *via* control of treasury bonds and other securities. Whilst (a) and (c) contradict the capitalist ethos, (b) and (d) have obvious negative implications for publicly funded civil commons.

Thirdly, of 192 member states of the UN, 160 are parties to the ICESCR and a further six have signed it, meaning that those states that have signed a treaty undertake not to undermine its object and purpose, pending ratification.[769] The State parties include states from all different geographical, legal, economic, cultural, and religious traditions at all levels of development, indicating shared recognition of the importance of economic, social, and cultural rights. Emblematically, after decades of negotiation, the Optional Protocol (OP-ICESCR) was unanimously adopted by the UN General Assembly in December 2008—just as world leaders were waking up to the depth of the current financial crisis. When opened for signature in September 2009, twenty-nine states immediately signed the protocol, indicating their support for the communications process. Since then and at the time of writing, a further four states have signed and two states have ratified it. The protocol will come into force when 10 states have ratified it, thus giving individuals and groups within those jurisdictions the right to bring communications indicating violations of their rights to the ESCR Committee.[770]

Fourthly, the ICESCR embodies paramount life-goals, consistent with McMurtry's understanding of value. The life-grounded character of the ICESCR is manifest already in its preamble, in which the vital dimensions of felt being and action are acknowledged as the goal to strive for: "the ideal of free human beings enjoying *freedom from fear or want*".[771] The ICESCR here refers explicitly to two of the "four freedoms" articulated by F.D.

Roosevelt in 1941, which formed the foundation of the UDHR.[772] The preamble of a treaty is not legally binding on State parties *per se*, but forms part of its context and indicates its object and purpose. Therefore, when interpreting the substantive articles, reference to the preamble can be made.[773] Each state is required to ensure the conditions that allow for moving in this direction, in other words "to take steps, individually and through international assistance and co-operation, especially economic and technical, to the maximum of its available resources, with a view to achieving progressively the full realization of the rights".[774]

No "freedom, justice and peace" can be attained if states fail in this task; and to secure their fulfilment is not charity; it is not an option; and it is not an expression of good will: it is a duty of states.[775] So crucial are these rights, that even individuals are said to be morally bound by them: not as charity, not as an option, not as an expression of good will, but as a moral duty to their fellow citizens: "The State Parties to the present Covenant... realiz[e] that the individual, having duties to other individuals and to the community to which he belongs, is under a responsibility to strive for the promotion and observance of the rights recognized in the present Covenant."[776]

Strengthening the life-centred tone of the covenant, article 1 of the ICESCR affirms that "[i]n no case may a people be deprived of its own means of subsistence." Article 7 speaks of "just and favourable conditions of work... A decent living for themselves and their families... Safe and healthy working conditions... Rest, leisure and reasonable limitation of working hours and periodic holidays with pay." Article 8 requires "the right of everyone to form trade unions and join the trade union of his choice", given their historical role in promoting equitable access to life-goods under democratic regimes.[777] Article 9 recognises "the right of everyone to social security, including social insurance." Article 10 acknowledges "[t]he widest possible protection and assistance... to the family... mothers... all children and young persons... [who] should be protected from economic and social exploitation... [e.g.] employment in work harmful to their morals or health or dangerous to life or likely to hamper their normal development." Article 11 identifies "adequate food, clothing and housing" as well as freedom "from hunger" and "an equitable distribution of world food supplies in relation to need" as key-factors in adhering to the covenant. Article 12 adds "physical and mental health... the reduction of the stillbirth-rate and of infant mortality... environmental and industrial hygiene... medical attention in the event of sickness." Articles 13 and 14 further acknowledge the thinking dimension of life by stressing "the right of everyone to education... Primary education... [to be made, if not already so,] compulsory and free to all", whilst "[s]econdary" and "[h]igher education" should "be made generally available and accessible to all." Similarly, article 15 highlights "the right of everyone... To take part in cultural life... enjoy the benefits of scientific progress and its applications... the conservation, the development and the diffusion of science and culture."

Human Rights as Duties of States

Labour standards, nutritional standards, health and safety regulations, living standards, education, healthcare provision, the promotion and diffusion of cultural activities and scientific knowledge: they all spring from the life-ground and, unsurprisingly, they are recognised as valuable by the international community. McMurtry himself emphasises the pivotal role that the rights enshrined in the ICESCR should play in rebuilding the life-fabric of meltdown-stricken societies, "because of their centrality to contemporary human life and their bridging across the received disjunction between economic and ethico-political rights in an integrated shape."[778]

As a matter of fact, life-value onto-axiology allows us to perceive that "the unifying principle of these rights is to protect and enable human life" which, as seen already in chapter 3, encompasses action (e.g. means of subsistence), felt being (e.g. mental health) and thought (e.g. education).[779] A counterfactual test may suffice to further substantiate this point: none of these rights can be sensibly described as intentionally, eminently or evidently prone to biocide or life-destructive agency, at least as long as life-value onto-axiology is adopted as a viable philosophical hermeneutic, that is, a creative, insightful, learned, and rigorous set of wide- and deep-reaching categories of interpretation of reality.

The ICESCR appears to be a clear case of civil commons. On the one hand, the rights addressed by the ICESCR are a conceptualisation of the "commons" upon which human communities stand and, possibly, flourish, e.g.: the short- and medium-term life-sustaining means that all members need (articles 1 and 11); the protection and generation of human life (article 12); its adequate care, socialisation and education (articles 10, 13 and 14); the long-term life-sustaining and life-enriching occupational, vocational and recreational opportunities of the physically and mentally fit members (articles 6, 7, 8 and 15); the humane and humanity-enhancing assistance due to those who are not fit (articles 9 and 12). On the other hand, the vast institutional consensus underpinning the ICESCR as a binding legal document requiring its parties to report regularly on the implementation of the covenant manifests that these commons are "civil" in the sense that they allow for civilisation to be and continue to be (articles 16 and 17).

The ICESCR shows vividly how the international community already possesses long-standing resources for interpreting and resolving life-threatening circumstances, despite the fact that even a legally binding international human rights treaty is difficult to enforce. One means of evaluating firm obligations and adjudicating violations is to set a minimum level below which the citizens of all nations should never be allowed to fall, which is what the ESCR Committee has defined as "minimum core" obligations.[780]

In this respect, McMurtry's understanding of human needs can serve as an example of where exactly one should set the threshold of the minimum core, at least as actual living persons—as distinguished from legal persons—are concerned. Progressive realisation of the ICESCR ought to be pursued without drastic short-term sacrifices that undermine the most rudimentary means of life in the present. A failure to guarantee the minimum core, the fundamental organic capacity of each person in a state's jurisdiction, constitutes a violation of the covenant unless the State can demonstrate "that every effort has been made to use all resources that are at its disposition in an effort to satisfy, as a matter of priority, those minimum obligations".[781]

The reduction of organic capacity can take many forms, be more or less expedite, and more or less rapidly fatal. Death is its most easily detectable indication, and it is in fact mentioned in the ICESCR itself (e.g. article 12). Still, it is possible to observe reduction of organic capacity long before that final stage, which is what the ICESCR presumes by its references, *inter alia*, to "the fundamental right of everyone to be free from hunger" (article 11(1)), and "the prevention, treatment and control of epidemic, endemic and occupational diseases" (article 12(2)(c)). Social scientists tracking rates of spousal abuses, nutritionists and social workers monitoring nutritional imbalances and poverty, public health experts reporting on pathological trends and their causes, whether aware of the covenant or not, are all engaged in a worldwide assessment of life-grounded phenomena that are pertinent to the aims of the ICESCR.[782]

Human Rights as Means of Life

As concerns the variety of ways in which reduction of organic capacity can happen, scientific standards are debatable and debated, as all human creations are, but are nevertheless employed daily by national public bodies and international authorities in determining, for example, the acceptable quality level of school meals (e.g. the US Department of Agriculture's (USDA) 1980s discussions on whether to assess ketchup as a vegetable), the new types of car engines that may be manufactured and sold (e.g. the EU emission standards), plausible grounds for separation or divorce (e.g. German judges' use of expert psychiatric opinions), literacy requirements for job applicants (e.g. British literacy and numeracy tests for aspiring civil servants), the regularity and fairness of democratic elections (e.g. regular monitoring of elections worldwide by the OECD). Consistently, the ESCR Committee requires State parties to submit detailed and disaggregated sociological data in its initial and periodic reports in order to review each state's situation in light of its obligations.[783]

In this connection, McMurtry offers his WBI, which was introduced in chapter 3, but is worth recalling here in its entirety, for it is said to comprise "the complete and universal set of needs which all humans require to be met in order to flourish", namely:

1. *breathable air, sense-open space, and daily light* (atmospheric means of life)
2. *clean water, nourishing foods and self-waste disposal* (bodily means of life)
3. *shelter space from the elements with ample provision to retire, sleep and function* (home means of life)
4. *environmental surroundings whose elements and contours contribute to the whole* (environmental means of life)
5. *intimate love, social inclusion, safety and healthcare when ill or infirm* (caring means of life)
6. *activities of language-logos/art-play to choose and learn from* (educational/recreational means of life)
7. *meaningful work or service to perform* (vocational means of life)
8. *self-governing choice in each's enjoyment consistent with each's provision* (just form of life)[784]

Debatable and perfectible—McMurtry himself has produced different versions of it—the WBI highlights several needs without meeting which human life, both individual and collective, would eventually disintegrate by accumulated physical and mental deficiencies. The WBI has a willing accomplice in the ESCR Committee's 2001 statement on poverty, in which the Committee attempts to integrate human rights in poverty eradication strategies. The statement addresses poverty in the following terms:

In the recent past, poverty was often defined as insufficient income to buy a minimum basket of goods and services.

Today, the term is usually understood more broadly as the lack of basic capabilities to live in dignity. This definition recognizes poverty's broader features, such as hunger, poor education, discrimination, vulnerability, and social exclusion. The Committee notes that this understanding of poverty corresponds with numerous provisions of the Covenant. In the light of the International Bill of Rights, poverty may be defined as a human condition characterized by sustained or chronic deprivation of the resources, capabilities, choices, security and power necessary for the enjoyment of an adequate standard of living and other civil, cultural, economic, political and social rights.[785]

Considering the WBI in light of the ICESCR and the work of the Committee, we can compare as follows:

1. *Atmospheric means of life*:

The ICESCR incorporates "the right of everyone to the enjoyment of the highest attainable standard of physical and mental health" (article 12(1)) and imparts a duty on states to take steps towards the "improvement of all aspects of environmental and industrial hygiene" (article 12(2)(b)) and ensure a "[s]afe and healthy working environment" (article 7(b)). In its General Comment No. 14 of 2000, the ESCR Committee recognises "a healthy environment" as a fundamental component of the right to health.[786]

2. *Bodily means of life*:

The ICESCR states: "The States Parties to the present Covenant recognize the right of everyone to an adequate standard of living for himself and his family, including adequate food, clothing, and housing, and to the continuous improvement of living conditions" (article 11(1)). Identified minimum core rights include the right not to be hungry and to have access to nutritionally and culturally adequate food and a safe water supply covering essential needs, with non-discriminatory, genuine and safe access to and equitable distribution of water facilities.[787] Indeed, article 11(2) of the ICESCR asserts that the State parties "recogniz[e]… the essential importance of international cooperation based on free consent".

With regard to the right to be free from hunger (as distinguished from the right to adequate food), State parties "recognizing the right of everyone to be free from hunger, shall take, individually and through international cooperation, the measures, including specific programmes, which are needed:" to improve food production, conservation and distribution and ensure an "equitable distribution" of food supplies (article 11(2)). "(Shall" is used to indicate a binding State obligation and the use of "everyone" indicates that the obligations of State parties are to all world inhabitants, not only those in the home state, nor even only those inhabitants living within other State parties.)

Also, the ESCR Committee goes further, relying on articles 55 and 56 as well as the ICESCR, in order to state that: "international cooperation for development and thus for the realization of economic, social, and cultural rights is an obligation of all States".[788] In other words, the Committee does not only claim that states should take the covenant into account when engaging in development cooperation but that development cooperation itself is an obligation, not a discretion for members of the UN.

3. *Home means of life*:

The right to be free from hunger is incorporated in article 11 and has a dedicated general comment, i.e. General Comment No. 4, issued in 1991. Additionally, "[b]asic shelter, housing and sanitation" are recognised as minimum core components of the right to health.[789] The right to social security crosses both bodily and home means of life, including, as the minimum core, that each have access to social security providing a "survival standard".[790]

4. *Environmental means of life*:

The ICESCR has a limited approach to the environment, recognising its value only where it contributes to the realisation of "human" rights. (More is said about it in a separate section at the end of this chapter.)

5. *Caring means of life*:

Article 10 of the ICESCR declares: "The widest possible protection and assistance should be accorded to the family, which is the natural and fundamental group unit of society, particularly for its establishment and while it is responsible for the care and education of dependent children… Special protection should be accorded to mothers during a reasonable period before and after childbirth". The ESCR Committee has highlighted the importance of family for persons with disabilities and older persons, groups whose members have historically found their rights to live in a supportive family environment constrained.[791] The Committee has a dedicated general comment on the right to health in which they identify the minimum core components of health-care, including non-discriminatory access to and equitable distribution of health-care services and essential drugs.[792]

6. *Educational/recreational means of life*:

Article 13(1) of the ICESCR affirms that States parties "recognize the right of everyone to education". This right is not only the right of children to schooling but to all individuals of all ages to education at a suitable level. The minimum core incorporates basic primary education and equality of access to all for education at other levels.[793] As clearly stated in article 13(2)(a) of the ICESCR, primary education must be "compulsory and available free to all"—implicitly including adults who lack basic numeracy and literacy skills—and this is the only provision for which the means for progressive realisation are spelt out in a distinct ICESCR article, number 14, which requires:

> *Each State Party to the present Covenant which, at the time of becoming a Party, has not been able to secure in its metropolitan territory or other territories under its jurisdiction compulsory primary education, free of charge, undertakes, within two years, to work out and adopt a detailed plan of action for the progressive implementation, within a reasonable number of years, to be fixed in the plan, of the principle of compulsory education free of charge for all.*

The minimum core of the right to "take part in cultural activities" (article 15) includes non-discriminatory access, free expression and choice as to whether to participate in cultural activities, and involvement of stakeholders in development of policies relating to cultural activities.[794] Further, States recognise, within the context of the right to work, the right of everyone to "[r]est, leisure and reasonable limitation of working hours and periodic holidays with pay, as well as remuneration for public holidays" (article 7(d)).

7. Vocational means of life:

The ICESCR states that "the States Parties to the present Covenant recognize the right to work, which includes the right of everyone to the opportunity to gain his living by work which he freely chooses or accepts, and will take appropriate steps to safeguard this right" (article 6(1)) and they "recognize the right of everyone to the enjoyment of just and favourable conditions of work" (article 7). Within the minimum core of the right to work are the fundamental principles of equal access to employment and non-discrimination.[795]

8. *Just forms of life*:

The indivisibility of the ICESCR and the ICCPR means that fundamental freedoms may not be sacrificed in order to fulfil basic needs or economic, social, and cultural right.[796] Thus, for example, is individual self-determination recognised as a central element of the right to health and coercive medical treatment is prohibited.[797]

In line with McMurtry's theory of value, rights are established by the ICESCR so that needs are met and life thus enabled to open towards wider ranges of:[798]

(a) action, e.g. stepping from sheer survival (the right not to be hungry as the minimum core) to adequate food, i.e. a nutritious, well-balanced diet (full realisation of the right to food);
(b) felt being, e.g. stepping from adequate food to adequate good food (food can possess an aesthetic dimension that encompasses several different levels of sentience); and
(c) thought, e.g. stepping from adequate good food to adequate, good, culturally significant food (traditions and local culture can be expressed and apprehended *via* food choices and food-related rituals).[799]

The ICESCR was not promulgated in order to specify only a floor below which nations may not fall. Rather, it was meant to provide its parties with defining principles and purposes concerning the sort of development desired by the international community. The "minimum core" obligations are merely a starting point. The distance from which each country still stands from fulfilling the covenant over 30 years after its entry into force, and, indeed, the regressive outcomes in a number of states, suggest that new conceptions of the factors that systematically oppose the ICESCR are needed. For instance, in blatant opposition to the life-aims of the ICESCR, primary education is not available for free to millions of African children[800] and labour unionisation in some developed countries has been reduced to a tiny fragment of the total workforce.[801] The time may have come for McMurtry's axiology to enter into the human rights mainstream.

In particular, McMurtry's WBI is his most conspicuous contribution to the alternative standards for the measurement of growth and wellbeing, such as the UN Human Development Index (HDI), the Genuine Progress Indicator (GPI) and the Statistics Canada System of Environmental and Resource Accounts, which have been championed in the recent past by a number of scholars and scientists, including Amartya Sen and Gene Shackman.[802] Some such alternative standards have already been used by leading international financial institutions, including the World Bank, in order to deal with the dimensions of human capital and natural capital and, more generally, to attempt to assess growth and decline in non-market-dependent ways.

To these all, McMurtry's WBI adds a theoretical foundation, i.e. life-value onto-axiology, which perhaps philosophy alone can produce. Still, it is significant that attempts have been made to evaluate performance in ways that differ from those of standard money-bound criteria, e.g. "full employment" in Keynesian economics. In any case, all these attempts are still far from being the leading parameters of evaluation actually employed by individual states and major international organisations *vis-à-vis* economic performance and inform most decisive aspects of policy.[803]

Almost without exception, what has appeared to be paramount to states in the end is growth or potential for economic growth, narrowly defined by life-blind money-value parameters, whilst human rights considerations have been left largely undersupplied. Were growth measured in this sense to correspond with progressive realisation of economic, social, and cultural rights, then the bare pursuit of growth would be a reasonable interpretation of the most "appropriate means" for a state to take to fulfil the Covenant. Yet, as highlighted by the current crisis, this does not seem to be the case at all.[804]

The Environment

Regularly, what has emerged from expert debates on the destabilisation of climate and hydrological cycles is that the type of growth pursued under the banners of globalisation and international trade has had systemic negative implications upon both human health and the environmental conditions of planetary survival. That is to say, globalisation and international trade have had systemic negative implications upon the integrity of life support systems at all levels, thus affecting the possibility of satisfying vital needs through generational time.[805]

There is actually *no* aspect whatsoever of the Earth's environment that has not been depleted in the processes of extraction, production, transportation, consumption, and disposal of the so-called "goods" enhancing today's mainstream conception of growth: the biosphere-protecting ozone layer, breathable-air producing and reproducing pluvial forests and oceanic life-systems, vegetal- and animal-life-supporting hydrologic cycles, self-regenerating water aquifers, nourishing-food-producing arable spaces, and natural-equilibrium-maintaining and science- and technology-inspiring biodiversity.[806] Denials of this dramatic situation are an exercise in intellectual dishonesty, as the causal link between the pursuit of profit in contemporary market economies and environmental degradation becomes visible every time environmental and health-and-safety regulation, or effective enforcement thereof, is resisted publicly as "too costly", "rigidifying" or "anti-competitive",[807] or is by-passed by illicit behaviour and/or by off-sourcing to countries that have actually little such regulation or none at all. (As the original article was being completed, news agencies reported of the $1.2m fine imposed on London-based Trafigura for illegally exporting toxic waste to Ivory Coast, thus causing illness to about 30,000 local inhabitants. Possibly, Trafigura had attempted to adhere to the impeccable economic logic sanctioned by Lawrence Summers in his notorious 1991 memorandum at the World Bank.)[808]

McMurtry's serving as Honorary Theme Editor for the philosophy section of UNESCO's EOLSS highlights the fact that one of the recurring concerns of his oeuvre is the acknowledgment that a healthy biosphere is valuable as such. By contrast, the ICESCR does not address environmental concerns for their own sake. For that reason, the ESCR Committee cannot make broad statements of law or policy on environmental issues but can only address the environment from a strict anthropocentric perspective.

In other words, under the ICESCR, the environment has no intrinsic value, but is only valuable to the extent that it maintains or improves humans' abilities to enjoy their economic, social, and cultural rights. As a result, the Committee has no self-standing general comment on the environment or the need for the development required to fulfil economic, social, and cultural rights to be "sustainable." Nevertheless, the perpetual validity of the ICESCR implies that immediate moves to fulfil its provisions must not come at the cost of future fulfilment.[809] Thus, the Committee recognises both the relevance of the environment for current enjoyment of human rights as well as the need for sustainability in the means chosen to realise human rights.[810]

A "healthy environment" is an integral factor in realising the highest attainable standard of health and explicitly addresses states' responsibilities to reduce workplace toxins that threaten the health of either employees or the general population.[811] The right to water requires control of pollutants and additional protection in times of crises, such as conflict or natural disasters.[812] The Committee adopts "respect for the environment" as one of the aims of education, with reference to the World Declaration on Education for All, and considers it "implicit in, and reflect[ing] a contemporary interpretation of article 13(1)".[813]

Sustainability was also addressed by the ESCR Committee in 1991 in the general comment on the right to adequate housing, which requires "sustainable access to natural and common resources, safe drinking water, energy for cooking, heating and light, sanitation and washing facilities, means of food storage, refuse disposal, site drainage and emergency services".[814] The concept came into its own in the context of the right to food when the Committee asserted that adequacy and sustainability are two sides of the same coin: "The notion of sustainability is intrinsically linked to the notion of adequate food or food security, implying food being accessible for both present and future generations".[815] The sustainability of food resources is considered to be so fundamental as to constitute an element of the minimum core of the right to adequate food.[816] On the same basis, sustainability is a crucial component of the right to water.[817]

These comments are particularly relevant for contemporary capitalist countries, the number of which has grown tremendously since the disappearance of Europe's Communist bloc, which also suffered from a poor environmental record. From a life-grounded standpoint, for example, a global free market that still causes scores of diseases due to pollutants, junk food, and addictive substances, while corporate pharmaceutical profits boom, is not a desirable development model, for it implies that such a market has been interested inherently in perpetuating or worsening such pathological circumstances rather than preventing them.[818]

On a global scale, as Hans Jonas' remarks anticipated in the previous chapter, growth in the orthodox economic sense may have even been pursued successfully for the past two decades, the ongoing international crisis notwithstanding. Yet, at the same, this narrowly conceived growth has been reducing the likelihood of planetary survival *via* depletion of the Earth's life support systems and the ability of States and the individuals within them to realise their economic, social, and cultural rights.

The environmental concerns of the ESCR Committee became much more overt in 2012, when the Committee took the opportunity of the Rio +20 summit to issue the "Statement in the context of the Rio+20 Conference on 'The Green Economy in the Context of Sustainable Development and Poverty Eradication'".[819] This statement was part of a loose package of human rights contributions to Rio emerging from the Office of the High Commission on Human Rights (OHCHR).[820] The statement is short (just two and a half pages) in contrast to the much lengthier general comments that the Committee is used to producing. It is therefore short on detail and this may have been a deliberate strategy to make it more appealing to busy Rio delegates.

The ESCR Committee demonstrates in this statement a genuine concern for the environment and recognises that the realisation of economic, social and cultural rights is dependent upon a healthy environment: one that can provide the necessities of life. Without adequate life support systems, the human rights upheld by the ICESCR and, *a fortiori*, by the international community as represented by the UN, cannot be plausibly attained on a universal scale. By demonstrating such a concern, the ESCR Committee implicitly acknowledges further the foundations of the ICESCR in the life-ground, hence being a token of civil commons.

The ESCR Committee's statement is reminiscent of the earlier environmental declarations of States at Stockholm and Rio by refusing to compromise human development.[821] The ESCR Committee cites "sustainable development" eleven times in only two and a half pages of text, including in the title, and sustainable development is indeed the key to its approach. This term came into common use with the Rio Declaration, of which the first principle is: "Human beings are at the centre of concerns for sustainable development. They are entitled to a healthy and productive life in harmony with nature."

A sustainable development approach views environmental protection as integral to, rather than in competition with, development. The Rio Declaration considers the right to development as the key to both human and environmental well-being. This perspective emerges from the negotiations twenty years prior, at Stockholm, during which States had agreed that in developing countries, environmental degradation was in most cases a result of underdevelopment and saw economic development as the key to better environmental conditions. With this in mind, the Stockholm Declaration called on developed states to increase financial and technical assistance to developed countries (principle 9).

The ESCR Committee encourages the States at Rio 2012 to integrate a human rights perspective more explicitly into environmental protection and into the final declaration in particular, with increased emphasis on the relationship between the green economy and sustainable development. Human rights and development are not interchangeable; each can lead to the other, but does not necessarily do so. The same considerations apply to sustainable development. Sustainable development, if poorly conceived, can lead to a diminution of human rights, including economic, social and cultural ones.

Far from being a purely academic hypothesis, this diminution has been frequently denounced by rights-holding indigenous populations[822] *vis-à-vis* the World Bank's self-professed "sustainable development" and "green growth" strategies,[823] which started being reviewed for this very reason.[824]

Noting first of all that "many provisions" of the ICESCR "link with environment and sustainable development", the fifth paragraph in the ESCR Committee's statement reminds the States parties of their general comments and other interchanges with States parties through the treaty monitoring process. The statement then points to the most relevant provisions of the ICESCR and goes beyond the bare text to remind States of circumstances that hinder both sustainable development and human rights fulfilment. These include a reminder of the provision of article 2(1) that encourages international cooperation to ensure economic, social and cultural rights as well as a call for sustainable development. With this in mind, and repeating many exchanges with States parties through the periodic reporting and monitoring process, the ESCR Committee recommends that States (though not solely developed States) devote 0.7% of GDP to international development assistance, in conjunction with a human rights approach to development.

The position of women is highlighted, both in terms of the positive contributions that they can bring to conservation, use and management of resources as well as their potential vulnerability when the environment becomes degraded. States are reminded of their treaty obligations to provide a healthy working environment. The right to food receives a little more detailed attention, recognising the obligation to ensure that traditional food sources are not unduly compromised by environmental damage but also to ensure that green technologies are not introduced blindly without assessment of adverse impacts on access to food and water. The right to health is addressed and the ESCR Committee underlines the dependency of human health on a healthy environment, pointing to rights to safe water and sanitation and the dangers posed by waste disposal.

The right to the highest attainable standard of health is also recognised in light of the opportunities offered by protecting biodiversity for developing pharmaceuticals, but the ESCR Committee reminds States that any exploitation must protect the cultural rights (intellectual property in Western-speak) of indigenous and other local communities. Indigenous and forest dwellers are further considered in light of their inherent rights to the land which they have traditionally used, the need for prior and informed consent to any other economic activities on these lands (such as logging), and the close relationship between these peoples and the habitats in which they live. The destruction of the habitat threatens the very existence of whole communities.

More generally, the ESCR Committee reminds States of the right to development and to ensure that development within a State is equitably enjoyed: paragraph 6h is adamant on the notion that "development efforts meet the beneficiaries of development". States are advised of their responsibility *vis á vis* private actors (in this case, the corporate sector) to exercise due diligence in regulating and monitoring non-State conduct to ensure that the rights of individuals are not compromised.[825] Environmental impact assessments have long been recognised as an essential element in environmental protection, but the ESCR Committee also urges States to undertake "human rights assessments" of their policies and gives the pertinent example of protecting communities from forced displacement based on ostensible environmental considerations.[826]

The statement concludes with a summary of four key principles that should be integrated into the Rio +20 outcome document: namely, to reaffirm the Rio Declaration 1992; to reaffirm the human right to development; to link the green economy closely to sustainable development; and to mainstream human rights, especially the rights recognised and endorsed by States parties to the ICESCR.

The ECSR Committee's statement is cautiously worded, but is summed up in more direct and dramatic fashion by the High

Commissioner:

> *Human rights matter to this debate [at Rio 2102]. The only way to ensure that the green economy is not a green-washed economy is to insist on a human-rights based approach, putting people and their rights, rather than government power or corporate profit, at the centre. In this heavy politicized discussion, human rights are not a regional bargaining chip, but rather a global imperative (P4 19 June a)... the difference between a green economy and a green-washed economy is a human-rights based approach.*[827]

The High Commissioner makes explicit that which can only be read between the lines of the ESCR Committee's statement: that ostensibly green measures may inadvertently impact negatively on human rights; but also that, at worst, green measures might be used as a smokescreen to deprive individuals and groups of their basic human rights by, for example, conversion of agricultural land to produce fuel and diversion of rivers from providing basic water supplies and fish to providing energy for corporate profit.

Significantly, the ESCR Committee recognises the symbiotic relationship between some groups living traditionally and the environment in which they live, referring twice to indigenous peoples and the dangers they face from unsustainable destruction of their homes and theft of their traditional knowledge. Whenever alleged development strategies, albeit sustainable or green in name, violate human rights, they fail a basic axiological test: they are no longer universal, for they benefit a group while damaging another. In this respect, they do not count as civil commons.

A Concluding Remark

Another lesson can be inferred from the fate of the indigenous peoples whose human rights may have been sacrificed to develop, perhaps at times even "sustainably" develop, the nations in which they happen to reside. The lesson is that growth, even of the green kind, can be pursued so that *some* may benefit at the expense of *others*. The appropriation of civil commons for class or elite benefit does not need to be confined to the realm of interactions between indigenous and non-indigenous groups. As planet-wide as well as local life support systems shrink in both present and future availability, while income inequality grows between and within countries, the fundamental human needs listed in McMurtry's WBI and addressed by several articles in the ICESCR can be attained by some, but not by all, human beings.[828] Depending on the needs at issue, this partial satisfaction translates into life for some, death for others.

Such an outcome may please social Darwinists and devotees of Nietzsche's superman, but human rights legislation is grounded neither in Herbert Spencer's (1820–1903) work nor in the philosophy of the author of *Also sprach Zarathustra: Ein Buch für Alle und Keinen*. Human rights, most certainly economic, social and cultural ones, are not only a matter of securing a better life for all human beings (e.g. labour standards, housing, access to higher education), but also a matter of securing life as such, that is, as opposed to death. If the rights sanctioned in the ICESCR are ever to enjoy a brighter future, then many governments, economists and business elites will have to prove themselves capable of undergoing a major value shift, which is what life-value onto-axiology has been offering for some time.

Chapter 8: Europe's Constitutions qua Civil Commons

On the 12th October 2005, while addressing the members of the National Italian American Foundation meeting in Washington D.C., Alan Greenspan (b. 1926), the long-time Chairman of the US Federal Reserve, stated openly and confidently: "recent regulatory reform [i.e. deregulation], coupled with innovative technologies, has stimulated the development of financial products, such as asset-backed securities, collateral loan obligations, and credit default swaps, that facilitate the dispersion of risk."[829] Writing three years before Greenspan's speech, financial mogul Warren Buffett (b. 1930) referred to the same products as "financial weapons of mass destruction".[830] Who was right?

Since then, such legally deregulated and technologically innovative products have caused the transnational banking network to freeze, the world's stock exchanges to crash and most countries to fall into an economic slump, which, depending on the country that is looked at, has taken the shapes of technical depression, mass unemployment, or reduced access to means of life for vast sectors of the population. It is no surprise that, three years after Greenspan's speech, the world's popular press as well as serious pundits did nickname all such products "toxic assets". (This term being the brainchild of Angelo Mozilo, founder of Countrywide Financial and having an indirect yet eerie echo of the sort of trade that Larry Summers' "impeccable" economic logic recommended *vis-à-vis* international waste disposal.)[831]

Despite its rather specific and institutionally circumscribed origin within the realm of deregulated, private, technologically intensive, global high finance, this realm's crisis, by disrupting the availability of credit for all kinds of businesses and opening vast opportunities for financial speculation, including bearish targeting of State bonds and currencies, has sent shockwaves throughout social bodies and institutions at large. Such were the eventual social results of the innovative creations of white-collar specialists in "Economics, Finance, and Insurance & Risk Management" that, at least until 2008, had been proudly called by some "the best and brightest".[832]

Even the typically aloof and fairly resilient sphere of constitutional law has been far from immune. Between 2008 and 2015, some European countries have either modified or tried to modify their constitutions in order to enshrine within them clearer, tighter budgetary rules. At the same time, constitutional *fora* have been busy addressing crisis-related laws and policies. In public debates and scholarly studies, many of these laws and policies have been referred to as "austerity" laws and policies, given their conspicuous consumption-reducing impact on citizens, particularly those already vulnerable and/or the less affluent members of society (e.g. youth's unemployment, wage cuts in the public sector, children's and elderly citizens' illness and/or premature death by reduced healthcare provision).[833]

In this chapter, I survey representative constitutional amendments in the EU area, whether attempted or accomplished, as well as significant adjudications by constitutional bodies. Then, I proceed to assess these legal phenomena in light of human rights jurisprudence. A pivotal reference is the 7th volume of the *Annuaire international des droits de l'homme* (AID), edited by G. Katrougalos, M. Figueiredo and P. Pararas under the aegis of the International Association of Constitutional Law.[834] Not only does this volume comprise the work of some of Europe's noted constitutionalists, it also addresses the constitutional matters central to this chapter in light of human rights jurisprudence, so as to answer the following question: have European constitutions continued to function *qua* civil commons in the crisis years?

Greece

Greece is possibly the most dramatically crisis-hit country in Europe, at least as regards demographic indicators such as HIV-infection, mental illness, suicide and overall mortality rates, all of which worsened considerably after the fatal intoxication of the international financial markets, the resulting collapse of Lehman Brothers, the subsequent disruption of the global economic regime, the opportunities for rampant financial speculation emerging therefrom, and the austerity measures taken by the Greek State in order to be granted new, dearer loans.[835]

Without these new, dearer loans transferring by definition an even bigger share of public wealth into private hands, the Greek State would have succumbed to speculation and possibly stepped into massive debt restructuring or even sovereign default. Both outcomes were resisted by State creditors,[836] for they would have meant:

(i) huge immediate losses for Greek as well as foreign private bondholders and investors;
(ii) sizeable gains for some foreign hedge funds speculating or betting directly upon such events;[837] and
(iii) a meltdown of the nation's financial and banking businesses akin to the one occurred in Iceland,
(iv) but this time within the Eurozone, hence foreboding major contagion risks on an international scale.[838]

Given its dramatic connotations, its systemic implications, and the publicity surrounding it, I focus here more upon the Greek experience than on the others following it. Besides, these additional experiences adhere to the same inherent socio-economic logic and debtor-creditor power aetiology outlined *vis-à-vis* Greece and its absentee owners who, as US economist Thorstein Veblen discussed almost one hundred years ago, can hold the nations' private businesses and public governments to ransom by means of actual and/or threatened financial sabotage of the real economy (e.g. reduction or suspension of credit provision, speculation upon State bonds and national currencies, mass capital outflow).[839]

The legal system of the Hellenic Republic does not include a constitutional court as such, but rather the Greek Council of State deals *qua* highest administrative court of the country with many, though not all, matters of a substantial constitutional character. As of 2008, this court has passed two decisions in relation to the 2010 and 2012 Economic Adjustment Programmes and the related "memoranda"[840] between the Greek State and the representatives of the IMF, the European Central Bank (ECB) and the European

Commission, i.e. the three international institutions representing creditor interests that the media dubbed the "Troika".[841]

Via the 2010 and 2012 bailout operations, the members of the Troika required the Greek government to adopt extensive sets of austerity laws and policies in order to obtain loans aimed at securing the solvency of the State, henceforth its ability to pay its creditors, as well as the effective continuation of the country's private financial and banking sectors. Such was at that point in history the will of the transnational institutional creditors, who had poured money far more easily, if not actually quite eagerly, into the Greek economy *before* 2008, irrespective of whatever notorious private corruption or public profligacy may have characterised that country.[842] As US investment giant Goldman Sachs is concerned, it even sold the Greek State highly profitable—for the former—and secretive financial derivatives in 2000–2002, thus allowing the latter to report misleading information on Greece's public finances.[843]

Analogously to the conditionalities that the IMF and the World Bank set in place for debtor countries in the so-called "Third World" over the 1980s and 1990s, these austerity policies have had a remarkably depressing effect on the Greek economy.[844] For one, they have generated a prolonged slump rather than the "higher growth and employment" indicated in the 2010 "Memorandum of Understanding of Economic and Financial Policies".[845] Three years later, the IMF's "Ex Post Evaluation of Exceptional Access under the 2010 Stand-By Arrangement" admitted that there had been "notable failures" with these policies, including the uneven way in which "the burden of adjustment" had been spread "across different strata of society".[846]

About 90% of the bailout money was used to repay or pay interest on loans from private lenders, Greek as well as non-Greek—*ergo* Goldman Sachs too—, also *via* eventual, partial debt restructuring in 2012.[847] So-called "haircuts" were made then, but the IMF and the institutional creditors that the IMF represents on international *fora* seem pleased with the overall result, which has so far prevented a sovereign default and preserved the bulk of creditors' claims: "Private creditors were able to significantly reduce their exposure" and "escape", whilst "[the] program… failed to achieve critical objectives, especially with regard to restoring growth, ensuring debt sustainability, and regaining market access", i.e. "put Greek public finances into safety".[848]

All these payments and repayments took place during, and in spite of, a worsening economic situation and, with it, vast socio-demographic losses, some of which beyond any possible compensation, such as death and children's loss of opportunities. Apparently, there was too little money to avoid them, the bailout funds serving the end of preventing major pecuniary losses to the State's bondholders as well as to private shareholders and investors of Greek private banks, these people being both Greek and non-Greek. Their claims did not vanish by way of sovereign default; their value was not annihilated thanks to the Troika's acting as intermediary and the State's wealth as guarantee; the interest payments to which they were entitled kept streaming unchanged, at least until 2012, and are still unfrozen; old, undesired claims were refunded; new ones were established at a higher premium for the willing. Meanwhile, the debt burden was shifted from private hands into public ones, which then reduced the provision of public goods and services at central and local levels, with dramatic effects for the population.[849]

As the 2010 Loan Agreements state, a "safety net" was promptly put and sternly kept in place, but "for the financial system",[850] not the population at large, who received instead "cuts in public sector salaries, bonuses… allowances, and steps to reduce health care spending".[851] Shifting the burden of the crisis onto States and their citizens, i.e. away from the private agents with whom it originated, is what the Bank of England's executive director Andrew Haldane (b. 1967) and economic analyst Piergiorgio Alessandri call "Banking on the State".[852] It is not a phenomenon limited to Greece alone: quite the opposite. As they wrote in 2009:

> *[Take] a snap-shot of the scale of intervention to support the banks in the UK, US and the euro-area during the current crisis. This totals over $14 trillion or almost a*

> *quarter of global GDP. It dwarfs any previous state support of the banking system. These interventions have been as imaginative as they have large, including liquidity and capital injections, debt guarantees, deposit insurance and asset purchase. The costs of this intervention are already being felt. As in the Middle Ages, perceived risks from lending to the state are larger than to some corporations. The price of default insurance is higher for some G7 governments than for McDonalds or the Campbell Soup Company. Yet there is one key difference between the situation today and that in the Middle Ages. Then, the biggest risk to the banks was from the sovereign. Today, perhaps the biggest risk to the sovereign comes from the banks. Causality has reversed.*[853]

Apart from recalling the experiences of developing yet never truly developed countries in recent decades, the chain of events observed in Greece has also proved consistent with the statement pronounced on the 9th May 2010 by Nogueira Batista, Brazil's executive director on the IMF board at the time of the first Greek bailout agreements. On that fateful occasion, Batista stated that the planned bailout process should "be seen *not* as a rescue of Greece, which will have to undergo a wrenching adjustment, but as a bailout of Greece's private debt holders, mainly European financial institutions."[854] As legal scholar Ellen Brown (b. 1945) succinctly explains: "ballooning Greek debt was incurred to save the very international banks to which it is now largely owed."[855] It should be noted that paying interest on pre-existing debt by taking on more debt is what the economist Gérard de Bernis (1928–2011) called "perpetual debt" or the "usury model" of Third-World countries.[856]

The inner economic logic revealed by references to Haldane, Alessandri, Batista, Brown and de Bernis is as clear as it is twisted. The nations' public wealth (e.g. State-owned utilities, tax revenues, citizen's pension money) and institutions (e.g. income taxation, debt-issuing treasuries, executive power) are used to keep afloat the transnational private financial sector, especially the over-indebted banks and funds that, in recent decades, created, traded and/or ballooned upon virtual assets that proved to be toxic in reality. These banks' and funds' debts and, in turn, these debts' toxicity caused an eventual systemic collapse. Then, and then only, did large-scale public intervention in the economy and novel regulation come to be advocated forcefully and operated factually, their prime aim being the rescue of the over-indebted private banks and funds (e.g. the US' TARP, the ECB's LTROs).[857]

At the time of writing of their original essay, the ECB had just handed out €1.1 trillion to the private financial industry in its latest round of quantitative easing, while impoverished Greek pensioners were going through the garbage in order to find something edible.[858] Yet this is only part of the twisted, indeed paradoxical logic at work. Such large-scale public intervention and novel regulation have occurred in spite of the free-market principles championed until 2008 by most Western governments since at least Margaret Thatcher's (1925–2013) first cabinet in the UK, as well as by the most eminent representatives of the private financial industry, which has been deregulated worldwide since the 1980s in line with the same principles.[859] Economic bankruptcy was averted by intellectual bankruptcy. As to the justification for suddenly abandoning these principles, it was argued that the transnational private financial sector, albeit culpable for the collapse, is uniquely necessary to provide credit to the real economy of the world. For instance, US President Barack Obama stated: "There are a lot of Americans who understandably think that government money would be better spent going directly to families and businesses instead of to banks… but the truth is that a dollar of capital in a bank can actually result in eight or ten dollar of loans to families and businesses."[860]

The real economy, however, has been largely deprived of credit since 2008, at least within the EU. The money that was made available most promptly to the private financial industry by Europe's as well as other major central banks did not go primarily to families and businesses. Rather, it has been used largely for worldwide speculation on financial assets.[861] This lack of outflowing productive credit has been lamented by the current ECB's president himself,

Mario Draghi, who has gone so far as to charge private banks for holding reserves at the ECB.[862]

Claims of the private financial sector's unique necessity, moreover, fly in the face of historical instances of constructive public credit provision, ranging from Bismarck's (1815–1898) Germany to today's North Dakota.[863] Desirable the private financial and banking sectors might be, certainly for private shareholders and top managers; but necessary they are not, at least factually. Neither are they necessary logically. If anything, the frequently heard official justification fails the principle of Ockham's (ca. 1287–1347) razor because of unneeded multiplication of agents. If public wealth is gathered *via* privatisation, taxation, budget cuts, etc. in order to be given to private agents, who then return it—for a fee—to the public, then it is simpler to skip the fee-charging intermediate agent and let the public manage the wealth it already possesses, e.g. by local or national public banks.

Rather than "necessity", Veblen's term "pecuniary opportunity" better describes the inner economic logic at work, albeit one that may be neither productive nor constructive.[864] Echoing Haldane and Alessandri, US economist and economic historian Michael Hudson (b. 1939) writes: "The [financial] rentier or monopolist masquerades as contributing to the production process so that its revenue appears to be earned rather than siphoned off in a zero-sum activity… In the case of financial parasitism, bankers and money managers have become more destructive over the centuries."[865]

It is within this broader systemic context that the Greek Council of State adjudicated case 668/2012 on whether the agreements with the Troika violated the constitutional principles of "proportionality, equality, the fair distribution of public burden and the right to property".[866] It determined that, given the "exceptional and urgent goals of general public interest as well as the need to guarantee the country's obligations towards the European Union and the International Monetary Fund", the agreements were acceptable, for "the need to serve the country's external funding and the enhancement of its financial credibility were crucial" at this stage.[867] It was a case of acknowledged *force majeure*, or an "*état d'exception*" [state of exception], under which "the need to effectively protect the public interest prevails temporarily over the full realization of rights and the executive is empowered towards the legislative and the judicial."[868]

Speaking of effective protection of people's interests by impeding the fulfilment of their rights may sound Orwellian, especially when this is coupled with the idea of skewing the balance among the three fundamental powers within the liberal paradigm. However, under international law, only slavery and torture are prohibited absolutely as *ius cogens* [compelling law], whilst in Europe, both inside and outside the EU, no State may take a citizen's life in peacetime either. All other rights, whether private property or freedom of assembly, can be weighed and must be balanced mutually in the interest of the public good. This is, for one, the constitutional ground for lawful withdrawal or redistribution of private property.

In an attempt to find the right equilibrium, in case 1685/2013 concerning whether the new taxes introduced because of the memoranda conflicted with article 78 § 2 of the Greek Constitution, which limits to one fiscal year any retroactive legislation imposing taxes upon Greek citizens, the court concluded that they were acceptable, "due to the need of protecting the public interest".[869] In what amounts to a patent acknowledgment of power relations under current economic conditions, the Greek Council of State concluded that, in order for "public interest" to be protected, resources should be withdrawn from the Greek citizenry so as to make sure that the creditors' interest payments kept flowing.

Some constitutional matters were dealt with by other courts, however, and they did not meet the same fate. The Greek Court of Auditors, "after reviewing the fourth… programmed cuts on the public sector pensions", issued an opinion on 20th February 2012 that condemned "these horizontal [i.e. across the board] and with no specific time limit reductions", for they [what follows is a direct translation of the opinion]: "violate the principle of the social state, but also lead to its destruction since they deteriorate the pensioners' situation in such a level, that the principle of *human dignity* according to the Constitution is jeopardized".[870]

Time had elapsed, elderly Greek citizens had been impoverished and their rights, especially social and economic ones, curtailed by repeated rounds of budget and pension cuts. The exceptional measures were becoming a new norm; henceforth, the balancing of rights in view of the public good required a move in the opposite direction, in order not to be disproportionate—indeed, in order not to violate the paramount principle of human dignity itself. As it is going to be explained, that is what the constitutional courts of other EU countries concluded as well during these years of crisis.

On 27th June 2014, the Greek Council of State in Plenum issued Decision 2307/2014, declaring all labour law measures implementing the second Memorandum of Understanding (MoU) in compliance with the Greek Constitution, the Treaty on the Functioning of the EU (articles 125 and 136), the European Court of Human Rights (ECHR; articles 11 and 1 of its 1st Additional Protocol), and ILO Conventions 87, 98 and 154, except those measures amending recourse to labour arbitration, which were found contrary to the principle of collective autonomy as guaranteed in the Greek Constitution (article 22, § 2). The Decision was the result of appeals lodged in March and April 2012 by nine trade unions, including the General Confederation of Workers of Greece, contesting the validity of Ministerial Act 6/2012 which implemented the austerity labour measures contained in the second MoU.[871]

One year later, a third bailout agreement was reached and, *via* the European Financial Stabilisation Mechanism, (EFSM) a €86 billion loan issued for the period 2015–2018, of which 25 were meant to recapitalise and resolve Greek banks (the first €10 billion disbursement was made available immediately for this purpose); further cuts introduced; a more onerous VAT system applied; recent laws undoing some of the previous austerity revoked; and a plan drafted to privatise about €50 billion of public assets. Additionally, EU aid to reduce unemployment and poverty was promised, by way of Jean-Claude Juncker's (b. 1954) European Commission's Investment Plan for Europe (EC IPE) over the period 2015–2017.[872]

Portugal

Together with Greece, other crisis-hit European countries came to be known in mainstream media as "PIIGS", i.e. a disparaging acronym that succinctly exemplifies how the victimisation of victims can take place on a vast public scale.[873] The first letter in the acronym, "P", stands for Portugal, which entered an Economic Adjustment Programme with the same Troika members as Greece in May 2011 and abandoned it voluntarily, without full disbursement of the planned loans, in June 2014.[874] It too comprised a "Memorandum of Economic and Financial Policies", a "Memorandum of Understanding on Specific Economic Policy Conditionality" and a "Technical Memorandum of Understanding".

Behind the decision to abandon the bailout plan lie three much-publicised rulings by the national Constitutional Court,[875] whose adjudications are binding on all public and private persons and bodies.[876] They concern cases 396/2011,[877] 353/2012[878] and 187/2013,[879] all pertaining to the constitutionality of severe cuts to public-sector wages and pensions.

In 2011, the court acknowledged "a compelling State interest in fiscal adjustment" and deemed constitutional "the contested salary cuts in the public sector", based upon considerations of adequacy, necessity and proportionality in view of "tangible results."[880] However, in 2012, the State budget had planned yet another round of vast cuts in the salaries and pensions of public employees, so as to gather resources to repay *in primis* its private creditors, but the court intervened: public-sector workers were being targeted in a way that was not applied to private-sector workers: the constitutional principle of *equality* was being denied.[881] (Perplexingly, such a principle has not been employed in previous rulings in order to secure private-sector workers' equality with public-sector ones in wages and pensions—the same consideration applies to the other EU countries where constitutional courts appealed to this principle.)

Similarly, in 2013, the principle of *equality* was called upon in order to condemn further cuts in the public sector as unconstitutional, adding to this notion a temporal and etiological component: "as time progresses... the reason to target public sector employees grows weaker since the cumulative effect of three years of pay cuts increases the weight of the burden placed specifically on their shoulders while... the Government had plenty of time to find workable alternatives to reduce public expenditure."[882] Finally, adjudication 413/2014 on articles 33, 75, 115 and 117 of Law no. 83-C/2013 cutting public-sector pay, pensions and welfare provisions was declared unconstitutional because of lack of *equality*, *proportionality* and *trust*.[883]

Italy

Italy has received no bailout funds yet and it has actually been the third biggest net contributor to the European Financial Stability Facility (EFSF), established in 2010 alongside the EFSM in order to loan funds to the States of Greece, Portugal and Ireland within the context of coordinated bailout programmes with other international financial institutions.[884] Italy has also been the third biggest net contributor to the EFSM's legal successor, i.e. the 2012 European Stability Mechanism (ESM).[885]

Nonetheless, the State's historically high public debt and the dubious "health" of some of its largest banks have made Italy a significant target of international financial speculation during the crisis years, so much that the president of the national entrepreneurs' syndicate *Confindustria*, Giorgio Squinzi (b. 1943), stated: "[b]y attacking Italy, financial speculation could really cause the euro-zone to break up".[886] In order to secure regular interest payments on its public debt and thereby reassure the international financial community, the country has been undergoing a prolonged period of austerity under four successive governments (i.e. Berlusconi IV, Monti, Letta, Renzi; of them, only the first was formed after a round of elections for the national Parliament).

Speculation-impairing limitation or suspension of free capital trade, as successfully operated in Malaysia during the 1997–1998 Asian crises or Iceland by the Emergency Act 125/2008,[887] was never truly considered by national leaders in connection with the

Eurozone troubles, despite its prime causal role[888] and the well-known absence of financial meltdowns in the Bretton Woods era.[889] Quite the opposite, austerity measures have been the standard solution across the board, thus displaying *ipso facto* the awesome power that international financial interests can have over national ones in current world affairs.[890]

Analogously to what occurred in Greece and Portugal, the Italian Constitutional Court was eventually involved in assessing some of the laws implementing such austerity policies. The rationale and the chronological evolution of the court's decisions have been analogous too. In 2010, assessing case 316/2010,[891] the court declared constitutional the State's recouping of resources *via* temporary cessation of the revaluation of the highest pensions of former State employees (i.e. above €90,000.00 *per* year). This recouping was called a "solidarity contribution", given the objectives of "a balanced budget" and the effectively "limited resources available" for the State at that time.[892]

Judgment 70/2015 of the Constitutional Court confirms unconstitutionality of the Monti government's (emergency) law decrees nos. 201 (6th December 2011) and 214 (22nd December 2011).[893] Pensioners' rights were unduly denied because of "unspecified financial needs" [*esigenze finanziarie non illustrate in dettaglio*]. Pension rights are said not to be untouchable, but more caution and clarity are required whenever touching them. One year later, however, dealing with case 116/2013,[894] the continued blockage of those pensions' revaluation was deemed unconstitutional, given also a previous decision of the same court on the salaries of public top managers (case 223/2012), in which it was determined that withholding due payments to public employees, whilst keeping those for equivalent private ones unaffected, violated the constitutional principle of *equality*.[895] As already seen in the opinions of the Portuguese constitutional court, the continued singling out of public-sector workers, past and present, violates their equal standing as right-bearing citizens of the State.[896]

An additional analogy is to be found with regard to those citizens that lie at the opposite end of the income spectrum, i.e. those who are so poor because of the ongoing crisis that a "right to nourishment" (the court's own formulation; case 10/2010) must be acknowledged openly and clearly to their benefit, in connection with the fundamental constitutional principle of the "*dignity of the human person*".[897] By so doing, the court recognises that "the extraordinary circumstances created by the crisis [are] a basis not to curtail rights, but to enhance their protection by upholding provisions that would otherwise be ruled unconstitutional".[898] Contrary to the 2012 decision of the Greek Council of State, the conditions of *force majeure*, i.e. the state of exception caused by the severe economic downturn, may actually justify unconventional policies to respect, protect and fulfil the citizens' rights, rather than curtailing them temporarily for the sake of meeting financial obligations with the State's creditors—as was also done, historically, in wartime periods.

"First things come first"; or, as even the liberal thinker Isaiah Berlin believed, they ought to.[899] If the State's interest payments are frozen, delayed or cancelled, an investor may lose some of her money, and hardly ever the principal. If the State's medical treatments are frozen, delayed or cancelled, a citizen may lose her one and only life, which can never be recovered. Economic, social and cultural rights may and can be prioritised over creditors' pressing demands, which may and can be postponed without harming or destroying citizens' livelihoods and lives. This prioritisation occurred in response to Iceland's 2008 meltdown, for instance, without it even causing a rift with the IMF.[900] Serious economic crisis is *ipso facto* the moral and legal justification for emergency lines of action.[901] It is precisely in gravely difficult times that legally acknowledged human rights become truly crucial *qua* means of shielding the individual from major life-harm and must therefore be respected, protected and fulfilled.[902]

Finally, under the umbrella-notion of austerity policies, Italy underwent a veritable constitutional change too. It was the introduction of a new constitutional principle, i.e. that of a "balanced budget" [*pareggio di bilancio*], through the constitutional law no. 1 of 20th April 2012, modifying articles 81 (State budget), 97 (Public Administration), 117 and 119 (regions and local authorities) of the

Italian Constitution.[903] This principle was introduced despite the ratified EU treaties, which allow for a 3% deficit over the national GDP, but in explicitly declared connection with the 2012 European Fiscal Compact among EU countries fixing the State's annual budget deficit to 0.5%, or 1% in case of the public debt being below 60% of the country's GDP.[904]

Taken in isolation, this new principle seems austere indeed, for it apparently contradicts the well-established notion and historical praxis whereby States grow and develop by means, *inter alia*, of public deficit. However, in the successive law of implementation (no. 243/2012),[905] a modicum of flexibility was immediately reintroduced, given previous pronunciations of the same court on matters of public finance (especially the decision 1/1966) and the explicit acknowledgment in the constitution of the simple but important fact of "contrary and favourable phases of the economic cycle" (article 81, al.1). Eighty years of macroeconomic science and experience were not suddenly obliterated. Rather, what was really new in connection with this constitutional change was the specification that the new principle has to be adhered to "in conformity with the normative order of the European Union" (article 97). To many commentators, this open reference to the EU did strike as a breach of national sovereignty.[906]

Ireland

Another country where constitutional changes have been discussed and/or passed is Ireland, i.e. the former much-celebrated "Celtic tiger" of free capital flows and low corporate taxation. Turned into a meeker creature, Ireland entered an Economic Adjustment Programme with the Troika in 2010, just like Greece and Portugal, given the implosion of its private banking sector in 2008.[907]

As already seen in Greece and Portugal, bailout programmes have regularly required austerity measures *qua* conditionality for the loans. Unlike Greece and Portugal, though, the Irish constitution requires popular votes to be held in connection with constitutional amendments. As a result, three referenda were held in Ireland on constitutional amendments that related palpably to the aftermath of the 2008 crisis. The first one was held on 27th October 2011 and allowed for the successive reduction of the wages for Irish judges, who therefore suffered a worse pecuniary fate than their Italian colleagues. The second was held on 31st May 2012 and allowed the Irish government to ratify the European Fiscal Compact. The third one was held on 4th October 2013 and rejected the abolition of the Seanad, i.e. the Irish upper house or Senate, which had been targeted for extinction by several politicians as a cost-saving move.[908]

Additionally, just before and then immediately after the 2008 worldwide collapse, Ireland's popular votes on constitutional amendments had already been in the news extensively, for the voting population had first rejected (12th June 2008) and then approved (2nd October 2009) the ratification of the Lisbon Treaty, which increased the level of institutional integration of the EU countries. Finally, three more popular votes have been held since 2008 that do not seem to be directly relatable to the crisis as such, the role played by the Irish banking sector or the deregulating governments of the former Celtic tiger in the early 2000s, or the austerity measures following the 2010 Economic Adjustment Programme. They consisted of: an October 2011 vote on the scope of investigative powers of Parliamentary commissions; a November 2012 vote on children's rights in the country; and an October 2013 vote on the introduction of a new Court of Appeal between the High Court and the Supreme Court.

A national Convention on the Constitution was held between 1st December 2012 and 31st March 2014, largely as a response to the crisis, as shown most clearly by the Convention's focus on economic, social and cultural rights.[909] For those who are not aware of the nature, composition and aims of this institution:

> *The Convention on the Constitution is a forum of 100 people, representative of Irish society and parliamentarians from the island of Ireland, with an independent Chairman. The Convention was established by Resolution of both*

> *Houses of the Oireachtas to consider and make recommendations on certain topics as possible future amendments to the Constitution. The Convention is to complete its work within 12 months. For its part, the Government has undertaken to respond to the Convention's recommendations within four months by way of debates in the Oireachtas and where it agrees with a particular recommendation to amend the Constitution, to include a timeframe for a referendum.*[910]

As regards the Irish constitutional court, however, not a lot has happened in the Irish courts directly related to the economic crisis. Education-related cases of the early 2000s set down such a conservative line on judicial enforcement of socio-economic rights, even those that are justiciable in the text, that it had a chilling effect on any possible litigation in this area. I write "conservative" because in other countries, most notably in South Africa, constitutional jurisprudence moved in the opposite direction, i.e. by facilitating the protection, respect and fulfilment of such human rights *via* judicial enforcement.[911] When the crisis erupted, it was pretty clear that the Irish courts were going to be highly unlikely to do anything with positive implications for resource policy or allocation. Certainly, there were some more procedural cases that sought to challenge some of the international agreements that Ireland signed up to during the crisis, but these were unsuccessful.[912]

Spain

Another country witnessing significant crisis-related constitutional changes has been Spain, which underwent a Financial Sector Adjustment Programme between 2012 and 2014, because of the precarious "health" of some of its biggest banks.[913]

In this kingdom, and in this crisis context, the national constitution was changed on 27th September 2011 without any popular vote on it, causing major protests at both national and local levels.[914] As in Italy, here too the so-called "*golden rule* of budgetary stability" was introduced into the constitution, this time by modifying article 135 and granting the central government new powers to "impose budgetary stability" over the largely autonomous communities of the kingdom.[915]

Only three Parliamentary votes on the national constitution have been held in Spain since 1978. One of them was already inspired by the European institutions and partners, i.e. the 1992 vote to ratify the Maastricht Treaty. The other vote was, in 1978, on the ratification of the constitution itself. Constitutional change, in Spain, is rare. Additionally, budgetary stability was already part of the Spanish constitutional order, given the Constitutional Court's judgment no. 134/2011 concerning laws 5/2001 and 18/2001.[916] These laws addressed and accepted a number of EU recommendations on budgetary stability within their member states. Why introduce the "golden rule" in such an atypical manner, then?

One likely answer that can be extrapolated from the 2011 Spanish constitutional text and context is the fear of the State's institutional creditors, especially large foreign financial holdings, of suffering pecuniary losses.

As the constitutional text is concerned, it could be argued that the 2011 constitutional amendment leaves the Spanish State, like its Italian counterpart, a modicum of room for technical manoeuvres aimed at implementing "budget stability" rather than a "balanced budget" *via* Keynesian responses to fluctuations of the economic cycle and/or at maintaining the "social sustainability" of the State itself.[917] Again, eighty years of macroeconomic science and experience could not be suddenly obliterated. Nonetheless, the constitutional amendment at issue states most blatantly that "*absolute priority*" must be given to the payment of sovereign debt and that "[t]hese appropriations may not be subject to amendment or modification" (article 135, comma 3).[918] *Ipso dicto*, the State's creditors, including foreign ones, are prioritised over its citizens.[919]

As the constitutional context is concerned, Spanish experts were left baffled, to say the least, by the fact that no popular vote was called on the 2011 amendment, no substantial Parliamentary debate was allowed (an *ad hoc* fast-track system conceded only *one* debate on the matter and this was deemed constitutional by the Constitutional Court) and, for the first time in Spanish history, no large consensus was sought in the national Parliament, since the two main Madrid- and Castile-based parties (i.e. the socialists and the Christian-democrats) had just enough votes to pass the amendment in accordance with formal requirements for constitutionality.[920] Considering the few previous, certainly consensus-based constitutional reforms, as well as the constitutionally acknowledged strong local autonomies, this third point remains a most striking aspect of the matter and may help explain the fervid resurgence of separatist parties in Catalonia, the Basque country and Valencia.[921]

On this last point, for the first time in Spanish history, municipalities lodged an action of unconstitutionality for breach of local competences. The law requires that 1,160 municipalities representing at least one-sixth of the Spanish population act together, i.e. about 7,8 million inhabitants; more than 3,000 municipalities cooperated in this case, about 850 of which from Catalonia. The municipalities oppose the reconfiguration of local social services carried out by the austerity laws 27/2013, whereby the management of social services can be transferred to the council of the province in municipalities of less than 20,000 inhabitants. Like the other actions against the Law 27/2013 of Rationalisation and Sustainability of the Local Administration, this action of unconstitutionality was pending of resolution by the Spanish Constitutional Court at the time of writing.[922]

Three More Cases

The former "Baltic tiger" of Latvia, between 2008 and 2012, underwent an Economic Adjustment Programme, which led in turn to major austerity measures, and joined eventually the Eurozone in 2014.[923] Austerity measures produced in turn severe impoverishment for large sectors of the population—especially the elderly—and mass emigration—especially the youth.

In this dire context, the nation's constitutional court issued a number of decision dealing with such austerity measures, some of which were deemed acceptable because of reduced State revenues, such as cases 2009-08-01 on pensions' indexing, 2009-44-01 on reduced child benefits, 2010-17-01 on reduced unemployment benefits, and 2010-21-01 on reduced future State pensions. Others, on the contrary, were deemed inacceptable, such as cases 2009-76-01 on the 70% reduction of retirement pensions of employees at the Ministry of Interiors, 2009-88-01 on the 10% reduction of retirement pensions for the Army, and 2010-60-01 on a wage freeze for the nation's judges. In the latter event, articles 1 (legitimate expectations and proportionality) and 109 (social rights) of the national constitution were regularly referred to in order to justify the negative judgment.[924] Even when deeming constitutional an early round of reduced old-age pension disbursements (i.e. case 2009-43-01), the court deemed it important to clarify: "even if the State reduces the pension disbursement amount for a period of time in the situation of rapid economic recession, there is still a definite body of *fundamental rights* that the State is not entitled to derogate from".[925]

Romania underwent as well a series of Financial Assistance Programmes over the years 2009–2011, 2011–2013 and 2013–2015.[926] They too translated into a number of austerity measures impoverishing what was under many accounts the poorest member of the EU.[927] On the one hand, cost-saving reforms of the national constitutions were attempted. First, the reduction of the houses of parliament to one and the introduction of the principle of the balanced budget in the constitutional text were proposed in 2011. Then, the former attempt having failed to gain enough political support, a new proposal comprising no fewer than 128 amendments of the constitution was presented in parliament in 2014 (no final decision had been taken at the time of writing). On the other hand, the Constitutional Court of Romania, *per* its decisions nos. 872 and 873, published in the Official Gazette no. 433 of 25th June 2010, pointed out that: "the state has a positive obligation to take all measures necessary to achieve that objective and to refrain from any conduct likely to encroach *the right to social security*".[928] Like their colleagues in the former "Baltic tiger", social and economic rights were being acknowledged by the constitutional court and the negative impact of austerity measures upon them condemned.

In Germany, finally, the constitutional "Court declared unconstitutional a law reducing benefits for social assistance, on the basis that the legislator had failed to respect the fundamental right to guarantee a subsistence minimum, which is derived by the principles of *human dignity and the social state*".[929] Emblematically, in the country that is regarded by most pundits as the politically most powerful member of the EU, both human dignity and the social State were highlighted by the constitutional court as essential benchmarks for the budgetary considerations of the State. It is not investors' confidence that legitimises State action, but its function *qua* constitutionally mandated civil commons.

Critical Remarks

Recessions happen. Crises happen. Depressions happen. Unlike tsunamis and earthquakes, however, it is not nature's tampered-with yet untamed power that causes them. Rather, they result from the combined responsibility of economic agents and the legal-political ones legislating upon, fostering, monitoring and sanctioning the former—or failing to do so.

Sometimes, the agents responsible for economic downturns are easier to spot than other times. As far as the 2008 crisis is concerned, the key-role played by gargantuan financial institutions under a deregulated normative framework has been clearly identified and denounced by *ad hoc* Parliamentary commissions[930] and top-level government officials (e.g. Giulio Tremonti). Yet, as the crisis deepened and expanded well beyond the borders of high finance, the brunt of the collapse has been borne by individuals that had hardly anything or nothing to do with high finance: poorer pensioners, poorer public employees, poorer disabled individuals, fired workers of private enterprises, and innocent children deprived of medical care and educational or cultural opportunities that will never come back, for, whatever improvement there may be in the future, their childhood will be over by then.[931]

Though rarely discussed in connection with the for-profit toxic assets that caused the ongoing crisis in the first place, innocent children are neither a rhetorical flourish nor merely some of the blameless victims of financial wizardry. They are the ontological precondition of the next generations in the world's communities. Civilised humanity is at stake here. This is no hyperbole. As shown in this account, more than one constitutional court claimed that the post-2008 crisis caused such socio-economic disruptions that not only well-established constitutional principles of equality and proportionality were endangered—and so were socio-economic rights too—but the very dignity of the human person had been encroached upon. Albeit somewhat vague, it is hard to imagine any stronger pronouncement coming from constitutional judges, who have come to confront, among other things, the malnutrition, destitution and death engendered by austerity laws and austerity policies over much of Europe.

As to applicable ethical criteria, I argued in my first volume for Northwest Passage Books that the whole logic inherent to the adjustment processes witnessed in Europe is nothing but cruel in the technical, philosophical sense of the term.[932] On the one hand, affluent private investors and shareholders are rescued from the losses caused by their own or their money-managers' bad market choices through the indebting of public bodies and the ensuing reduction of social goods provision, whilst private banks enjoy ECB's special credit lines (e.g. 2008, 2011 and 2012 LTROs), which have been used *inter alia* to speculate on EU-based public debt instead of lending money to the shrinking real economy. On the other hand, no such ample and prompt credit is provided to the populations, for such a provision might be inflationary, while Europe's peoples are left to suffer both psychologically and physically, not just economically, for their health is negatively affected, the growth of their offspring reduced[1] in quality and opportunity, and the lives of some ended under avoidable circumstances.

First things are not coming first. Quite the opposite, the relentless crushing of livelihoods and lives goes on for the sake of continued money-accruing. As the current Pope of the Church of Rome has recently written on this point: "The worldwide crisis affecting finance and the economy lays bare their imbalances and, above all, their lack of real concern for human beings", thus adding to the "persistent injustice, evil, indifference and *cruelty*" that we witness "all around us".[933] As he continues: "The thirst for power and possessions knows no limits. In this system, which tends to devour everything which stands in the way of increased profits, whatever is fragile, like the environment, is defenseless before the interests of a deified market, which become the only rule."[934] No less forcefully does Greek constitutional lawyer Giorgios Kasimatis state (emphasis added):

> *The Loan Agreements (the Loan Facility Agreement; the Memorandum of Understanding between Greece and the Euro-area Member States and the agreement with the IMF for the Participation of Greece in the European Financial Stabilization Mechanism to the purpose of obtaining the approval of a Stand-by arrangement by the International Monetary Fund) form a system of international treaties the likes of which... the* cruelty *of the terms and the extent of breach of fundamental legal rights and principles... have never been enacted in the heart of Europe and the European completion; not since the World War II.*[935]

But who is the cruel invader here?

There are no tanks, no armed divisions in view. We invite the reader to reflect on a statement that the former President of the German Central Bank, Hans Tietmeyer (1931–2016), made during the 1990s, as the Europe-wide process of liberalisation of financial markets was being implemented and the Euro was in the process of being launched: "*the financial markets will become the gendarmes of the nations*";[936] or, in a slightly longer version quoted by Uruguay's famous novelist Eduardo Galeano: "Financial markets more and more play the role of gendarmes. *Politicians should understand that from now on they are under the control of financial markets.*"[937]

Meant as a metaphor, Tietmeyer's paradigm evokes a military occupation, which is what Kasimatis refers to: the Second World War, to be precise. The cruel invader is transnational private finance, as embodied by the "European financial institutions" that the Troika set itself to rescue through the nation-wrenching bailout programme foreshadowed by the aforementioned Brazilian IMF board director Batista in 2010. In this connection, signs of an evolving "supranational economic constitution" serving the wishes of large transnational creditor institutions are detected by some of Europe's noted constitutionalists.[938] These legal scholars have no hesitation in regarding such a development as a silent *coup d'état* directed against "national democracy", e.g. by means of "ultra vires" decisions on matters well "outside EU competencies" in the memoranda between the Greek State and its institutional creditors (e.g. Decision 2010/320/EU).[939]

Also, as already seen in this book, Italy's former finance minister and current conservative Senator of the Republic Giulio Tremonti dubs the political clout of the private financial sector *"financial fascism"*, whereby the money-preferences of transnational financial institutions trump the constitutional rights of Europe's citizens. Politicians use even stronger language than constitutional judges. Yet, it is not only European financial institutions that are engendering a "supranational economic constitution" that caters to their wants. In a May 2013 public report entitled "The Euro Area Adjustment: about halfway there", the Europe Economic Research Team of US financial giant J.P. Morgan openly laments that Europe's national "Constitutions tend to show a strong socialist influence, reflecting the political strength that left wing parties gained after the defeat of fascism", thus allowing *inter alia* for "constitutional protection of labor rights" and "the right to protest if unwelcome changes are made to the political status quo", both of which prevent these nations from undergoing "fiscal and economic reform agendas" meeting their creditors' desiderata.[940]

"Portugal", "Spain", "Italy and Greece" are singled out in particular as having constitutions that constrain governmental action in this sense, as though the democratic constitutions emerged after the Second World War were not an affirmation of those freed peoples' national self-determination, but the source of "deep seated political problems" that impede the European Monetary Union (EMU) "to function properly".⁹⁴¹ To put it bluntly, the world's gendarmes do not like democracy, at least when it does not produce the results desired by J.P. Morgan's shareholders and investors. Moreover, as these gendarmes criticise constitutions that were born after, and as a result of, Europe's bitter struggle against fascism, they exemplify and substantiate Tremonti's observation regarding an emergent financial fascism, which prioritises creditor interests over citizens' rights.⁹⁴² It might not be merely a matter of strong words, then.

Nonetheless, whatever J.P. Morgan's expert team may be upset with, European human rights jurisprudence is pretty straightforward on who comes first. In a pivotal adjudication of the ECHR, i.e. *Capital Bank AD v. Bulgaria* no. 49429/99 (24ᵗʰ November 2005 §§ 110–1), it is made clear that States' obligations under human rights conventions and their protocols persist, no matter what subsequent obligations States may agree upon with international institutions such as, in this case, the IMF.⁹⁴³ This is the case despite the right to private property being enshrined in the first protocol of the European Council's Convention of Human Rights⁹⁴⁴ and the ECHR being primarily *not* about social and economic rights, but rather civil and political ones.

Precedents making the same point exist, though perhaps in not so explicit a manner, in abundant number, e.g.: *Prince Adam II of Lichtenstein v. Germany* [GC], no. 42527/98, §§ 47–8, ECHR 2001-VIII; and *Bosphorus Hava Yollari Turzim ve Ticaret Anonim Sirketi v. Ireland* [GC], no. 45036/98, §§ 153–4, ECHR 2005; *Matthews v. the United* Kingdom [GC], no. 24833/94, ECHR 1999-I; *Waite and Kennedy v.* Germany [GC], no. 26083/94, ECHR 1999-I; *Beer and Regan v. Germany* [GC], no. 28934/95, 18 February 1999; *Al-Adani v. the United* Kingdom [GC], no. 35763/97, ECHR 2001-XI.⁹⁴⁵ This case could become even stronger by including additional sources of human rights legislation that bind all European countries, both within and outside the EU, but their inclusion is not needed: the

ECHR's jurisprudence is more than adequate and eloquent here, since it is EU countries that are being dealt with.

Human rights are what the cited constitutional judges and experts claim to be at stake. Human rights explain and underpin the official constitutional rejection of some of the laws passed in the context of austerity policies, cutting public expenditures to scoop up resources for institutional creditors and *a fortiori* private banks' shareholders and investors. If unemployment, poverty and reduced social provisions by the State increase dramatically, then the fundamental human right of personal dignity is denied, not to mention human rights to adequate nutritional standards, as exemplified in case 10/2010 of Italy's constitutional court.[946] If public-sector workers, whether current or former, are singled out for prolonged or repeated cuts, freezes and "solidarity contributions", proportionality and equality are also being denied. By holding against the power of institutional creditors and *eventually* reminding the legislator and the executive of their paramount human rights obligations,[947] the constitutional bodies of Europe are being true to their life-serving function as civil commons.

In an abstract philosophical debate, we could conceive of anarchists, libertarians, objectivists, Stalinists or National-socialists arguing that no such human rights and constitutional principles ought to exist. Yet, in concrete and civilised legal or political debates, at least as Europe is concerned, these rights do exist and must be respected, protected and fulfilled. The day that we should find ourselves outside the human rights treaties signed and ratified by our States, and the previous "socialist" constitutions criticised by J.P. Morgan's specialists superseded by new ones negating them, then such intellectual stances may be considered and the relevant human rights thoroughly denied. More often than not, if we look at human history, such rights have been denied; but that happened in previous stages of human civilisation, including the fascist one. As for whether the mounting financial fascism denounced by Tremonti will emerge victorious, that is likely to be today's challenge for anyone who cares about human rights, which are themselves but a signpost for the means of life that citizens ought to have access to.

As Cicero (106–43 BC) had already realised long ago, that access is the ultimate ground for the legitimacy of public policy and legislation: *"Ollis salus populi suprema lex esto"*.[948]

Chapter 9: Iceland and the Crises

In this chapter, I provide two succinct and inevitably selective pictures—one small, another big—of the much-televised 2008 economic crisis that took place in Iceland, or *kreppa*, as it is called locally. The small picture is a three-step account of what led essentially to the economic crisis, what this crisis consisted primarily in, and what followed it that induced a recovery. I focus in particular upon the third step, since it is less known internationally than the prior ones. The big picture is a brief twofold reflection on how the Icelandic experience fits within larger global trends, that is, I assess its *kreppa* from an economic-historical perspective and from an axiological one.

The Small Picture

What preceded the crisis was a fairly long phase of transformation of the country's laws and economy, spearheaded by the governing Independence Party and its leader: "Prime Minister David Oddsson".[949] Writing in 2004, Oddsson's personal friend, policy advisor, fellow Central Bank board member, Mont Pelerin Society vice-president and long-time university professor Hannes H. Gissurarson (b. 1953) describes him as "the longest serving leader in the Western world, having formed his first government in 1991", to whom "[m]uch of the credit goes" for launching "a radical and comprehensive course of liberalization that mirrors similar reforms in Thatcher's Britain, New Zealand and Chile".[950]

What Gissurarson depicts and praises as a "[m]iracle on Iceland" is a set of policies truly analogous to those seen in Thatcher's Britain and Pinochet's (1915–2006) Chile, such as: "cut[ting] extensive direct and indirect government subsidies early on, mainly by dissolving some public investment funds and privatizing others"; "stabiliz[ing] the economy with monetary and fiscal restraint"; "privatizing… small companies, later turning to large fish-processing plants, factories and financial companies"; "deregulat[ing] the economy [by] target[ing] the special privileges of groups such as pharmacists, and, more importantly, allow[ing] the free transfer of capital in and out of the country and competition in the telecommunications sector... creating conditions for competition in Iceland's hydro-electrical system by bringing in foreign investors"; "reduc[ing] the corporate income tax to 30% from 50% and abolish[ing] a special tax on company turnover... [and later] further... cutting the corporate income tax to 18%... phas[ing out] [t]he net-wealth tax... and... greatly reduc[ing] the estate tax"; and "strengthening private property rights, both to capital and natural resources".[951]

Joining the European Economic Area and weakening the trade unions' bargaining power could be added too, but Gissurarson laments that "much remains to be done", since "[t]he health and education systems are publicly operated, and so are the utilities, some broadcasting stations, and the hydro-electric power system."[952] Between 2004 and 2008, part of what was left to be done was done, including tuition-charging private universities, which received State subsidies as well.[953] Despite such a blatant example of corporate socialism, the ideological inspiration of the country's transformation over the 1990s and early 2000s is described plainly as non-socialist: "Free-market economists like Friedrich von Hayek, Milton Friedman and James M. Buchanan all visited the country in the 1980s, influencing not only Mr. Oddsson but many of his generation. In the battle of ideas here, the right won."[954] The aim of this transformation is also not difficult to identify, i.e. to let Iceland be among "the richest countries in terms of GDP per capita".[955]

Gissurarson's article does not focus upon the privatisation of the country's three largest banks, which was concluded in 2003 and that, five years later, proved to be the pivotal cause of the nation's sudden and spectacular crisis.[956] Back then, the privatisation of the largest banks in the country was opposed in Parliament by only one minor left-wing political party (the "Left-Green") orbiting around 8% of the popular vote, which indicates a rather widespread popular approval of the self-declared free-market right-wing course of action that Gissurarson dubs a "[m]iracle".[957] Although Iceland enjoyed already in the 1980s very high standards in education, health, cultural and recreational life, most voting Icelanders might have dreamed of something else: fancy cars, high-tech gadgets, bigger houses and a life "American-style", high private indebtedness included.[958]

As commonplace in the history of several countries that underwent analogous transformations after the end of the Bretton Woods system, Iceland's alleged miracle into a meltdown. Elaine Byrne and Huginn F. Þorsteinsson write:

> *[I]n October 2008. Within a span of less than a week, the entire financial sector, ten times the gross domestic product (GDP) of Iceland, went bust. The stock market was nearly wiped out. The economic outlook was not favourable. Interest rates and inflation were at 18 per cent. Unemployment sharply rose from 1 per cent to 9 per cent. Government revenue was rapidly evaporating but government expenditure had surged. The Icelandic króna (ISK) was in free fall and the reputation of the country was in absolute tatters. The entire financial sector had collapsed lock, stock and barrel.*[959]

The Viking Tiger, just like the Asian, Latin-American, Baltic and Celtic ones, discovered itself to be a sacrificial lamb upon the altar of free trans-national capital trade. Rather than shining like a new wealthy "Luxembourg",[960] Iceland's boom-bust cycle mirrored the events that have repeatedly taken place in a plethora of former Western colonies since the 1980s and a number of post-communist countries since the 1990s.[961]

In this specific case, the crash of the derivatives-filled financial market in the US—the private toxic assets that somehow have already disappeared from mainstream public discourse and the mass media *in lieu* of public debt and nations suddenly living beyond their means—produced a "credit crunch".[962] In essence, not knowing how "toxic" another's books could be, private banks stopped lending to each other for fear of facing major losses, both nationally and internationally. As a consequence, it became impossible to continue to refinance the massively leveraged (i.e. debt-based) and poorly collateralised growth of Iceland's "three main banks, Glitnir, Kaupthing Bank and Landsbanki."⁹⁶³

Caught with their pants down, if I can use a crude but vivid expression worthy of a finance minister, the recently privatised banks "collapsed creating significant turmoil in the financial markets. This in effect shut down the foreign exchange market and caused a dramatic depreciation of the *króna*. The immediate consequences were the nationalisation of these three banks, which accounted for 85 per cent of the banking system. The International Monetary Fund immediately intervened with a $2.1 billion package in order to avert a further meltdown of the Icelandic economy."⁹⁶⁴

Such a vertical and critical collapse led to a modicum of soul-searching, which found a bulky and permanent expression in the 2010 Report of the Special Investigation Commission of the Icelandic Parliament, part of which has been translated into English. In it, the technical details of the banks' collapse are presented at length, as well as the many anti-competitive and anti-meritocratic practices occurring within the country's financial sector, the impotence of under-funded regulatory bodies, and the unethical complacency of much of the nation's media, academia and political class.⁹⁶⁵

Among the protagonists of these sectors of Icelandic society, *Time* magazine singles out former Prime Minister David Oddsson as one of "The 25 People to Blame for the Crisis" worldwide, since he had not only promoted the "experiment in free-market economics" discussed above, but also been at the helm of the country's Central Bank since 2005, just in time to fail to prevent the meltdown from occurring.⁹⁶⁶ Indeed, such a vertical and critical collapse led to street protests too and what was later named Iceland's "Kitchenware Revolution", which made us "[t]he first country to throw its government out of office as a result of the global financial crisis".⁹⁶⁷

The change of government meant that, for the first time in decades, the conservative party would not steer the course of the nation's fate. A left-wing government was formed, inside which the formerly minor 8% political party opposing the privatisation of the

State's banking sector had grown into a two-digit strategic player, especially *via* "Iceland's finance minister, Steingrimur J. Sigfusson, a lifelong leftist".[968] Iceland did not turn into a Nordic Cuba, though.

Quite the opposite, over the following three years, Iceland pursued economic policies "in close contact with the I.M.F.'s representative [t]here" that included "sharp cuts in health spending and higher gas prices... [h]igher interest rates", cuts to culture and education, and further "severe economic restrictions that the country has been forced to endure to qualify for more money from the I.M.F. and other Nordic lenders."[969] The tax revenue from the ballooning financial sector had evaporated, while the bill for unemployment benefits had soared at the same time: pressured by its historic Nordic partners, Norway *in primis*, the options on the government's table seemed limited. Far from challenging orthodoxy, the new government followed "the fund's recommendation that [they] maintain high interest rates as well as capital controls — a prescription [Steingrimur J. Sigfusson] describes as similar to wearing a belt and suspenders at the same time."[970]

As peculiar as such a statement may sound, the pants were up this time; and so they have stayed thus far. As Elaine Byrne and Huginn F. Þorsteinsson report:

> *[I]n the three years since the 2008 Icelandic collapse, the Nordic country has made a remarkable and noteworthy economic recovery. The IMF approved the final loan tranche in August 2011, marking the end to a 33-month rescue package. The Finance Minister, Steingrímur Sigfússon, subsequently announced that 'All the program objectives have been achieved.' Nemat Shafik, IMF Deputy Managing Director and Acting Chair, likewise stated 'Key objectives have been met: public finances are on a sustainable path, the exchange rate has stabilized, and the financial sector has been restructured.' The economy has stabilised, fiscal adjustment has been successful, economic growth is picking up and the sovereign financed itself successfully in the bond market in May 2011 on what were*

considered good terms.[971]

Were high interest rates and severe budget cuts the crucial recipes of this second Icelandic miracle?

Yes and no. Orthodoxy did play a role, but so did heterodoxy, starting with capital controls, which the IMF, a long-time enemy of them, regarded as necessary on this occasion.[972] On top of these controls, which made Iceland reminiscent of the Bretton Woods' days, the new Icelandic government pursued: the re-nationalisation of the recently privatised banks; their dismantling into viable good banks (thus saving domestic depositors) and bankrupted bad banks (thus causing shareholders and foreign investors to lose their risk capital); the steering of the banks' credit in support of domestic entrepreneurship and employment; the regular consultations among the government, the employers' associations and the trade unions in order to keep joblessness under control; a new markedly progressive taxation of income; and the principle that the regressive measures, i.e. the many painful cuts to public investment, should be done in a progressive manner.[973] Thus, unlike the 1st letter of intent with the IMF, which was passed before the "Kitchenware Revolution", the 2nd letter of intent with the IMF made it clear that Iceland would retain its Nordic Welfare model.[974] (I believe this explicit reference to welfare *qua* conditionality for the IMF intervention to be the first and only in the IMF's history.)

Additional factors played an equally important role: the depreciated national currency led to a surge in the country's export of goods and incoming tourism; the people of Iceland rejected twice the so-called *Icesave* agreements with Holland and the UK, which would have burdened the country's public budget with new loans to repay the Dutch and British customers of foreign branches of now bankrupt Icelandic private banks (Icelanders voted the latter time against the advice of nearly all parties, both left and right of the political spectrum); and the curious fact that the orthodox IMF recipes of sweeping liberalisation and privatisation could not be applied, since they had already taken place in the seventeen years before the eventual meltdown. So-called "free-market economics" could not come to the rescue, for it had been the cause of the country's shipwreck.

The Big Picture

Sub sole nihil novum est. On a national level, the Icelandic crisis did tread along the lines of the notorious 1929 Wall Street crash and successive US financial collapses (e.g. the savings & loans crises after the 1986 tax reforms, the 2000 dot-com bubble). All of the key-ingredients discussed in John Kenneth Galbraith's 1955 classic study of the 1929 Great Crash were there:[975] financial speculation prevailing over genuine productive investment; media-inflated irrational euphoria; private over-indebtedness by easy credit; blind, biased and bought punditry; irritated dismissal of critical voices; successful corporate lobbying for lax regulation; endemic corruption across private and public sectors; business-friendly legislation for businesses befriending legislators through generous campaign donations and revolving-doors incentives; reduced taxation on higher incomes.[976]

Even Galbraith's main fear *vis-à-vis* modern economies was there: the sheer ignorance of and/or wilful blindness to the lessons of economic history; could things be really different this time?[977] Had Icelanders found a special, Viking way of doing business, as a colleague once told me with great pride before 2008?[978] As Galbraith would quip: "The oldest Galbraith rule is that when you hear that a new era has dawned, you should take cover."[979]

On an international level, the Icelandic crisis did tread along the lines of innumerable post-Bretton-Woods meltdowns. Latin America, Sub-Saharan Africa, Pakistan, South-East Asia and post-communist Europe have given ample testimony to the chaos that Cornelius Castoriadis predicted *qua* inevitable outcome of the re-introduction of free capital trade worldwide: only a "planetary casino" could emerge from "the absolute freedom of capital movements".[980]

As to the British and Dutch attempts to impose onto Iceland *via Icesave* agreements a system of self-perpetuating debt, that is precisely what the already-cited de Bernis calls the "usury model" of the Third World, whereby national governments find themselves burdened by such amounts of debt that, apart from reducing all forms of public spending, they service their debt by taking on more debt, which in turn has to be serviced in the same way.

What is conspicuously different in the Icelandic case are some rather unusual outcomes of the crisis: banks i.e. shareholders were not bailed out. For once, the laws of competition were applied, though possibly out of inability to do the opposite, given the disproportion between the banks' losses and the country's GDP. Also, sweeping reforms were implemented, but in a protectionist sense, e.g. by re-nationalising recently privatised banks and protecting local depositors. Above all, free capital trade was suspended since the emergency laws were passed in response to the 2008 meltdown (again, at least in part, out of sheer necessity) and reintroduced only in 2017. Finally, further privatisations and fire-sale handovers to foreign investors were avoided, at least until now.[981]

Do note however that performing a second miracle on Iceland was not enough for the 2009 governmental coalition to win the 2013 elections, which brought the so-called "crisis parties" back to power. Not to mention that the second miracle itself might have seemed dubious to many Icelanders, whose private debts have endured *qua* assets of the new "good" banks capitalised after the demise of the old "bad" ones, while their purchasing power fell together with the national currency and the dreams of a fancy way of life—the kind of life that so many TV programmes, movies and adverts have been showing to them on a daily basis. On top of that, many Icelanders might have wanted to reward the one and only party opposing the *Icesave* agreements on both national referenda, while also campaigning for a large-scale private-debt write-off (the "Progressive Party").[982]

As McMurtry observes in the second edition of his *Cancer Stage of Capitalism*, Iceland and, for that matter, all meltdown countries are cases of societies turned into means to multiply the money demand of private money possessors as the supreme goal of the economy and society itself. In all these cases, with no exception whatsoever, the countries' economy and, which is constitutionally worse, the State's life-protective functions were and are turned into means to this lifeless end, whether by hijacking the State to reset to business-serving functions (e.g. competitiveness-aimed new public management) or by selecting out life-serving functions not subordinated to this end (e.g. budget cuts to public care for the disabled and to public cultural activities).

This macro-law of the money-sequence axiology is revealed whenever performance and success, both individual and collective (e.g. of States), are measured regularly and primarily in terms of money-value alone (e.g. American-style consumer goodies, paychecks, bonuses, growth, RoE, FDI) rather than by well-being indicators (e.g. Bhutan's pioneering 1972 Gross National Happiness metrics, the UNDP's 1997 Human Poverty Index, the Council of Europe's 2005 Social Cohesion Indicators) or fulfilment of human-rights standards of sufficient nutrition, access to education and healthcare, democratic participation and freedom to form and/or join a trade union.

As Gissurarson's "Miracle on Iceland" reveals, what justified politically and axiologically the possibly miraculous transformation over the years 1991–2008 was to let Iceland be among "the richest countries in terms of GDP per capita". When this *reductio ad pecuniam* happens, then money becomes *de facto* the guiding supreme value, which determines individual choices (e.g. one's 'sensible' studies and 'rational' career moves) as well as collective ones (e.g. 'sound' governmental policies), above and/or beneath cultural traditions and constitutional duties. It is not happiness that counts above all else; not health; not children's well-being; not human rights; not nature's pristine continuation and provision of life-supporting conditions; not stability; not secure and full employment. Money alone does.

Iceland is not isolated in this modern form of fetishism, which Castoriadis regarded as a token of pseudo-rationality; i.e. rational behaviour is assumed to be the one that promotes economic growth, but no valid rational justification is given for this unqualified growth to be taken as primary.[983] McMurtry dubs such a presupposed rationality "moronic" and poignantly remarks: "no place on the balance sheets is provided for doing good for others, or even providing for anyone's life need."[984]

Concluding Remarks

The world at large testifies to this inane accounting deficit, which threatens the sustainability of civilisation itself.[985] Across today's Europe, for one, States act regularly as though they were to serve money-value alone (e.g. recurrent references to the "will" and "sentiment" of "investors", the TINA-esque must of "competitiveness", the desirability of unqualified "growth"), while their citizens are either a resource (i.e. a means to an end) or an obstacle (e.g. "costs", "expenditures", "unproductive" classes). However, the citizens' wellbeing, as captured for instance in human-rights jurisprudence, is the actual aim and justification of State power under all existing constitutional arrangements. People are meant to be safe, healthy, educated, socialised, acculturated and enjoying progressively better living conditions. Money-value is a means to these ends, which embody and exemplify higher values (e.g. cultural identity, happiness, family life). In a successful society, people enjoy better and better psycho-physical well-being and opportunities for intelligent self-realisation. If the economy facilitates that, then it is good. It is bad if it hampers such goals, e.g. by making people's livelihood insecure, their minds and bodies ill, their understanding bamboozled by media propaganda, i.e. regular features of today's global consumer market societies.

Not to mention the depletion of the Earth's life support systems. Unlike actual people, money-value does not need pristine environments, clean air and potable water; hence it either turns them into priced goods that only moneyed consumers can purchase, or destroys them in the pursuit of other profitable activities. Modern meltdowns, like the environmental crisis of our age, are not unforeseen natural disasters akin to tsunamis, but the inevitable result of an economic system that aims at money-value maximisation, not at life-sustenance and amelioration. As McMurtry stated long before the 2008 crisis—and as seen in chapter 7

—"financial crises always follow from money-value delinked from real value, which has many names but no understanding of the principle at its deepest levels."

Chapter 10: Eight Noble Opinions and the Economic Crisis: Four Literary-philosophical sketches à la Eduardo Galeano

I.

Until control of the issue of currency and credit is restored to government and recognised as its most conspicuous and sacred responsibility, all talk of the sovereignty of Parliament and of democracy is idle and futile... Once a nation parts with control of its credit, it matters not who makes the nation's laws... Usury once in control will wreck any nation.

- William Lyon Mackenzie King

Since the real purpose of socialism is precisely to overcome and advance beyond the predatory phase of human development, economic science in its present state can throw little light on the socialist society of the future.

- Albert Einstein

Philosophers are often and rightly accused of dealing too much with the past, pondering endlessly upon origins, reasons and causes, and too little with the future, leaving hardly any room to proposals, solutions, or calls to arms. To prove myself capable of the latter kind of activity, and despite the unavoidably old noble opinions quoted above, I shall keep Minerva's owl nailed to a perch. Though Pythonesque, this little cruelty should delay any backward-looking blathering of mine, which is to come eventually in the other sketches.

After all, we are facing a dramatic twofold crisis, ecological and economic, which even uninfluential public figures like the current UN Secretary and US President have acknowledged and denounced as deadly. As for the title under which I allow myself to do so, I shall be content with declaring myself a professor of philosophy who has studied value for some time, i.e. what is important and what is not. In this pursuit, which I regard as valuable, I have reached a fairly simple conclusion: that which keeps all of us and our descendants alive and well is very, very important indeed. Those who deny it or claim my claim to be unscientific can do so because they are tacitly doing all that is necessary in order to stay alive and well enough to be able to talk a lot of nonsense.

But let us dwell no further on this simple subject, about which I have written around fifteen complicated essays in the past ten years—I need another nail… Worthy of Epicurus, I can offer a *tetrapharmakos* to today's world, confident to be received by no-one in useful time, for that seems to be the fate for all who dare criticise—as I am going to do—large-scale private banking, the profit motive as paramount, the private ownership of strategic resources, deregulation, and the managerial mind. Some may even call me a "socialist", as though it were a derogatory and disqualifying term, similar to "criminal", "pervert" or "rascal". Probably, given the notoriety of Italians and academics, "old pig" or "bore" would be more fitting insults. Politically, however, I would describe myself as "life-grounded", not "socialist". Still, I shall not mind and endure the epitaph with grace, even gratefulness. I shall keep company with Claude Henri de Rouvroy, Comte of Saint-Simon, Albert Einstein, and Bertrand Russell. An aristocrat, a physicist, and a logician…

(1)

First, fundamental medication, upon which all else depends: nations should establish, or in most cases re-establish, good public banks. Why? Well, here is something that should have become obvious to anyone who has eyes to see and a fat wallet. As stated by Russian President Vladimir Putin when speaking last year at the World Economic Forum in Davos, the economic crisis that we are witnessing today has destroyed, in about one year, approximately twenty-five years of pecuniary wealth, i.e. the sort of wealth that our intrepid yet "virtual" capitalists were aimed to produce in the first place. Private banks and financial institutions, left to their own devices by prolonged tidal waves of worldwide deregulation, brought themselves down and, with them, much of the world's "real" economy. Do you remember the real economy? If it goes down, down go also the starving children of unemployed sub-Saharan family fathers. Down into the earth they go, whilst shareholders moan for lost profits and fire a few more people to ease their pain.

Clearly, many private banks cannot do their job unaided. As they were busy concocting mathematically byzantine derivatives and variously vehicled securisation packages in the deregulated shadow of global finance, they forgot about honest bookkeeping, sound reserves, mutual trust, and other basic old-fashioned principles of chronically anachronistic banking. They even forgot about that primitive slave invention, morality. Alas! Such is the genius of the invisible hand free from State direction or, as Icelandic philosopher Mikael Karlsson dubs it, "the invisible brain." This is not meant to be an insult to anyone, unlike "socialist" or "pervert". The so-called "Free Market" promoted by "deregulators" has no visible brain, insofar as State-centred social and public planning is regularly rejected as anathema. Still, who came to the rescue of self- (and other-) destructive private banks? The State.

Turned into the banks' pork-barrel, the State has thrown trillions at the banks in order to keep them afloat—in the Land of the Free, in Great Britain, in Benelux. Was it necessary? No, for the State could have simply taken over the banks. Was it desirable? No, for public banks, still run in communist countries such as China and North Dakota, can spur development, employment, and take far fewer risks than private ones.

It must be emphasised that it is not enough for the State to own the banks; these must be run like public banks i.e. banks for the public good. Some morality is required in the process. Prudently restricted by various strings, these public banks can respond more easily to the needs and aims of actual populations, rather than to the whims and fancies of absentee owners or of their volatile servants, that is to say their bonus-benefitting managers.

What am I saying? Have public banks and run them as such. They must spur real development, not inflate bubbles that transfer wealth from the bottom to the top. Will it hurt the shareholders and wealthier customers of private banks? Certainly. They have already enjoyed the State's helping hand; it may be time to repay the State with gratitude. Doesn't anyone remember how to do it? Read history books, study the European Payments Union of the 1950s, ask retired Italian or French bank managers, use your imagination. A few rules of thumb may assist those who lack enough imagination:

(a) Ban financial and currency speculation, at least within and *via* public banks: the casino belongs to "competitive" gamblers. Yes, people who used to claim that they would succeed or fail like Promethean heroes… Before they all asked for help to the Great Nanny, of course, lost as they were on their er-Rand. And please, let the State never again salvage these hypocrites from their own myopic greed. They are now trying to wash their guilty conscience by returning one hundredth of what they have received from the public purse, whilst re-filling their pockets at the State's expense, with fierce bearish appetite.

(b) Lubricate the real economy, if forward-looking, so as to launch much-needed public works, create long-term employment, and generate steady streams of income within the nation. Public banks can do so, at low interest rates: they must be profitable, but not at all costs.

(c) Monitor inbound and outbound capital flows, so as to direct investments to socially beneficial areas, and counter tax evasion as well as tax avoidance: far too much has been denied in the past to the very public purse that has then saved the incompetent affluent from themselves. And remember that a stable currency and genuine economic sovereignty can only be secured by abandoning the disastrous freedom of capital flows that has flooded the world with crisis upon crisis since the 1980s: tequila, vodka, whiskey or brennivín, ouzo, they all taste the same.

(d) Secure reserves by compelling the capitals of public bodies, pension and social security savings, and the revenues of public banks to be invested in the public banks themselves. The State must be as free as possible from the bondage and the blackmail of its current masters, i.e. foreign direct investment and international bondholders.

(e) Pay bank managers State salaries comparable to those of other leading promoters of public wellbeing—surgeons, health-&-safety inspectors, judges—and avoid attracting the covetous, self-indulging, big-jet and big-penthouse penis-length-comparing "best and brightest" who plunged the world into a massive crisis. Communities need not such beastly best and brittle brightness. Forget them and their barbaric macho ethos—made of turrets of money, performance-enhancing bonuses (as though they alone were working), fee-demanding buddies-consultants, and PR companies using invariably words like "aggressively" and "targets".

Finally, do not underestimate the fact that it is difficult to deal with cronyism by voting new governments into office. Yet it is much more difficult to do the same thing by waiting for anonymous and short-lived shareholders to reform their servants, who are so free from supervision as to jot down any number they like in the books without anyone finding out. As Adam Smith forewarned us some time ago, the corporation is amongst the least competitive and the most corruptible of human institutions, hence amongst the most damaging to the proper functioning of capitalism.

And inflation? Don't worry. Nobody talks about it— a sudden silence. After all, common people are no longer able to buy anything, not even on credit. If anything, the real problem to come will be deflation. Besides, more than 90% of the money circulating around the globe is the result of financial leverage by private institutions. Still, old-fashioned, knee-jerk reactions may be reoccurring soon: pensions and salaries must not go up, for the poor must repay the money lost by the rich; States must rein in public expenditures, which they have been doing for thirty years, unless there was a war to be fought; public assets must be privatised, so as to further enrich the incompetent and further weaken their only saviour; cheap money must stop (now), lest we tax the wealthy to give some jobs to the restless youth, etc. By the way, how is it that bonuses for bank managers could always go up? It must be the same people who think that only private firms can be valid multipliers...

It is ironic that, after two decades during which we had been told that the State and, for that matter, its independent Central Banks could not issue money for schools, hospitals, public works and social projects, quite mysteriously they started printing so much money. Sure, they now tell us that we need private banks to keep credit flowing, for credit is the life-blood of the economy. Without it, there shall be no green-spanning across the meadows. And yet, enterprises and households worldwide are still struggling to get the credit that they need. In truth, the selectively generous Central Banks' cheap money benefits financial speculation, which is where the trouble started in the first place. How could ever a heartless economy pump any actual life-blood?

Indeed, in California, the local government is at risk of being terminated by the refusal of private banks to subscribe local public bonds because "unsafe" i.e. the State of California could go bankrupt. "What a cheek!" my mother would say, and she has dealt with banks for most of her life. The banks refusing to purchase these sunny bonds today are the same banks that were saved by public money yesterday, when it was raining. But there is more.

Were even these banks to provide enterprises, households and public authorities with the credit they need, they would not do it for free, for the common good, or for a little interest; they would do it for profit, and for as much of it as they can get. Thus, things would be so arranged and, sadly enough, they are being so arranged, as to have public money given very prodigally to private banks, so that these banks may give it to the public far less prodigally.

What is more, in order to be worthy of the bailed-out banks' money:

- Enterprises have been reducing their workforce to be more "competitive"
- Households have been returning their homes to banks that had sold highly reliable mortgages towards the purchase of… homes
- The State has been thinning out its already skinny body in order to

be attractive to the banks, which the State has just rescued from themselves

After decades of TINA-like reduction of all that is public, public money is being given to glaringly incompetent private banks so that their losses be made public and their profits, which were always private, recover and be still private. In the process, public money is not used to counter dwindling employment, secure houses, and, say, fund hospitals, schools, university research, care for the elderly and the mentally ill, public gardens, public football fields, archaeological preservation programmes, amelioration of penal institutions, better garbage collection, sanitation and, why not, aid to starving children. How many tramps will get trapped in the revolving doors of the wealthy's tower?

That the State may have money for the bankrupt banks but not for its own social functions, it is something that defies imagination, morality, and even legal obligations. Many of them ratified the International Covenant on Economics, Social and Cultural Rights, didn't they?

(2)

Second, life-saving medication: if you skip the middle man, operate good public banks, and have money to use for the common good, then launch a vast programme of green public works. More severe and threatening than the economic crisis itself is the ecological crisis. Ask the United Nations about that. The former crisis threatens fat wallets at the top and starving children at the bottom, yet at different degrees of dangerousness. The latter crisis threatens all equally with death. The grim reaper is the great leveller. Since so much private enterprise has caused the ecological crisis in the first place—the smoky days of the Industrial Revolution—and has continued it in the face of scientific alarm calls as old as Britney Spears, then it is advisable that the State be able and willing to step in and, both by regulation and by direct economic action, reverse the tide.

Forget speculative carbon emission quotas and reduce carbon emissions; ban outright or force rapid conversion of the most obvious forms of life-destructive economic activity; tax the remaining polluting activities and de-tax non- or less-polluting ones; have a major public company undertaking proper refitting of houses on a massive scale so as to make them less energy-consuming; create large public recycling facilities so as to counter illegal dumping of waste at large; found and fund new public research centres for the development of green technologies, free from the yoke of short-term corporate desiderata; ration carbon-based power and use it only for vital and life-enhancing activities…

There are so many tokens of environmentally constructive planning, yet so few that have not been resisted as "too costly", "too rigid", "too much for us, who have already done so much", etc. Were only the people uttering such phrases to consider seriously the fact that they can be so garrulous because the environment is still, barely, able to support them, their bodies, their minds, and the natural and social infrastructures that have allowed them to grow, socialise and, limitedly, mature…

In addition to a life-enabling aim and a counter-cyclical alternative to depressing austerity, politics would also regain its dignity by having a green mission. Strangled by powerful yet incompetent lobbies, and fettered by incompetent yet powerful central banks, politics has been reduced for far too long a time to day-to-day management of production costs in the domestic market and salesmanship in the foreign ones.

(3)

Third, important medication: since some neighbours may not like your policies and your currency, then they might respect your resources. States should increase or secure public control of strategic assets: water, oil, gas, the knowledge of its own population—this knowledge having been fostered by public education, healthcare provision, and cultural activities.

Whether by safeguarding the revenues originating in natural

resources that would otherwise enrich few and often foreign shareholders, or by reclaiming a knowledge-based industry that would otherwise be outsourced by corporate giants, the State must secure a steady source of income for itself and for the nation's economy. This income alone should help democratic governments to respond to their constitutional sovereigns, not to rating agencies and "markets" whose lords regularly reside offshore.

As Norway's long experience in State-run oil extraction and refining illustrates, it is the one and only "trickle-down" strategy that has produced tangible results for an entire nation. States' assets are not a factor of market distortion, but a factor of production—and one that can help businesses to grow by providing cheap goods and services, as opposed to the endless and costly bloodsucking of postmodern privatised economies. Ideally, it would be good for States to regain control over money-creating central banks, but there are limits even to one's dreams.

Incidentally, even the many wars paid by the American public purse to secure control over other nations' oil, or at least force its trade in US dollars, indicate that the public control of strategic assets is not so foolish an idea. And yes, also that getting bombed may be a risk for the nations pursuing the path recommended hereby. Apart from the landowners, cunning agents and financial moguls who have charged prices well over any real cost of production, for all others there is no such thing as a free lunch—Miltons have always known the devil very well.

(4)

Fourth, integrative medication: since some powers-that-are may not be pleased with your plans, make sure you can deal with them. Create a just fiscal and regulatory framework, which empowers the population at large and weakens the usual lobbies: close tax loopholes and tax breaks for the usual lobbies; withdraw passports and freeze assets of tax fugitives; tax rents (land, inheritances, capital gains) and de-tax hard work, so as to reward merit and distinguish sharply between earned and unearned income; end subsidies, legal privileges (e.g. limited liability) and tax-breaks to private companies, lest they never compete in a truly free market; nationalise the companies that are too big to fail, as John Kenneth Galbraith advised us to do long ago; reclaim research and development grants and whichever other public credit given to private firms leaving the country; confiscate the assets of companies outsourcing to countries with lower labour and environmental standards; put regulatory agencies and grassroots associations on the boards of private and public companies to fight corruption; inspect constantly and reward those inspectors who discover illicit activities.

Taxes matter. Especially when there is an ever-richer tiny elite of super-rich whose fortune comes as a long free lunch over accumulated wealth, whether in property or capital. They hardly ever pay taxes. They pay fewer than most, since someone else paid taxes before them: those who actually earned that property or capital in the first place. In truth, they may quite simply avoid taxes by shoring their assets off to tiny islands or Alpine valleys. The members of this tiny elite are above and beyond the common citizen, whilst their trusted and highly paid managers rarely go to jail when guilty of fraud or cheating. Above-and-beyondness is a transferrable asset too. If and when hijacked by this elite, States are likely to commit suicide by taxing those who work instead. And if the people sweating and bleeding don't have enough money, then State activities are to be reduced in the name of, say, the Big Society--of the hopeless and of their hopeless resilience.

In brief, internalise costs that have been externalised regularly and mercilessly at the expense of natural and societal well-being; and effectively re-regulate the disastrously de-regulated playground of the free enterprise--especially but not exclusively of the virtual type —whose only known freedom is that which cages every possible aspect of reality into the life-blind logic of profit-making.

Will anyone undergo this cure? History will tell. And history is full of surprises. Who would have ever thought, for example, that little furry animals could outlive giant dinosaurs and become the first species ever capable of destroying the ecological structures that allow them to live!

II.

Speculators may do no harm as bubbles on a steady stream of enterprise. But the position is serious when enterprise becomes the bubble on a whirlpool of speculation.
— John Maynard Keynes

There are two ways of conquering a foreign nation. One is to gain control of its people by force of arms. The other is to gain control of its economy by financial means.
— John Foster Dulles

In the year 2003 I published a review of *Value Wars*, written by Canada's leading value theorist John McMurtry. In it I provided an account of the stunning whistle-blowing by World Bank Chief Economist Joseph Stiglitz *vis-à-vis* "deregulation" and "globalisation", two terms that had been dominating economic and political discourse for some time. Quite unexpectedly, and rather shockingly, a well-connected, mainstream, Nobel-prize-winning economist denounced the World Bank and the International Monetary Fund for implementing over a period of at least twenty years a merciless four-step process of re-colonisation of independent nations by international private capital. This was the sort of suspicion that radicals like pop singer Bono Vox and Polish actor Karol Woitila, better known as Pope John Paul II, had been voicing for a long time. As for John McMurtry, he took due notice, since Stiglitz's revelation was consistent with his own description of world affairs as directed by the profit-motive of the few *versus* the vital interests of all others. Preferring truth to originality, I endeavoured to spread this description of world affairs around me. In fact, I had given lectures about it, also in Iceland, before 2003.

Nobody seemed to care, however, at least here in the north. Stiglitz's views were not widely discussed and even less were they taught at the university level, except by a few—sometimes foreign— eccentrics. McMurtry's views, hadn't it been for the same eccentrics, would have been left to gather dust in local libraries. Meanwhile, the policies of deregulation and enthusiastic participation in globalisation were not halted. On the contrary, in the year 2003, the three largest public banks were privatised. Immediately, they started to sail the seas of international speculation, never seen before in Icelandic history. "Carry trades" and "financial leverage" became mantras recited on the first page of all newspapers, whilst the businessmen who were dubbed the "new Vikings" set out to raid foreign banks, enterprises, supermarkets, and football clubs, with money that they did not have. But such is late- (or post-) modern capitalism, or "the Icelandic way of doing business", as I was told back then. Besides, it would appear that only professional economists are entitled to teach about why they, unlike a mere philosopher like McMurtry, got it so wrong. And there's so much to learn!

What did Stiglitz's whistle-blowing describe? And how does it apply to the Icelandic case?

First, the permeability of the nation's borders to private foreign capital is increased by deregulating capital trade and privatising strategic national assets. Barriers, bottlenecks, and "obsolete" protections are removed, whether material or immaterial. Nobody quite remembers why they were there, and even fewer wonder why. Above all else, money must flow. That's the consensus, at least in the District of Columbia, which is obviously populated by zealous reformers. Their principles are crystal-clear: "public is bad, private is good." They believe in "The Free Market", whatever that may be thought to be; and they believe in it so ardently and unflinchingly that Stiglitz and others refer to them as "market fundamentalists." They even set complicated rules at roundtables to force dissenting markets to be free. Anyhow, this very first step, which may take some time, is achieved by lubricating slow-moving and slow-thinking local politicians, business leaders, present and future ideologues with adequate amounts of grease. Grease, yes, such as co-opting these people into the international jet- and yacht-set, promising or securing that they will have their own golden toilets, washing their brains at spectacular conferences and exclusive think-tank meetings, baptising their best and brightest first-borns in the sacred founts at the sacred shrines, stirring their simmering jingoistic sentiments, or bribing them straightforwardly—indeed Stiglitz talks of this process as "briberization".

Secondly, money flows into the country. A bubble ensues; in fact, a cyst. Depending on the country's economic conditions, the cyst can take different forms, but all of them eventually become painful. In the case of a reasonably well-off country, glittering streams of foreign capital inundate the land, turning modest entrepreneurial fields into a glorious harvest of unprecedented projects. Thus refreshed, the local currency and the local shares pupate into surprisingly light-winged and seemingly fertile young fairies, whose well is said to be full of diamonds. Moreover, the nation's financial institutions become large fountains that can quench the thirst of anyone who is eager to drink from them, including those who do not need it, but have the misfortune to possess a belly. New buildings spring up like mushrooms in the vast new wetlands, luxury and consumer spending—mostly dependent upon credit—fly high like gleaming droplets out of a geyser's mouth. So mesmerising is this sight, that more permeability is actively sought.

Then, the cyst bursts. As swiftly as it flew in, so does the money flow out. A rumour, a token of gossip, an unfortunate diplomatic incident, a well-paid expert report, or a speculator's premeditated signal to his colleagues rapidly reverses the tide. The flood ends. A drought follows. Projects—and buildings—remain unfinished, half-mast, like flags at a funeral. The wombs of local currency and local shares reveal themselves sterile; it was all make-up, they now say, even the wings; you should never trust the books. The well in the garden is dry, and full of stones. Moreover, the fountains are dry too. Around them, stunned, jobless, emaciated peons, indebted up to their eyeballs, drown into whirling sand clutching their plasma TV sets. And their TV heroes have not come to save them, be they crusading party leaders or Viking raiders. Who will?

Nobody is without friends, especially after having become part of the international jet- and yacht-set, educating his own children in the best schools, or attending eye-opening conferences and meetings.

Not to mention those friends who have already proven so generous in the past. In truth, after having advised on how to render the country prosperous, they now spare no saliva explaining what can be done in order to rescue it from its unfortunate plight. Thus, money is poured back into the nation. High interest rates are, however, *de rigueur*. One does not give much to drink too easily to a friend who has already drunk too much. What kind of a friend would he be?

The third step is therefore to make up for the mistakes of the past and repay one's generous friends. Whatever wealth remains must be scrupulously collected so as to honour the debt—or so as to secure further loans. Debt gives salvation from debt, as gamblers understand so well. Certainly, the wealth of the wealthy is better left untouched: they are the producers, the life-givers, blessed fountainheads of the nation's wellbeing, which needs them so badly under the burning sun of the new sad day. They must be treated kindly, lest they or their wealth be forced to flee by too rapacious and visible a hand—some have already fled, they whisper. The wealth of the poor—or of the poor-to-be—is a better starting point. After all, they may have little, but there are many of them. Besides, since they have little, they cannot flee as easily as the rich, nor can their wealth flee. And whereas the wealthy can go bankrupt and be resurrected cleansed of their debt, like the imperishable Phoenix, ordinary mortals honour their debts, willingly or not. They may protest, but law and order are the last two public sectors whose resources are cut off, unless successful ways are found to privatise them too.

Finally, as the nation struggles in debt and turmoil, groaning so loudly as to disturb its neighbours, the generous friends come back to help. They cannot remain untouched in the face of so much poverty and violence. They have new "plans", "strategies" and "packages" to sort things out. Yet, to implement them, national borders must be removed completely and an iron framework of conditions for investment and development must be imposed in order for the nation to become a proud participant in fully liberalised, multinational free trade. For example, its tax environment must be suited to foreign investors—may God bless them—and its population as flexible as unthinking reeds in gushing new brooks, to which they contribute sweat and tears.

By the way, where does Iceland stand now? Probably it stands at the threshold of deciding whether to plunge headlong into step three, with signs of the fourth step already lurking behind the waterfalls harnessed for hydropower.

III.

In all normal civilisations the trader existed and must exist. But in all normal civilisations the trader was the exception; certainly he was never the rule; and most certainly he was never the ruler. The predominance which he has gained in the modern world is the cause of all the disasters of the modern world.

- Gilbert Keith Chesterton

The economic logic behind dumping a load of toxic waste in the lowest wage country is impeccable, and we should face up to that.

- Lawrence "Larry" Summers

It has been long known that Europe catches a cold whenever the United States sneezes. Yet things get even worse when the immune system of rules and restrictions to international capital and currency trade has been removed altogether. Iceland and some young, yet already former, free-market miracles on the Baltic Sea did catch pneumonia this time. Ironic indeed, as they are just another group of market miracles turned into meltdowns—Asia had a few of them in the 1990s. Miracles seem short-lived these past few decades... Though if truth be told, even Lazarus died, after having been brought back to life.

Historians of the future, if there shall be any and if they will be honest, are going to wonder and ponder upon how such intelligent and highly educated "knowledge economies", capable of the finest mathematical-financial wizardry via the fanciest computer technologies, could bestow upon themselves so much avoidable pain, destroying in the process not solely further scores of planetary life support systems, but also man-made social infrastructures that have generated, depending on the country, genuine welfare for up to three or four generations. These future historians will be at pains to conceive of powerful, well-off, democratically elected representatives who listened to foreign bankers, and not to their own citizens, rushing to implement, whenever they could, multilateral agreements on investment robbing their own cabinets of much of their power.

These future historians will probably fail to empathise with and understand such bizarre people, very much like Voltaire, who could not really explain why our forefathers were willing to slaughter one another over the correct interpretation of the Holy Trinity. After all, they had never seen it (or them?) and Jesus himself had never said anything clear, if anything, about it (or them?). Not to mention the centuries that humankind spent warring, raping, disembowelling, burning, maiming, chaining, flogging and excommunicating one another because of errors of interpretation. Obtuseness is incredibly resilient. And we are not so different today. Check the Athenian cradle of our civilisation if you don't believe it.

Yes, embodied and expressed by the very same conventional people at the helm of the world's public and private financial affairs, the wisdom arising from the ashes of the current crisis is astoundingly similar to the one that caused the crisis. Are you indebted? Take on another loan. The private banking sector has betrayed you? Restore it with public money and run it as before. The world's economy is a gilded cage run on behest of under-taxed oligopolists, tax-evading rentiers and idle absentee owners that squeeze money out of the real economy through banking charges, debt repayments, service fees, monopoly and land rents? Keep it going and call it a "free market". People are suffering, jobless, and with their tax money siphoned to the creditors that inflated the bubble? Show them tough love and deprive them of further healthcare, education, culture, wages, pensions, childcare, subsidised water and power. Austerity measures turn a crisis into a depression?

Implement more of the same measures. The environment is running amok in the so-called free-market environment? The market will fix it; in the meantime, profit will keep being extracted from increased prices in oil, gas, polluting consumer goods, and cancer treatments due to the ecological collapse of the planet. Apparently, the only green rules acceptable are those that transfer further money from the public purse into private pockets. All others are resisted as "costly", "distorting", "rigidifying", "liberticidal", which may be true—and good. The one and only truly binding international environmental regulation that, so far, has saved us from extinction, preventing excessive UV-irradiation, was a top-down imposition from Montreal.

But life, not to mention a happy and healthy life, has never been the paramount goal of the pursuit of profit. War was and still is a major source of profit, towards which public subsidies to private firms are given generously… Well, they call them "research & development" grants or "national security" strategies… Disease-causing pollution has been mostly an externality that had nothing to do with profit, until pharmaceutical conglomerates found a way to exploit that too. Slaves and their children were most profitable for many, many centuries. Wage slaves… Oops! The flexible working poor and their children are very profitable today too.

And for what must all this wisdom be endured? To give money to people who have money. They have enough, one would believe. They should start communicating it to those who have nothing… little… less. Jesus and Aquinas regarded this as obvious. No, it is not obvious. Money is never enough, especially to those who need yet another fancy dress. But why are these people non-satiable? Why do they complain, lobby and shift electoral allegiance whenever taxation on capital gains is vented? Why do they transfer their fiscal residence to tax havens, whilst benefitting from handouts of the State they are deserting? Why do they outsource productive structures to countries squeezing labour out of turnips, if youngsters are not available? Why do they say that "they have already done enough" whenever life-saving regulation is discussed? Why do they care more about the interest rate they can get, than they care about how their money is invested? Why do they oppose healthcare, old-age pensions, education and culture for all, while they enjoy it for themselves?

It is competition, they answer. There isn't enough around for all of us, only for the really tough ones, who can then live in much-deserved luxury. But why do people compete for having more for themselves, instead of, say, competing for beauty, generosity, selflessness, equal distribution, full employment? There can be so many different and more constructive competitive aims in life: just look around. Nuns, school teachers, barefoot physicians, rocket scientists, marine biologists, old fishermen, young artists... They may not all dislike some cash, but they do not live for it, or at least they try not to. Since Divine Will is out of fashion, and if you press them long enough, the luxury-deserving competitors are going to tell you, eventually, that *we* are cruel wolves. How naïve was I! I thought that *they* were cruel wolves... The world is a cruel place—those ferocious nuns... Nobody waits for those left behind—and they don't. The market forces accept no barrier. As one of their fairest ideologues so frequently stated, there is no alternative; it is human nature. A hidden philosophical anthropology...

And yet, none less than their poorly understood hero Adam Smith taught us long ago something very different in the opening page of his greatest book, *The Theory of Moral Sentiments*:

> *How selfish soever man may be supposed, there are evidently some principles in his nature, which interest him in the fortune of others, and render their happiness necessary to him, though he derives nothing from it except the pleasure of seeing it. Of this kind is pity or compassion, the emotion which we feel for the misery of others, when we either see it, or are made to conceive it in a very lively manner. That we often derive sorrow from the sorrow of others, is a matter of fact too obvious to require any instances to prove it; for this sentiment, like all the other original passions of human nature, is by no means confined to the virtuous and humane, though they perhaps may feel it with the most exquisite sensibility. The greatest ruffian, the most hardened violator*

of the laws of society, is not altogether without it.

This is certainly not the one and only betrayal of Smith by current capitalism. After all, his market was meant to be free from rentiers, who now run the show. Anyhow, why so much mercilessness, then? Have we become worse human beings? Have we lost our humanity? Have we found ways to outcruel the cruel, underfed, superstitious peasants, who, when not breaking skulls in the name of God or King or Country, killed and maimed animals on a farm? Well, as modern and proud of our science-technology as we can be... Well, yes... Overall, subtly, we have. The thinning of solidarity that embraces the whole humankind, which a German-sounding French warmonger studied in depth, is a weaker barrier to the undergoing evil drives.

Or, at least, we have done our best to train impressionable young minds to being ordinarily callous and participating in the most spectacularly life-destructive economic system ever seen on Earth—a system that, as denounced by the scientific community for the past thirty years, has turned the survival of our species into a big question mark. Much is done in this direction, routinely, thousands of times a day, so that our youth may become more beastly than ruffians and more abrasive than criminals. But how? Simple. We (mis-)educate them, and we have tools for (mis-)education that no emperor or church of old has ever owned or mastered. Only a couple of totalitarian dictators gave it a go or two in the blood-drenched century of Charlie Chaplin and Woody Allen... But how, where? Open your eyes. Watch.

Our TVs and media are replete with commercials. They are meant to accompany you from the cradle to the grave. Selectively and scientifically trained marketing strategists, creative psychologists and advertising gurus are paid to induce desires in the subtlest and most effective manners, starting with our children's delicate souls. These desires will blossom into poisonous "new needs", as these "experts" call them. These weed-like flowers being sheer wants perceived as genuine individual needs, the delayed satisfaction of which is to generate a sense of inadequacy, anguish, frustration, isolation, or envy towards those who do satisfy them. And these are the only flowers that must grow; hence they are everywhere. Children no longer need an imagination. Marketing strategists make sure that the only pictures that children can have in their mind are those that sell. They speak already like TVs: why shouldn't they replicate TVs in their brain? Eventually, as grown-ups, these children will be branded, like slaves of old, or cattle still is today. Perhaps, like the slaves of old, they will enjoy freedom one day a year. Or maybe all the days will have been taken away by marketing strategists, who wish to celebrate the sales of Valentine's Day, Mother's day, Father's Day, Marketing Strategist's Day…

You don't believe me? Go to any primary school and you will meet hordes of little creatures dressed according to the latest fashion code, or pestering their parents to be so dressed. Those who are not there, because they are busy sewing the actual fashion items, may well try to rob them from the horde one day. These little brats! They want and want and want scores of items that they do not need, the possession of which, moreover, does not grant happiness at all, despite the glittering promises. Were it so, no new purchase would be "needed", and that would be bad for business. Certainly, one may learn to control such a powerful impetus, but it takes years of self-re-training. Not even hunger and utter destitution placate it. Not even the full awareness of not being able to afford those consumer goods. Nothing will ever erase the deep-rooted psychological mechanisms implanted into our souls when we were little. Is this enough? No, there is more to it.

Our TVs and media are replete with role models—and the medium is the message. Rich and wannabe-rich people of all sorts shine even when performing the most ordinary activities, such as shaving or concealing their stench with perfume. From slutty heiresses to pimping rappers, from cosmetically mummified bad actors to ignorant footballers, from divorce-addict hair-died tycoons to soon-to-be-millionaires answering questions or showing their private parts in public—these are the saints and blessed inspirers of the modern secular creed. They may be confessing their own sins to a TV host, confident that their words will be forgotten. What remains, instead, is the scent of money that perspires through their placenta-creamed pores. A powerful aura.

The same aura surrounding the action hero, who fights, kills and kidnaps for the sake of justice, peace and freedom... There he comes! Dressed in an Armani suit, he jumps out of a Mercedes, talking briefly on his Nokia. He checks his Rolex, then gets into a Ferrari and drives to Chez Maxim's. There, he meets a beautiful young lady, whose Valentino dress will soon be ripped at the Hilton's. And there he'll kick the guts out of the villain, smashing his Patek Philippe and ruining forever his Dolce & Gabbana jacket... Justice is served. Peace is conquered. Freedom triumphs. That's the message, isn't it? And if not much of the beautiful young lady is shown, then children can watch too.

Poor people are less frequently shown. They don't sell as well as our hero. Moreover, they don't buy. There exist notable exceptions, though. Poor men and poor women are sometimes on display, like animals at the zoo, to be observed, mocked and, on Christmas day, to feel sorry for. Other times, they are actively humiliated on screen by policemen, judges and other masters of entertainment. Crime, ignorance, savagery: what a show! Once again, as long as it sells, keep it up. There, in the spotlight, for less than fifteen minutes and amidst commercial ads, the poor can shine like greasy piglets on spits, or like the tin their most unfortunate children collect in garbage dumps.

What is the result of this *Blendungsroman*? Go to any secondary school and you will meet cell-phone-talking walking replicas of the rich, parading themselves in the corridors. Give them an opportunity to put down a "loser", and they will savour it like their own parents, whose SUVs and triple-mortgaged houses are punches into the Joneses' stomachs. Even poverty is a risk worth taking to cast the rich's aura.

The silent walking replicas of the poor are usually in other schools, unless they have dropped out of school already to find a job that will secure their poverty. Some are hiding in the toilets. They are poor and they know it. They look poor. It is not only their clothes that say it, but their bodies. They have bad teeth, small tits, big noses. Their parents have wrinkles. They can't get fixed, like those people on TV, or their replicas and the replicas' parents. To cope with this obvious inferiority, they breathe in. In Italy, they sniff cocaine to think that they too are rich. In Rumania, they sniff glue to think that they too are sniffing cocaine.

Either way, none of these kids must worry about being politically active. It is too dangerous. Yes, youngsters still remember how to bark: they haven't been beaten up into silent submission, yet. Some will have to be locked up, so that trade be free. Don't give them any wrong ideas. That's socialism—or any bad "ism" of the day. Don't give them hope. That's socialism. Politics is best left to corporate employees, who siphon public money to their shareholders and, God be gracious, to their own bank accounts. That's the free market. These employees alone are capable of understanding why unemployment is natural and inequality good. They've got talent. They've got the degrees that get you good jobs. Therefore, unless they are corporate employees, not even the kids' parents have to worry about politics. Like these happy few, the kids' parents can take happy pills too or, if pills are too expensive, drink themselves out blind.

Drunk, the poor parents can cope better with the trauma of seeing their children die. Each country has its own special way of sending new winged angels to God. In high-tech market-miracle India, they die of cholera in open-air sewers, where they were looking for edible scraps. In coup-idity-ruled Honduras they die poisoned by pesticides in a free-market plantation, so that the bananas people eat in Canada be not too pricy. In revolutionary France they die stabbed by an angry pusher in a dark alley, but they were not really French after all. In peace-loving America, they die fighting for human rights in another country, since their own country denied them a future. How was it possible? They had trained them at killing people since they were three, on a stolen X-box… Maybe they should have trained them at doing something else, but there is no videogame that teaches you how to free a political party from corporate diktats or join a trade union… Is this enough? No, there is more.

Our TVs and media are replete with experts telling us that greed is good. They are the most interviewed and consulted members of the intelligentsia of our community. Sometimes they even become our presidents, ministers, mayors and godfathers. Go to any university. Some of them feed on tenure and enjoy healthcare and pension benefits, whilst arguing that you shouldn't have them. You will discover that there is an entire discipline built upon that notion.

If truth be told, a few of its adherents do remind their students, on leap years, that the profit-motive of the *homunculus œconomicus* is just one drive amongst many. This drive becomes one and insatiable for the sake of toying with mathematical formulae, not for the sake of describing reality, which never works quite like the models do. Facts can be so obstinate. Theory is much more flexible. Occasionally, on elective days, these beautiful souls mention even mysterious, metaphysical, unscientific words: "ethics", "morality", "duty", "respect", "goodness", "virtue", "governance", "responsibility"… They don't fully grasp them, though, for they slip out of books and balance sheets. Sometimes they even get their students to learn some history, thus half-stuttering what sort of devastation this homunculus and its *leit*-motive have caused. Still, these are exceptions, divagations, and the students, between the end of their studies and the beginning of their careers, know it very well.

Our MBAs and the many branches of science and engineering dependent upon private sponsors and future corporate employers are the convent-barracks where our crusading novices, more or less geeky and asocial, are told that only numbers really matter. The fate of a *paterfamilias* and of his family does not. They are told that persons are not persons: they are costs, opportunities, capital, markets… They are all sorts of things that can be converted into monetary units—numbers, in fact—though most definitively they are not persons. In fact, such things, be they free individuals or free communities, can turn into dependent variables. And if some of these things are laid off by a firm that rationalises an otherwise irrational workplace—what a madness it must have been!—then it may be time to invest money in that firm. If the right numbers go up, then things are just as they should be. If they don't, they can be massaged. If they still don't, they can be fixed. If they still refuse to go up, then a couple of hospitals plus half a university, as long as they are public, can be sacrificed to a return to growth.

In the streamlined world there can be recoveries without jobs, business opportunities in famines, increased flexibility via insecurity of employment and future bread, full employment at the natural unemployment rate, goods that do a lot of bad things, and market miracles that melt into destitution because of something bad but the pious market. What lesson is learnt? Everything in the world exists in order to maximise the money of investors and/or their managers. Even old, wrinkly countries must be attractive to such people or face their own demise. Make the rich richer. That is the one and paramount commandment. Such merciless *homunculi* are no fiction; they are science-fiction: they drive around in Dalek machines. Indeed, to those who do not simply rob and run, being merciless is a fiduciary duty. Apart from this, everything else goes.

Yes, everything else, unless you get caught and cannot pay the best lawyers—what a shame. Business words of the business world tell no lies: lack of scruples is "determination", mercilessness is "having balls", inhumanity is "being committed", callousness is "professionalism", locust-like behaviour is a "hedging", stealing traditional knowledge is a "patent", depriving people of knowledge is a "copyright", poisoning the destitute is "mutually beneficial trade", taking public-sector resources to guarantee private profits is "hard work", threatening employees with unemployment is "personnel management", gambling is "trading futures" and other cabalistic formulae "over the counter", oligopolies are "economies of scale" and cartels are "free markets", sending knowingly drivers to die because of a few faulty cars is a "cost-saving measure", sending knowingly air passengers to die because of reduced safety controls is a "cost-saving measure", corruption of inspectors is a "cost-saving measure", corruption of politicians is "lobbying", and rent-exacting parasites are "the productive class". The list goes on and on. Read the news and enjoy the game: destroying peoples is "restructuring", keeping them poor is "preventing inflation", colonising a nation is "opening markets", withdrawing rights is "reform"… By the end of it, you almost believe what they say.

Has any student still doubts or feels uneasy? Then he is told that all is well, for all ends well. Yes, those things that we unscientifically call "people" may seem to be suffering, poor things. And the others, crony criminals who have nothing to do with the free market, are the exception, though the rule just wants to be like them. After all, those exceptional exceptions were on the cover of glossy magazines like *Capital*, the *Cosmopolitan* of people who "have balls"... Don't worry. Everything will be alright. Just wait—that's what my old priest and the party commissar would say... The invisible hand of the self-regulating market is going to look after all of them. Free from State intervention and from trade unions—for only capitals may associate and go on strike if they don't like a government—the invisible hand is to generate endless bounty for all—the invisible bounty? Most of the world's trade is virtual, after all...

Such is orthodoxy today, for which even a Pope's distribution chests are heresy, utter *hilaireous bellocs*... If you claim that small is beautiful, the giants get angry: go make your shoes elsewhere! Today, you no longer need to be red to be a danger. It is enough to be as white as a dove. The Market God likes hawks, whose endless preying is the source of all that is good. His transparent hand turns into water all the blood that these hawks spill. As to the tallest shrines, they are no longer erected for the glory of the Sun, Athena or Almighty God, but for the likes of Morgan Stanley. Behind all this, a hidden theology... Maybe Divine Will should be in fashion again.

IV.

The measure of the restoration lies in the extent to which we apply social values more noble than mere monetary profit.

Franklin Delano Roosevelt

To avoid glaring inequality or widespread misery I am ready to sacrifice some, or all, of my freedom... I should be guilt-stricken, and rightly so, if I were not.

- Isaiah Berlin

The child empathises with the dying bird. The adult empathises with the starving child. The nurse attempts to ease the pain of the terminal patient. The teacher smiles patiently at the pupils playing in the courtyard. The schoolmaster hides his unease as the ancient oak is felled. The gardener watches wildlife documentaries on the TV. The mayor goes on holiday to his cottage on the lakeside. None of them likes to be ill. All of them fear death. All of them experienced curiosity or elation as they held a newly born creature in their arms. All of them have been compassionate at some point. All religions have praised divinity as the fountainhead of all that is. Whether physically, emotionally or mentally, all of the above have exemplified the ultimate source of all values.

Years of research about value have led me to conclude that nothing is more valuable than that which allows value itself to emerge: life. Without life—biological, emotional and mental—there can be no value, whether ethical, aesthetic, economic or political. Those that deem life's value instrumental acknowledge its value nevertheless. Besides, none of them seems likely to prefer beauty or other values to eating every day and being in good health: take away their bread, and they will sell their dearest painting… Of all crazy philosophers ever alive, only a handful rejected life as a value and one alone behaved in a way that denounced actual indifference to life: Pyrrho the sceptic, whom his friends prevented from walking under carts and falling off cliffs. One. As for the few who told us that life is a valley of tears and an endless stream of horrors, none of them ever stopped eating, drinking, and philosophising, i.e. one of the activities that they clearly enjoyed the most. But what can the lives of crazy philosophers teach us about economic matters?

As usual, philosophy can reveal the heart of an issue. If life is so crucial, indeed the source of all values, then it can be inferred that a successful economic system provides universal access to vital goods across generations. Economic efficiency means that the lives of all benefit from it and nothing is spoiled to the point that those who come after us may not benefit too: resources are left for others the way in which we would like to have them left for us, if not better. Improvement is a possibility. An economic system that achieves its vital aims more effectively, thus opening the door to a richer fulfilment of planetary and human potential, is yet a better system. On the contrary, an economic system that does not fulfil its vital aims, either because access is limited to few or some, past or present, or because it delivers goods that are deadly, detrimental to life or irrelevant to life needs, whilst leaving some of these needs unanswered, is a failure.

The current economic system is a failure. As repeatedly denounced by the international scientific community at its highest and most representative levels, human civilisation has become for the first time in its history a threat to the planetary environment that allows for humanity's own existence. There is no aspect of the Earth's environment that has not been depleted in the three centuries that have seen the affirmation of capitalism worldwide: the biosphere-protecting Ozone-layer, breathable-air-producing and reproducing pluvial forests and oceanic life-systems, self-regenerating water aquifers, nourishing-food-producing arable spaces, and natural-equilibrium-maintaining and science- and technology-inspiring biodiversity. The continuation of life as we know and enjoy it is at risk.

Much has already been destroyed beyond repair, to the point that bioengineering is being discussed as a tool to cope with the most tragic consequences of "development" awaiting us. Emblematically, one nation of the world is planning already the purchase of land in India in order to transfer its entire population there upon the day when the ocean will have swallowed their ancestral islands. And yet, in the face of current profit losses, all this is treated as secondary. Just read the news and you shall see that the focus of collective action is upon a "return to growth", as though the sad and deadly harvest of greed were not still vivid before our eyes.

What is more, the mantra of competition goes on unchallenged. But competition for what? To generate profits? And why? Why should rich people become richer? There's more than enough to go around. Even more ludicrous is the idea that schools, healthcare, free time, old-age security, peace of mind and all those gains for life that people acquired in decades of blood and humanity should be dismantled so that competition be won. By whom? What sort of victory is the augmentation of the money heaps of people who already have it, whilst the quality of life and the living conditions of most are worsened?

F.D. Roosevelt told us seventy years ago that greed is not only bad morals, it is also bad business. When business' sole purpose is to make as much money as possible as soon as possible, then the somewhat constructive role that business may play in society disappears altogether. It doesn't matter if any private business actually makes a lot more money, gets bigger internationally or pervades even more diffusely the lives of millions: the standards of evaluation and appreciation for the constructive role of private business belong to the sphere of public wellbeing. And public wellbeing cares about long-term indicators: happy workers retiring in good health, healthy mothers making plans for their children's education, educated youngsters looking forward to playing on the beach with their grandchildren. If this horizon disappears, then you'd better start to worry. Private business is known to have played far too often a destructive role, as everything, the long-term survival of private business included, can be sacrificed to man-eating Baal.

Short-termism, combined with the relentless pursuit of profit, characterised roaming Goths, wooden-legged pirates and cigar-loving gangsters. The entrepreneur, the glorious creation of modern capitalism, has always been expected to be something different. Restrained by family and personal pride, religious morals, annual dividends, trade unions and other 20th-century legal suasions, his horizon has been defined as a somewhat distant future, his playground the real world of flesh-and-bone persons like him, his reward the admiration of affluent or fully employed fellow citizens that participate in and benefit from his endeavours.

As long as alternative economic systems were either widely discussed or experimented with, the entrepreneur had to justify his existence by creating some tangible, albeit sometimes debatable, token of social worth, such as employment, community networks, or nice new gadgets. Only the speculator, hardly distinguishable from fraudsters, trotted relentlessly upon a different path. But speculators were said to be the exception, not the rule…

Yet the day came when Gordon Gekko and his friends got to control more than three quarters of what is still incautiously dubbed "world trade". The decades of my life, infested by Maggies, Wall-Street yuppies and wall-less oligarchs, launched "The Financial Revolution", a pivotal process in contemporary history that no historian has yet so baptised: let this label be my grand legacy to international scholarship.

An equally bombastic historian used this term in the 1960s to describe the emergence of public creditors in 18th-century England… It doesn't quite compare, I'm sorry. We've just witnessed thirty long years of national barriers coming down—and how long it took for both nations and their barriers to come into existence!—so as to allow for a gigantic flood of miraculously leveraged liquidity springing out of… books and vast pools of capital formed by privatising public money in all of its shapes, squeezing profit from de-unionised workforces threatened by—what a coincidence!—unbarred international competition, and such ingenious tokens of financial engineering that only professional mathematicians could make sense of them. All this money travelling much faster than any good or service ever before: computers have replaced the pens and ink of old. The world of Gekko and other reptilian inhabitants of city hedges and wall streets is indeed a very bizarre world.

Originally, these creatures were meant to trade pieces of paper granting a share of the profits made by fairly large private companies. It is something that had begun in Genoa a long time ago and that their trading partners, the Dutch, had brought to the North Sea around the year 1600, sailing thence to the New World, another Genoese discovery… But a share of the profits may be less remunerative than profiting from shares. Gekko's forefathers started betting on rises and falls in the price of those pieces of paper, sometimes causing them by moving massive amounts of money or dropping a few words into the nearest ear…

In the days of poor old Nixon, in the Big Apple, they traded about 20 million stocks every day. Today they trade 1600 million or so—and there's more fruit in the basket than just a big apple. Also, as of

Nixon's time, they started playing games with the world's currencies, namely the money with which common people buy their bread. Again, they started slowly, about 20 billion USD a day, but now, after "freeing" trade worldwide, they are up to 2 trillion. It is by far the largest chunk of trade in the world and it has one severe drawback: it makes the form of trade that normal people think of when they hear the world "trade"—buying and selling bananas, timber, cars, computers, etc.—much more complicated. Not to mention buying bread. But the reptiles don't worry: they own the future. They buy and sell it.

Actually, they take bets—only a tiny fraction of trade in existing "futures" fulfils the official excuse that these are ways to hedge against risks on purchases of actual goods—on nearly anything that can be grown, mined or brought into existence, influencing the price of all sorts of goods, including the bread that common people wish to buy. Still, since even this casino was not big enough, the reptiles added onto the table the so-called "derivatives", which are pieces of paper whose value is derived—hence the name—from something else, whether another piece of paper or a price arising from combining a few of them. Anything goes. Also because you can buy or sell these pieces of paper any way you like—over the counter, under the counter, beside the counter… You can actually buy and sell the option to buy or sell them, for short-termism can be so short that, to spare time, it allows certain persons to sell what they don't have.

Is this too complicated? Too silly? Well, today, around the globe, there's an ocean of derivatives, for a value of about 500 trillion USD. It is a lot of money… Strangely enough, however, the reptiles that invented them also felt the need to insure themselves against any risk that may ensue from trading in… derivative paper. So they started buying "credit default swaps" from insurance companies and let their friends and colleagues, the bankers, pile them up as assets, claiming that these "swaps" were as sound and good as gold itself. Probably they would have started taking major bets on them as well, had the entire mathematically engineered and economic-science-backed system failed from collapsing under its own virtual weight. Too much genius had been spent for the business world to bear.

Under so much talent and foresight, the reptiles' joints felt suddenly empty of market force. Amazingly, the invisible hand was nowhere to be seen. Fortunately, the State ran to their rescue and gave them a visible, reinvigorating bailout with other people's money, lest the bank's own mouthpiece uttered "BBB" or some other silly rating. And that's where we stand today. The real suffering surrounding us, from the unemployed Spanish worker to the starving Senegalese farmer, is due to a virtual catastrophe. And if the starving Senegalese farmer tries to move to Spain, he shall meet a wall and possibly drown in the sea, while frustrated unemployed Spaniards, trained by modern corporate journalists, will hate guts those that didn't. Strangely enough, these migrants are to be loathed, not the freely migrating virtual capital that cannibalised both Senegal and Spain.

Like all human endeavours, business can be either good or bad. To know what makes it good or bad, what is nobler than money, means to know how to measure real growth, real development, real utility, real goodness. Who, though, after Pareto's Protagorean reinvention of economics, is allowed to know what real value is? Certainly not serious economists, who can only acknowledge preferences... The Pope may know, perhaps. He claims to be right like no-one else and that's maybe why so many people cannot stand him: who likes an old moralising grandpa, in an age in which we are told by our media gurus to give into any juvenile urge of ours that can make them a buck?

Or maybe any living creature knows: they're all God's creatures, after all. Yes, even by watching slugs and bugs we can evince something important, which degree-honoured geeks may have neglected while sitting in front of an inanimate computer screen. They are not forgivable, though: no matter how much you masturbate, avatars are not human beings. Here comes the slap; Zen masters should love it: entomology can rescue economics from its value slumber. *Vade ad formicam.* What a twist! Or maybe not. It all started with Mandeville's bees, to be honest...

Let me be brief and clear on this. What consistent pattern of behaviour can be observed amongst slugs and bugs? Watch them in your garden, if you have one. Or go and watch them in a public garden, if it hasn't been sold to developers. As small and allegedly stupid as they are believed to be, all invertebrates try to do their best to survive at all times. And when they take risks, it is because they either look for food, shelter, safety, or attempt to ensure the survival of their species. As economically irrational as animals can be, these small beings can even sacrifice individual utility—one's safety, food or head—for the sake of keeping, indeed at times just making, their young. Future generations matter, to them. Some seem even to care for their fellows in the anthill, hive or nest in which they live… Life, in truth, matters to living creatures, and yet life can be sacrificed, for more life may thus ensue. The only higher value that life acknowledges is, in fact, life.

And yet, in today's world, money is still prioritised over life. Listen to our leaders, and with the exception of a pair of Caribbean politicians that corporate media describe regularly as lunatics, what matters most to most who matter most is to keep "growth" going. Capitalism or the "free market", as they like labelling it despite its dictatorial logic, must keep generating profit, free from State intervention, which does not serve that one paramount end. All this is held, despite the well-known biocide implications of such a process. Yes, capitalism is responsible for the ecological degradation that we are living in with, and leaving to, our children. Has nobody really put together the Industrial Revolution and the collapse of the planet's life support systems?

I shall help you: the causal link between the pursuit of profit and environmental degradation becomes visible every time environmental regulation is resisted as "too costly" or by-passed by illicit behaviour or by off-sourcing to countries that have actually little such regulation or none at all. Unless business is forced forcefully to comply with existing regulation, which is much more difficult in a barrier-free worldwide market, common praxes show that the primacy of profit persists over, say, not killing other people by dumping toxic waste onto them.

Indeed, in economics, it is methodologically impossible to address the environmental preconditions that make life possible and can secure its long-term flourishing. To the eyes of the economic observer, bread is as much and legitimately a "good" as nuclear waste, as long as a lawful market exists for both of them. It is only through direct State intervention that a bad "good" becomes officially what it is: a bad—and that is just the first step, for enforcement is yet to be secured from lobbying and bribes.

States alone can ban slavery, organ trafficking, child labour, exploitation, air pollution or aquifer poisoning as the bads they are. States alone can make the real economy and earned income primary, and the virtual economy and unearned income secondary. There is nothing intrinsic to market mechanisms leading to that and we have known it for nearly two hundreds of years. Read Charles Dickens' subversive novels to get a clearly bleak picture. Also, ecosystems are "externalities", as the language of economics reveals, at least as long as they are not turned into a cost by environmental legislation, into a loss of profit by reduction in reputation *and* actual sales, or into a market opportunity by persistent spoliation of it—see the oxygen cans sold in the subway in Tokyo.

Protecting life and the environment is something that runs against the logic of profit, even if some business leaders may themselves desire it ardently. Profit can only relate to the value of life instrumentally: as a means to further profit. Money is a fetish, and one that eats living creatures and their dwelling spaces if that generates revenue. Nothing leads profit-driven "rational" agents to doing that which is necessary for planetary survival and, for that matter, for a decent social life on a vast scale. Even public health, the most obvious case of socially beneficial public agency, is opposed as unprofitable hence bad. Not to mention all the money that is made by "growth" via sales of carcinogenic "goods".

As the world's money is controlled by gargantuan private institutions and managed to enrich their rich shareholders, even if it means strangling debt-ridden public authorities and diverting resources from public sewers to private coffers, there is little hope that the dominating logic may change. Some used to argue that money should be controlled by public authorities and managed for the public good, as written in certain constitutions… But we have already talked about such a peculiar notion. For the moment, let's see whether the Philosopher-Kings of Greece will crumble because of the Goths, after being failed by Chelsea-resident haven-seekers and the advice of Goldmen-sackers.

Endnotes

[1] Francis Fukuyama, *The End of History and the Last Man*, New York: Free Press, 1992. As also done in my previous volumes for Northwest Passage Books, I use "liberal" and "liberalism" *à la* European, i.e. not in the progressive American sense, which would better translate in Europe as "democratic socialism" and "social democrat".

[2] Milton Friedman, "Free Markets and the End of History", *New Perspectives Quarterly*, 23(1), 2006, http://www.digitalnpq.org/archive/2006_winter/friedman.html.

[3] Cf. Hanhee Lee, "Foreign Direct Investment in North Korea and the Effect of Special Economic Zones: Learning from Transition Economies", *Journal of Economic Development*, 40(2), 2015, 35–56.

[4] Cornelius Castoriadis, "The Crisis of the Identification Process", *The Rising Tide of Insignificancy (The Big Sleep)*, 2003, 219, <http://www.notbored.org/RTI.html> (the English translations of Castoriadis' works available on this website are anonymous and provided as a public service. Their quality and, above all, their accessibility, are higher than the alternatives available; hence my choice of them as cited references in this book).

[5] John Kenneth Galbraith, "The 1929 Parallel", *The Atlantic Monthly*, 1, 1987, https://www.theatlantic.com/magazine/archive/1987/01/the-1929-parallel/304903/

[6] Regarding the present endnotes, I make use of the Chicago Style Citation standard, i.e. the most common among Anglophone academic philosophers, though purged of some of its most quixotic aspects.

[7] Cf. FBI, *FBI Records: The Vault*, Bufile numbers 61-7099, n.d.a, <http://vault.fbi.gov/Albert%20Einstein>.

[8] Ibid.

[9] Ibid. "CP" stands for "Communist Party".

[10] Cf. Hans-Joseph Küpper, *Albert Einstein in the World Wide Web*, 2000–2015, <http://www.einstein-website.de/indexhtml.html>.

[11] Cf. Thomas Levenson, *Einstein in Berlin*, New York: Bantam Books, 2003.

[12] Cf. Hubert Gönner, *Einstein in Berlin. 1914–1933,* München: C.H. Beck, 2005.

[13] Cf. Ze'ev Rosenkranz *et al.* (eds.), *Einstein Archives Online*, 2002–2013, <http://www.alberteinstein.info/> (Archival call numbers are made up of two parts: the microfilms' reel number and the sequential number within that reel; for the sake of brevity, after a first extended bibliographic entry, I refer to them by their call numbers).

[14] Cf. Diana K. Buchwald *et al.* (eds.), *Einstein Papers Project*, 2005–2015, <http://www.einstein.caltech.edu/>.

[15] Cf. Albert Einstein, "On Internationalism", *New York Evening Post*, 26th March 1921, in *Einstein on Politics: His Private Thoughts and Public Stands on Nationalism, Zionism, War, Peace, and the Bomb*, edited by D.E. Rowe and R. Schulmann, Princeton: Princeton University Press, 2007, 88–90 (published originally under the title "How Einstein, Thinking in Terms of the Universe, Lives from Day to Day"; when possible, I make use of the English translations of Einstein's German-language documents comprised in Rowe's and Schulmann's book).

[16] Cf. Albert Einstein, "Undelivered message to the World", April 1955; EA 28-1098.

[17] Cf. Albert Einstein, "Letter to Franklin Delano Roosevelt", 2nd August 1939; EA 33-088.

[18] Cf. Albert Einstein, "Letter to Michele Besso", 21st April 1946; EA 7-381.

[19] Cf. David E. Rowe and Robert Schulmann, *Einstein on Politics*.

[20] Issue 61(1), 55–61, to which I refer here.

[21] Albert Einstein, "Why socialism?", 55.

[22] Ibid.

[23] Ibid.

[24] Cf. David Reisman, *The Social Economics of Thorstein Veblen*, Cheltenham: E. Elgar, 2012.

[25] Albert Einstein, "Why socialism?", 55. Veblen's earlier stage or phase of human development is the "savage" one, when nature's overpowering force made life so precarious that human beings could only cooperate within small communities in order to survive, and nobody would attempt predatory behaviour upon her fellows for fear of injury or death.

[26] Ibid., 56.

[27] Ibid.

[28] Ibid.

[29] Ibid.

[30] Ibid.

[31] Ibid., 57.

[32] Ibid.

[33] Ibid.

[34] Ibid., 58.

[35] Ibid., 59.

[36] Ibid.; emphasis added.

[37] Ibid.

[38] Ibid.

[39] Ibid., 60.

[40] Ibid.

[41] Ibid., 60–1.

[42] Ibid., 61.

[43] Both World Wars were initiated by countries that had economies patently based upon private property and political systems formally based upon liberal constitutions. It is unlikely that such considerations should have escaped Einstein's mind, as preoccupied as he was by the twin issues of war and peace, also in Palestine.

[44] Cf. Peter Marshall, *Demanding the Impossible: A History of Anarchism*, Oakland: PM Press, 2010.

[45] Thorstein Veblen, *The Theory of Business Enterprise*, New York: Charles Scribner's Sons, 1904, 338.

[46] Cf. John Wood, *The Life of Thorstein Veblen and Perspectives on his Thought*, New York: Routledge, 1993.

[47] Albert Einstein, "Remarks on Bertrand Russell's Theory of Knowledge", in *The Philosophy of Bertrand Russell*, edited by P.A. Schilpp, La Salle: Open Court, 1944, 279.

[48] William T. Ganley analyses the connection between Einstein and Thorstein Veblen, but finds clear analogies and plausible reverberations *vis-à-vis* their understanding of natural science, rather than economics, politics or social and moral issues (cf. "Institutional Economics and Neoclassicism in the Early Twentieth Century: The Role of Physics", *Journal of Economic Issues*, 29(2), 1995, 397–406; and "Note on the Intellectual Connection between Albert Einstein and Thorstein Veblen", *Journal of Economic Issues*, 31(1), 1997, 245–51).

[49] For an introduction to Polanyi's work, cf. Mark T. Mitchell, *Michael Polanyi. The Art of Knowing*, Chicago: ISI Books, 2006.

[50] Albert Einstein, "To the Society 'A Guaranteed Subsistence for All'", 12th December 1918; EA 32-754.

[51] Albert Einstein, "On the Fifth Anniversary of Lenin's Death", 6th January 1929; EA 47-471.

[52] Albert Einstein, "On a Document Collection from Russian Prisons", 1925; EA 28-029.

[53] Albert Einstein, "Letter to Henri Barbusse", 17th June 1932; EA 34-546.

[54] Albert Einstein, "Statement for the Amsterdam Peace Congress", in David E. Rowe and Robert Schulmann, *Einstein on Politics*, 426.

[55] The same conclusion had been reached in those years by Michael Polanyi's brother Karl, cf. his classic 1944 study in economic history, *The Great Transformation* (New York: Farrar & Reinhart).

[56] Albert Einstein, "Thoughts on Forming a Council of the Wise", 14th March 1939; EA 28-473.

[57] E.g. Claude Henri de Rouvroy, Comte de Saint-Simon, "Industry" (1817), in *Henri de Saint Simon, 1760–1825: Selected writings on science, industry and social organization*, New York: Holmes & Meier, 1975, 158–61.

[58] Cf. Alexander Bogdanov, *Essays in Tektology: The General Science of Organization*, Seaside, CA: Intersystems Publications, 1980.

[59] Albert Einstein, "Letter to John Dudzic", 8th March 1948; EA 58-108. This statement casts doubt on the conclusion reached by Schulmann, according to whom Einstein's socialism is so un-Marxist as to be nothing but liberalism, in line with his Swiss youth's ideals (cf. "Einstein and Socialism", *Physics Today*, 62(10), 2009, 12). Like many contemporary Anglophone commentators, Schulmann is perplexed that Einstein may have chosen such a 'radical' and socially unapproved term as "socialism" to describe his own political views.

[60] EA 58-108.

[61] For one, the *CCPA Monitor* published in September 2007 various excerpts from Einstein's "Why Socialism?" ("Take it from *Time*'s 'Person of the Century': Socialism offers the only hope for true, humane democracy", 14(4), 27).

[62] As I have argued in my third volume for Northwest Passage Books, the *a priori* unfalsifiable assumption of the free market's beneficial character, which allows economic failures to be blamed upon external shocks and forms of agency that cannot but be present in real-world economic life (e.g. State 'interference', individual cases of excessive greed, faulty national character leading to cronyism), leaves ample room for such self-exculpatory intellectual manoeuvres. Whether because of his training as an empirical scientist or of his own sense of personal and intellectual integrity, Einstein did not pursue this self-exonerating line of thinking.

[63] My references here are to the 1992 republication of his talk in *Cornelius Castoriadis, Political and Social Writings*, Volume 3, 1961–1979, edited by David Ames Curtis, Minneapolis: University of Minnesota Press, 106–17.

[64] E.g. Cornelius Castoriadis, "The 'Rationality' of Capitalism", in *Figures of the Thinkable. Including Passion and Knowledge*, 2005, 81–122, <http://www.notbored.org/FTPK.pdf>.

[65] Cornelius Castoriadis, "The Crisis of Modern Society", 106.

[66] Ibid., 107.

[67] Ibid.

[68] Ibid.

[69] Cf. Cornelius Castoriadis, "The Crisis of Culture and the State", in *Philosophy, Politics, Autonomy*, edited by David Ames Curtis, New York: Oxford University Press, 1991, 219–42; "Un mond à venir", *La République Internationale des Lettres*, 4, June 1994, 4–5; and "Entretien avec Cornelius Castoriadis", *Pratiques de formation*, 25–6, April 1993, 43–63.

[70] Cited in the introduction.

[71] Cornelius Castoriadis, "The Crisis of Modern Society", 107.

[72] Ibid.

[73] Ibid., 108.

[74] Ibid.

[75] Ibid.

[76] Ibid.

[77] Ibid., 109; emphasis added. Readers familiar with Castoriadis' work can certainly recognise here a theme that was to gain prominence in his later intellectual production (cf. *The Rising Tide of Insignificancy*).

[78] Ibid.

[79] Ibid.

[80] Cornelius Castoriadis, "The Rising Tide of Insignificancy", *The Rising Tide of Insignificancy*, 125.
[81] Cornelius Castoriadis, "The Crisis of Modern Society", 110.
[82] Ibid., 111.
[83] Ibid.
[84] Ibid., 112.
[85] Ibid.
[86] Ibid.
[87] Ibid.
[88] Ibid.
[89] Ibid.
[90] Ibid., 113.
[91] Ibid.
[92] Ibid.
[93] Ibid.
[94] Ibid., 114.
[95] Ibid.
[96] Ibid.
[97] Ibid.
[98] Ibid.
[99] Ibid., 115.
[100] Ibid.
[101] Ibid.
[102] Ibid.
[103] Ibid.
[104] Ibid., 116.
[105] Ibid., 117.
[106] Ibid.
[107] Ibid.
[108] I explored Castoriadis' understanding of mortality in my first volume for Northwest Passage Books (2017).
[109] Cf. John Kenneth Galbraith, *The Affluent Society*, Boston: Houghton Mifflin, 1958; and *The New Industrial State*, Princeton: Princeton University Press, 2007 (reissued 4th ed.; originally published in 1967); as well as Thorstein Veblen, *The Vested Interests and the State of the Industrial Arts*, New York: B.W. Huebsch, 1919.
[110] Cornelius Castoriadis, "The Rising Tide of Insignificancy", 135.
[111] Hans Jonas, "Sul razzismo", *Il concetto di Dio dopo Auscwitz. Una voce ebraica*, translated by Carlo Angelino, Genoa: Il melangolo, 1993, 48–9. Unless otherwise indicated, as in the case of the present note, all translations from Italian into English to be found in the present book are mine.
[112] E.g. A. Aziz and I. Bajwa, "Erroneous Mass Transit System and Its Tended Relationship with Motor Vehicular Air Pollution (An integrated approach for reduction of urban air pollution in Lahore)", *Environmental Monitoring and Assessment*, 137(1–3), 2008, 25–33.

[113] Cf. R. Loeppke, "The Value of Health and the Power of Prevention", *International Journal of Workplace Health Management*, 1(2), 2008, 95–108; and World Health Organisation, *Obesity and Overweight*. 2009, <http://www.who.int/dietphysicalactivity/publications/facts/obesity/en/print.html>.

[114] E.g. N.S. Agar *et al.*, "The Basal Layer in Human Squamous Tumors Harbors More UVA than UVB Fingerprint Mutations: A role for UVA in human skin carcinogenesis", *Proceedings of the National Academy of Science of the U.S.A.*, 101(14), 4954–9.

[115] Union of Concerned Scientists, *World Scientists' Call for Action* (Document presented at the 1997 Kyoto Summit on climate change), § 3, <http://www.eolss.net>.

[116] Cf. UNESCO, *Encyclopedia of Life Support Systems*, Paris & Oxford: Eolss Publishers, <http://www.eolss.net>.

[117] The environmental record of Soviet Union and its European satellites was far from positive (cf. M. Deutsch, M. Feschbach and A. Friendly Jr., *Ecocide in the USSR: The Looming Disaster in Soviet Health and Environment*, New York: Basic Books, 1968; and C.E. Ziegler, *Environmental Policy in the USSR*, Amherst: University of Massachusetts Press, 1990). After their demise, liberal capitalism was adopted in all of these countries, yet without improvement *vis-à-vis* crucial vital parameters. On the contrary, the Russian Federation experienced an unprecedented peacetime depopulation (cf. I.B. Zagaitov and L.B. Yanovskii, "The population of the Russian Federation: Solvency dynamics and depopulation", *Studies on Russian Economic Development*, 18 (1), 2007, 94–101) and tuberculosis became a widespread threat due to the intervention of the International Monetary Fund, whose chief aim was to restructure the banking sector and the new states' public budgets along profitable lines, thus suffocating prevention programmes (cf. D. Stuckler, L.P. King and S. Basu, "International Monetary Fund Programs and Tuberculosis Outcomes in Post-communist Countries", *PLoS Medicine*, 5(7), 2008,.<doi:e143.doi:10.1371/journal.pmed.0050143>) that had been commonplace in the days of so-called "real socialism".

[118] Cf. P. Boffetta, "Human Cancer from Environmental Pollutants: The epidemiological evidence", *Mutation Research/Genetic Toxicology and Environmental Mutagenesis*, 608(2), 2006, 157–62.

[119] Cf. Joseph Stiglitz, *Freefall: Free Markets and the Sinking of the Global Economy*, London: Allen Lane, 2010. In accordance with the superstitious, non-falsifiable hypothesis of self-regulating free markets (cf. Paul Oslington, "Divine Action, Providence and Adam Smith's Invisible Hand" (Paper presented at the 21st conference of the history of economic thought society of Australia, Rosehill, NSW, 9–11 July 2008)), these packages were designed by highly paid mathematical wizards, whose unfettered selfish pursuits should have generated the nations' wealth, eventually and providentially, or at least accrued the stockholders' invested wealth (cf. D.T. Wargo, N. Baglini and K. Nelson, "The Global Financial Crisis—Caused by Greed, Moral Meltdown and Public Policy Disasters", *Forum on Public Policy Online*, 1, 2009, <http://www.forumonpublicpolicy.com/spring09papers/archivespr09/wargo.pdf>). "Shock[ingly]", neither end was attained (Alan Greenspan, "Quotes of 2008", *The Independent*, 1st January 2009, <http://www.independent.co.uk/news/business/analysis-and-features/quotes-of-2008-we-are-in-a-state-of-shocked-disbelief-1220057.html>).

[120] Cf. UNESCO, *Encyclopedia of Life Support Systems*.

[121] E.g. R.K. Pachauri and A. Reisinger (eds.), *Climate Change 2007*, Geneva: IPCC, 2007, <http://www.ipcc.ch/publications_and_data/publications_ipcc_fourth_assessment_report_synthesis_report.htm>.

[122] Ki-moon Ban, "UN Secretary-General Ban Ki-moon's message for the World Environment Day", 22nd May 2009, <http://www.un.org/News/Press/docs/2009/sgsm12265.doc.htm>.

[123] Cf. John McMurtry, *Unequal Freedoms: The Global Market as an Ethical System*, Toronto: Garamond Press, 1998.

[124] Cf. David Korten, *When Corporations Rule the World*, Herndon: Kumarian Press, 2001 (2nd ed.).

[125] Cf. Jennifer Sumner, "From Academic Imperialism to the Civil Commons: Institutional possibilities for responding to the United Nations decade of education for sustainable development", *Interchange: A Quarterly Review of Education*, 39(1), 2008, 77–94.

[126] Cf. Tim Jackson, *Prosperity without Growth. Economics for a finite planet*, London: Earthscan, 2009.

[127] E.g. M. Gaggi, "Ibm e i big Usa: chi ha paura del Barack 'statalista'", *Corriere della Sera*, 7th November 2008, <http://rassegna.governo.it/rs_pdf/pdf/JSM/JSMF0.pdf>.

[128] Cf. L.C. Backer, "Values, Economics, Theology and Legitimacy: Catholic social thought and its implications for legal regulatory systems", *Economics, Management, and Financial Markets*, 5(2), 2010, 17–56.

[129] Cf. Andrew Glyn, *Capitalism Unleashed. Finance, globalization, and welfare*, Oxford: Oxford University Press, 2006; and International Labour Organization (ILO), *Labour Inspection 2006* (General surveys by the committee of experts on the application of conventions and recommendations), 2006, <http://www.ilo.org/public/english/support/lib/resource/subject/labourinsp.htm>.

[130] Cf. Joseph Stiglitz, *Freefall*.

[131] Cf. Serge Halimi, "Thinking the Unthinkable", *Le Monde Diplomatique*, November 2008, 1A & 5A.

[132] Cf. "Threat of Inflation Sky High", *The Washington Times*, 22nd March 2009, <http://www.washingtontimes.com/news/2009/mar/22/threat-of-inflation-sky-high/>.

[133] Slavoj Zizek claims these tokens of international law to be as binding as the governments' interests allow them to be, for they are not backed by any non- and super-human source of authority, such as the Biblical God of old (cf. *The Fragile Absolute: Or, why is the Christian legacy worth fighting for?*, London: Verso, 2001).

[134] UNESCO, *Encyclopedia of Life Support Systems*, "Definitions", § 2.

[135] John McMurtry, "What is Good? What is Bad? The Value of All Values across Time, Place and Theories", *Encyclopedia of Life Support Systems*, 2009–2010, § 5.34.10.

[136] Ibid., § 6.3; emphasis removed.

[137] John McMurtry, *The Cancer Stage of Capitalism*, London: Pluto, 1999, 206–7.

[138] John McMurtry, "What is Good? What is Bad?", Glossary.

[139] Ibid., § 6.2.1; emphasis in the original.

[140] Cf. David Humphreys, "Life Protective or Carcinogenic Challenge? Global forests governance under advanced capitalism", *Global Environmental Politics*, 3(2), 2003, 40–55.

[141] Cf. Jeff Noonan, *Democratic Society and Human Needs*, Montreal and Kingston: McGill-Queen's University Press, 2006.

[142] Cf. Chapter 8.

[143] John McMurtry, *Value Wars: The Global Market versus the Life Economy*, London: Pluto Press, 2002, 156; emphasis removed.

[144] John McMurtry, "What is Good? What is Bad?", § 10.10.4. In the course of the last decade, McMurtry has offered slightly different versions of the WBI. Because of it, Jordan has argued that the WBI is bound to be undecided, because biological needs are invariant, whilst the emotional and intellectual ones are not (cf. "Growth to Freedom or Support to Life?", *Res Publica*, 10(2), 2004, 193–205). Probably, as countered by Rubino, Jordan confuses invariant emotional and intellectual needs with the varying awareness of them that we possess, as well as with the varying means available for their satisfaction (cf. *Assiologia dominante: Struttura del neoliberismo tra scienza e superstizione* (*Laurea* degree thesis defended at the University of Genoa, Italy), 2010). In addition, as Rubino also suggests, Jordan fails to appreciate the openness of the WBI to empirical rectification and theoretical clarification. What is most important, though, is that the WBI does undoubtedly identify actual vital needs, the missed satisfaction of which would eventually disintegrate any individual and/or collective life by compounding physical and mental deficiencies. Who would reasonably and in good conscience ever assert that the prolonged absence of breathable air, clean water, adequate shelter, non-alienating surroundings, human affection, spontaneous interaction, or secure and humane employment does not generate devastating life-disruption, whether in the form of irreparable psychosis, physical illness, or even of the most expedite death?

[145] John McMurtry, *Value Wars*, 156. McMurtry writes more about "life capacities" than "life capabilities". He thereby chooses to focus upon the ontological ground out of which emerge the life-capabilities responsible for life's flourishing.

[146] John McMurtry, *Unequal Freedoms*, 164; emphasis added.

[147] In *Democratic Society and Human Needs*, McMurtry scholar Jeff Noonan adds to this understanding of human needs the notion that they balance mutually. For example, the need for water is balanced out by the need to urinate; whilst the need to be educated can only turn into pathological solipsism if it is not balanced out by the needs to rest and socialise. Needs are satiable, unlike standard economics' desires or preferences, which can be distinguished sharply from true needs. First of all, "deprivation of needs always leads to harm whereas deprivation of wants is only harmful in light of revisable self-interpretation." (xiv). Secondly, "needs are satiable whereas wants are not" (57).

[148] Cf. G. Shackman, *Understanding the World Today* (Website of the Global Social Change Research Project), 2006–2009, <http://gsociology.icaap.org/>.

[149] Cf. Worldwatch Institute, *State of the World 2009*, Washington, D.C: The Worldwatch Institute Press, 2009.

[150] Cf. Vladimir Putin, "Prime minister Vladimir Putin's speech at the opening ceremony of the 39th World Economic Forum in Davos, Switzerland", 28th January 2009, <http://www.weforum.org/pdf/AM_2009/OpeningAddress_VladimirPutin.pdf>; and Nicolas Sarkozy, "Speech by M. Nicolas Sarkozy President of the French Republic at the 40th World Economic Forum in Davos, Switzerland", 27th January 2010, <http://www.elysee.fr/documents/index.php?mode=viewandlang=frandcat_id=7andpress_id=3303>.

[151] John Barry, "'Choose Life' Not Economic Growth: Critical social theory for people, planet and flourishing in the 'age of nature'", *Current Perspectives in Social Theory*, 26, 2009, 93.

[152] Cf. "Troppi pesticidi nell'acqua", *La Repubblica*, 19th December 2008, <http://www.repubblica.it/2007/06/sezioni/ambiente/goletta-verde/rapporto-ispra-acqua/rapporto-ispra-acqua.html>.

[153] Cf. "Budget Cuts Threaten Opera House Future", *ThinkSpain*, 26th December 2008, <http://www.thinkspain.com/news-spain/15876/budget-cuts-threaten-opera-house-future>.

[154] Cf. "Allarme mense, qualità a rischio", *La Repubblica*, 12th November 2008, <http://www.repubblica.it/2008/11/sezioni/cronaca/mense-rischi/mense-rischi/mense-rischi.html>.

[155] Cf. D. Stuckler, L.P. King and S. Basu, "International Monetary Fund Programs and Tuberculosis Outcomes in Post-communist Countries".

[156] Cf. J.W.E. Sheptycki, *In Search of Transnational Policing*. Aldershot: Ashgate, 2002.

[157] Cf. L. Elliott and D. Atkinson, *The Gods that Failed. How blind faith in markets has cost us our future*. London: The Bodley Head, 2008.

[158] Cf. M. Bunting, *Willing Slaves. How the overwork culture is ruling our lives*. London: Harper Collins, 2004.

[159] Cf. M. Florio, *The Great Divestiture. Evaluating the welfare impact of the British privatizations 1979–1997*, Cambridge, Mass. and London, UK: The MIT Press, 2004.

[160] Cf. David Humphreys, "Life Protective or Carcinogenic Challenge?".

[161] Cf. John Barry, "'Choose Life' Not Economic Growth"; and Jeff Noonan, *Democratic Society and Human Needs*.

[162] Martha C. Nussbaum, *Not for Profit. Why democracy needs the humanities*. Princeton: Princeton University Press, 2010, 1–2.

[163] Ibid., 2.

[164] Ibid., 23.

[165] Ibid., 2; emphasis added.

[166] Ibid., 9; emphasis added.

[167] Ibid., 15.

[168] Ibid., 77.

[169] Ibid., 94.

[170] Ibid., 15.

[171] Ibid., 27.

[172] Ibid., 80.

[173] Ibid., 29, 38 & 43. It should be noted that Adam Smith was a trained philosopher and taught logic, rhetoric, literature, philosophy of law and moral philosophy at Glasgow University, of which he later became Lord Rector. Idolised in the business world as the prophet of capitalism, he was a humanist of the highest calibre.

[174] Pietro Verri, *Meditazioni sulla economia politica*. Livorno: Stamperia dell'enciclopedia, 1771, 149.

[175] D.D. Avant, *The Market for Force: The Consequences of Privatizing Security*. Cambridge: Cambridge University Press, 2005.

[176] Norman Roessler, "Do as I Say, Not as I Do", *Broad Street Review*, 26th August 2010, <http://www.broadstreetreview.com/index.php/main/article/martha_nussbaum_defends_the_humanities/>.

[177] Cf. Troy Jollimore, "On Why Democracy Needs the Humanities", *Truthdig*, 23th April 2010, <http://www.law.uchicago.edu/news/nussbaum042310>.

[178] Martha C. Nussbaum, *Not for Profit*, 77.

[179] OECD, "Country notes. Finland", in *Economic Policy Reforms: Going for Growth*, 2010, <http://www.oecd.org/dataoecd/17/54/44651474.pdf>.

[180] Cf. PISA., *OECD Programme for International Student Assessment*, 1997–2010, <http://www.pisa.oecd.org/pages/0,2987,en_32252351_32235731_1_1_1_1_1,00.html>.

[181] Martha C. Nussbaum, *Not for Profit*, 127.

[182] Edmund Burke, *Reflections on the Revolution in France*, 1791, § 134, <http://bartelby.org/24/3/>. It should be added that for Burke, religion was also very important as part of the substratum of learning and proper moral dispositions that made society and *a fortiori* commerce possible. Nussbaum is more sceptical on this point, particularly as she draws from India's great poet, Rabrindanath Tagore (1861–1941), and his assessment of religious conflict in southern Asia.

[183] Isaiah Berlin, *Four Essays on Liberty*, Oxford: Oxford University Press, 1969, 124.
[184] Ibid., 125.
[185] Martha C. Nussbaum, *Sex and Social Justice*, Oxford: Oxford University Press, 1999, 34; emphasis added.
[186] Ibid., 39.
[187] Ibid., 39–40.
[188] Ibid., 41–2.
[189] Ibid., 44.
[190] Ibid.
[191] Ibid. Nussbaum's insistence on the importance of having in place institutions whereby to actually make possible the enjoyment of life capabilities by each and every person is what makes me enlist her among the socialists, who have been promoting the establishment of such institutions as their paramount socio-political and legal mission.
[192] Martha C. Nussbaum, *Sex and Social Justice*, 57.
[193] Ibid., 62.
[194] *International Covenant on Economic, Social and Cultural Rights* (adopted 16 Dec. 1966, G.A. Res. 2200A, U.N. GAOR, 21st Sess., Supp. No. 16, at 49, U.N. Doc. A/6316 (1966), entered into force Jan. 3, 1976), article 2(1), <http://www2.ohchr.org/english/law/cescr.htm>. *Via* the Universal Declaration of Human Rights (UDHR), the ICESCR draws on the ground-breaking 1941 "four freedoms" speech by F.D. Roosevelt (cf. D.J. Whelan and J. Donnelly, "The West, Economic and Social Rights, and the Global Human Rights Regime: Setting the record straight", *Human Rights Quarterly,* 29(4), 2007, 908–49).
[195] Ibid., Preamble.
[196] Ibid.
[197] Cf. Alþingi, *Report of the Parliamentary Commission on the Banking Collapse, 2008*, Vol. 8, 2010, <http://rna.althingi.is/pdf/RNABindi8.pdf>.
[198] Jagdish Bhagwati, "Coping with Antiglobalization", *Foreign Affairs*, 81(1), 2002, 2–3; emphasis added.
[199] Johan Norberg, *In Defence of Global Capitalism,* New Delhi: Academic Foundation, 30.
[200] As cited in Z. He *et al., An intellectual history of China*. Beijing: Foreign Languages Press, 1991, 186.
[201] Cf. George Soros, *The Crisis of Global Capitalism: Open Society Endangered*, Jackson: Public Affairs, 1998. On this matter, John Kenneth Galbraith advocated long ago the nationalisation of "too-big-to-fail" private companies that constitute *de facto* market-distorting oligopolies, for they generate private profits irrespective of actual competition and socialise their losses at will (cf. *The New Industrial State*).
[202] Robert Nozick, *Anarchy, State, and Utopia*, New York: Basic Books, 1974, 179.
[203] UN Committee on Economic, Social and Cultural Rights (ESCR), *Report on the Twenty-fifth, Twenty-sixth and Twenty-seventh Sessions* (U.N. ESCOR, Comm. On Econ., Soc. and Cultural Rts., 58th Sess., Supp. No. 2, U.N. Doc. E/2002/22), § 176, <http://tb.ohchr.org/default.aspx>.

[204] Ibid.

[205] John McMurtry, *Value Wars*, 156.

[206] John McMurtry, "Principles of the Good Life: The primary theorems of economic reason" (Unpublished manuscript circulated amongst EOLSS contributors to the encyclopaedia entitled "Philosophy and World Problems"), 2005.

[207] Cf. "Le Maldive risparmiano per comprarsi una nuova 'patria'", *La Stampa*, 10th November 2008, <http://www.lastampa.it/redazione/cmsSezioni/esteri/200811articoli/38055girata.asp>.

[208] A. Felton *et al.*, "Replacing Coniferous Monocultures with Mixed-species Production Stands: An assessment of the potential benefits for forest biodiversity in northern Europe", *Forest Ecology and Management*, 260(6), 2010, 939–47.

[209] J.C. Escudero, "What Is Said, What Is Silenced, What Is Obscured: The report of the commission on the social determinants of health", *Social Medicine*, 4(3), 2009, 183.

[210] Lawrence H. Summers, "The Memo" (Internal World Bank memorandum circulated on 12th December 1991), <http://www.whirledbank.org/ourwords/summers.html>; cf. also Kevin Smith, "'Obscenity' of Carbon Trading", *BBC News*, 4th April 2007, <http://news.bbc.co.uk/2/hi/science/nature/6132826.stm>; emphasis added.

[211] The history of Summers's notorious memorandum is intriguing (cf. "The Memo"). After the memo was leaked to the public in February 1992, Brazil's Secretary of the Environment José Lutzenburger (1926–2002) sent the following comments to Summers, who was back then at the helm of the economists' team at the World Bank: "Your reasoning is perfectly logical but totally insane... Your thoughts [provide] a concrete example of the unbelievable alienation, reductionist thinking, social ruthlessness and the arrogant ignorance of many conventional 'economists' concerning the nature of the world we live in... If the World Bank keeps you as vice president it will lose all credibility." (Lawrence H. Summers, "The Memo") Lutzenburger lost his job shortly after writing his letter. Larry Summers, instead, was appointed in 1999 the U.S. Treasury Secretary, and later became President of his *alma mater*. Nonetheless, facing prolonged media inquiries and some political backlash, Summers has been trying to disavow it (cf. "Harvard Students Rip New President Lawrence Summers on Toxic Waste Memo", *Boston Globe*, 13th March 2001). Specifically, in the late 1990s, a former young member of Summers' staff at the World Bank and soon-to-be colleague of his at Harvard—the economist Lant Pritchett—claimed to be the actual author of the memo, which he had merely shown and given to Summers to sign, its tone being sarcastic, its aim being to spur internal debate, and its leaked version having been used malevolently to discredit Summers and the World Bank (cf. "Toxic Memo", *Harvard Magazine*, 5th January 2001). Whatever the case, which resembles in its intricacy the popular TV series *House of Cards*, the memo crystallises poignantly the callous character of *laissez-faire* liberalism and, whether sarcastic or not, it has been taken seriously by many scholars, including economists affiliated with the libertarian Cato Institute (cf. Jay Johnson, Gary Pecquet and Leon Taylor, "Potential Gains from Trade in Dirty Industries: Revisiting Lawrence Summers' Memo", *Cato Journal*, 27, 3, 2007, 397–410).

[212] Mario Draghi, "Giornata mondiale del risparmio del 2008" (Presentation by the Governor of the Bank of Italy at the national meeting of ACRI on the annual world day for savings, 31st October 2008).

[213] Cf. Law no. 173/2008, article 7; Law no. 70/2009, article 18.

[214] Cf. "Allarme mense".

[215] Cf. "RFA tracks increased speculation in corn markets, predicts 'more exaggerated' market", *Biofuels Digest*, 10th September 2010, <http://biofuelsdigest.com/bdigest/2010/09/10/rfa-tracks-increased-speculation-in-corn-markets-predicts-more-exaggerated-market/>.

[216] Martha C. Nussbaum, *Not for Profit*, 17.

[217] Aulis Aarnio, "Statutory Interpretation in Finland", in *Interpreting Statutes. A Comparative Study*, edited by D.N. MacCormick and R.S. Summers, Aldershot: Dartmouth, 1991, 131.

[218] Cf. OECD, "Why a Global Standard for a stronger, cleaner, fairer economy?", 2009, <http://www.oecd.org/general/whyaglobalstandardforastrongercleanerfairereconomy.htm>.

[219] Cf. Giulio Tremonti, *La paura e la speranza. Europa: la crisi globale che si avvicina e la via per superarla*, Milan: Mondadori, 2008; *Rischi fatali. L'Europa vecchia, la Cina, il mercatismo suicida. Come reagire*, Milan: Mondadori, 2005; and Francesco Galgano, Sabino Cassese, Giulio Tremonti and Tiziano Treu, *Nazioni senza ricchezza, ricchezze senza nazione*, Bologna: il Mulino, 1993.

[220] Cf. Giulio Tremonti, "Discorso inaugurale all'Università Cattolica di Milano, mercoledì 19 novembre 2008", <http://www2.unicatt.it/pls/catnews/consultazione.mostra_pagina?id_pagina=14218>.

[221] Cf. Giulio Tremonti, *Rischi fatali*.

[222] Giulio Tremonti, *Uscita di sicurezza*, Milan: Rizzoli, 2012, 19.

[223] Ibid., 35.

[224] Ibid., 14.

[225] Ibid., 69; emphasis removed.

[226] Ibid., 84.

[227] Ibid., 151.

[228] Ibid., 167.

[229] Ibid., 173.

[230] Ibid., 177.

[231] Ibid., 40.

[232] Ibid., 14 & 120; emphasis removed.

[233] Ibid., 8.

[234] Ibid., 27.

[235] Cf. Georg Diez, "Habermas, the Last European. A Philosopher's Mission to Save the EU", *Der Spiegel Online*, 25th November 2011, <http://www.spiegel.de/international/europe/habermas-the-last-european-a-philosopher-s-mission-to-save-the-eu-a-799237.html>.

[236] Giulio Tremonti, *Uscita di sicurezza*, 38.

[237] Ibid., 12.

[238] As cited in Luciano Gallino, *Con i soldi degli altri*, Milan: Einaudi, 2009, i.

[239] Cf. John Kenneth Galbraith, *The New Industrial State*.

[240] Cf. John Kenneth Galbraith, *The Economics of Innocent Fraud,* Boston: Houghton Mifflin, 2004.
[241] Cf. Giulio Tremonti, *Uscita di sicurezza*, 29–31.
[242] Ibid., 16 n4.
[243] Ibid., 168.
[244] Ibid., 14 & 120.
[245] Ibid., 70.
[246] Cf. Michael D. Bordo, "The Globalization of Financial Markets: What Can History Teach Us?" (Paper prepared for the conference "International Financial Markets: The Challenge of Globalization", 31st March 2000, Texas M and A University, College Station Texas), <http://econweb.rutgers.edu/bordo/global.pdf>.
[247] Giulio Tremonti, *Uscita di sicurezza*, 22.
[248] Ibid., 23.
[249] Ibid., 22 n5.
[250] Cf. John Kenneth Galbraith, *The Economics of Innocent Fraud.*
[251] Giulio Tremonti, *Uscita di sicurezza*, 168.
[252] The original version, *Wirtschaftsethik* (Bonn: Scientia Humana Institut, 1994), is available online (<http://www.stiftung-utz.de/file/1/Sozialethik-IV.pdf>). All English translations of and from Utz's works, titles included, are mine. I cannot claim major proficiency in German, but I believe my competence to be adequate to the present task. Moreover, I also consulted existing Italian, French and Spanish translations.
[253] Born in Basel, Utz grew up in Germany and became a Swiss citizen in the 1950s (cf. Wolfgang Hariolf Spindler, "Arthur Fridolin Utz", *Thomistenlexicon*, Bonn: Nova & Vetera, 2007, 677–84).
[254] Utz was a member of the *Ordinis Praedicatorum* i.e. the Dominican Order. His *Social Ethics* is neither confessional nor clerical, however. It is philosophical, and specifically Thomist.
[255] To my knowledge, Utz's only English-language publication was "The Principle of Subsidiarity and Contemporary Natural Law", *Natural Law Forum*, 3(1), 1958, 170–83. An English-language brief account of his thought can be found in Helen Alford's excellent essay "The Influence of Thomistic Thought in Contemporary Business Ethics", in *Handbook of the Philosophical Foundations of Business Ethics*, vol. 2, edited by Christoph Luetge, Dordrecht: Springer, 2013, 227–50.
[256] Utz's most widely translated books are the eleven volumes of his monumental *Bibliographie der Sozialethik* (Freiburg: Herder, 1960–80). Extensive bibliographies and e-texts of Utz's works can be found on the websites *Helmut Zenz: Arthur Fridolin Utz im Internet* (<http://www.helmut-zenz.de/hzutz.html>) and *Stiftung Professor Dr. A. F. Utz* (<http://www.stiftung-utz.de/index.php?cID=1>).

[257] Koslowski knew of Utz's research. Koslowski's *Principles of Ethical Economy* (Dordrecht: Kluwer, 2001) refer to the 1982 collection of essays entitled *Kann der Christ Marxist sein? Muß er Kapitalist sein?*, edited by Utz (Bonn: Scientia Humana, 1982); "The Common Good of the Firm as the Fiduciary Duty of the Manager", i.e. his contribution to the 2005 book *Business and Religion: A Clash of Civilisations?* (edited by N. Capaldi; Salem: M. & M. Scrivener Press, 301–12), refers to Utz's 1958 first instalment of the *Sozialethik*; his essay "Public Interest and Self-Interest in the Market and the Democratic Process" (*International Centre for Economic Research*, Working Paper no. 9, 2004, <ftp://ftp.repec.org/opt/ReDIF/RePEc/icr/wp2004/Koslowski9-04.pdf>) includes another to B. Kettern's 1992 monograph on Utz, entitled *Sozialethik und Gemeinwohl. Die Begründung einer realistischen Sozialethik bei Arthur F. Utz* (Berlin: Duncker & Humblot). Also, Koslowski and Utz took part in a collaborative project on economic ethics (cf. Peter Koslowski & Yunquan Chen (eds.), *Sozialistische Marktwirtschaft und Soziale Marktwirtschaft. Theorie und Ethik der Wirtschaftsordnung in China und Deutschland* (Dordrecht: Physica Verlag, 1996), from the book series *Ethische Ökonomie. Beiträge zur Wirtschaftsethik und Wirtschaftskultur*, directed and co-edited by Koslowski). As to Utz himself, his *Economic Ethics* alone mentions five times Koslowski, whose work figures prominently in the bibliography.

[258] Based on the older Catholic Union for Social and Economic Studies (est. 1885), the institute was affiliated with the University of Fribourg between 1946 and 1978; afterwards it became autonomous. Utz was also the director of the Institute for Social Sciences Walberberg (1966–1993) and the president of the International Foundation Humanum (1976–1998).

[259] Domènec Melé states: "Utz and Messner have made an outstanding contribution to social and economic ethics from a Thomistic approach." ("Scholastic Thought and Business Ethics: An Overview", in *Handbook of the Philosophical Foundations of Business Ethics*, vol. 2, 137). Thomists, clergymen and key-contributors to the Social Doctrine of the Church, these two thinkers agreed on all crucial conceptual issues, while disagreeing on the details. Their divergences in matters of economic ethics are addressed by Utz in his *Economic Ethics*. Firstly, Utz adopts a stricter notion of human freedom than Messner (1.2.4; except for the book's preface, for which I make use of page numbers in the original German edition, in-text references are provided by way of numbers separated by full stops: the first number indicates the chapter, the second the section, the third the sub-section and the fourth the sub-sub-section; I owe the idea to Giovanni Salmeri and Angelo Lanzoni, the Italian translators of Utz's volumes 4 and 5, which in the original editions employ respectively, though somewhat idiosyncratically, worded numerals, Roman numerals, Arabic numerals and letters of the Latin alphabet.) Secondly, albeit praising him for his "unsurpassed... systematic exposition of economic ethics", Utz criticises Messner for not distinguishing sharply between the level of the "abstract... theory of value" applying to all forms of "social ethics" and the level of the "economic order" best reflecting "the natural or quasi-natural behaviour of social members" (1.2.5.3). Utz and Messner engaged in a rich intellectual dialogue that lasted for several decades, the former editing as well a collection of essays in honour of the latter (*Der Sozialethiker und Recthsphilosoph Johannes Messner. Leben und Werk*, Bonn: Scientia Humana Institut, 1980).

[260] Utz had direct contact with several Popes, before and during their pontificates, especially Pius XII, John Paul II (who nominated Utz founding member of the Papal Academy of Social Sciences) and Benedict XVI (cf. Spindler, "Arthur Fridolin Utz", and Herbert Schambeck, "The History of the Pontifical Academy of Social Sciences", *Sustainable Humanity, Sustainable Nature: Our Responsibility*, Rome: Pontifical Academy of Sciences, 2014, 1–8). Important in this connection are also Utz's 1963 extensive commentary on Pope John XXIII's encyclical *Pacem in Terris* (*Die Friedensenzyklika Papst Johannes' XXIII. Pacem in Terris*, Basel: Herder, 1963) and the many volumes on the SDC that he authored, co-authored and edited, such as *Die katholische Sozialdoktrin in ihrer geschichtlichen Entfaltung* (Aachen: Scientia Humana Institut, 1976), *Was ist katholische Soziallehre?* (Köln: J.B. Bachem, 1978), and *Die katholische Soziallehre und die Wirtschaftsordnung* (Trier: Paulinus, 1991).

[261] Utz received in 1968 West Germany's Federal Cross of Honour.

[262] Utz received in 1991 Austria's Great Golden Medal.

[263] Other key-members were Joseph Höffner (1906–1987) and Oswald Nell-Brüning (1890–1991). Utz is also known as part of the Walberberg intellectual circle, which comprised four more Dominicans: Laurentius Siemer (1888–1956), Eberhard Welty (1902–1965), Edgar Nawroth (1912–2010) and Basilius Streithofen (1925–2006) (cf. Wolfgang Ockenfels, "The Walberberg Circle. The Social Ethics of the German Dominicans", in *Preaching Justice: Dominican Contributions to Social Ethics in the Twentieth Century*, edited by Francesco Compagnoni, Dublin: Dominican Publications, 2007, 330–55).

²⁶⁴ All original versions and partial Japanese translations of volume 5 are available online (<http://www.stiftung-utz.de/index.php?cID=9>).

²⁶⁵ An anonymous reviewer of the Italian translation of Utz's *Political Ethics* describes his style as "compact, schematic, clear, assertive", whilst also praising "the absence of polemics" and concluding: "this style of thought and expression is something that only old wise persons can afford." (cf. FASS, 2008, <http://win.scienze-politiche.org/ep/html/indexpiu.html>) The same can be said of Utz's *Economic Ethics*, which reads like a series of calm yet trenchant logical steps following from the adoption of the Thomist ethical perspective and its application to economic affairs. Utz observes and comments upon them in a way that is aloof from current intellectual fashions, priorities and prejudices. Looking at modernity from, so to speak, the 13ᵗʰ century, leads to remarkable lucidity.

²⁶⁶ Cf. Arthur F. Utz, *Economic Ethics*, 6.1.3.2.

²⁶⁷ Cf. Enrico Pattaro, "An Overview on Practical Reason in Aquinas", *Stockholm Institute of Scandinavian Law*, 2010, 252–67, <http://www.scandinavianlaw.se/pdf/48-16.pdf>).

²⁶⁸ Arthur F. Utz, *Economic Ethics*, 3.3.2.

²⁶⁹ Ibid., 5.3 & 5.4.

²⁷⁰ Ibid., 1.2.3.

²⁷¹ Ibid., 1.2.4.

²⁷² Helen Alford, "The Influence of Thomistic Thought in Contemporary Business Ethics", 238.

²⁷³ Arthur F. Utz, *Economic Ethics*, 1.2.6.2.

²⁷⁴ Helen Alford, "The Influence of Thomistic Thought in Contemporary Business Ethics", 239.

²⁷⁵ Arthur F. Utz, *Economic Ethics*, 4.1.

²⁷⁶ Ibid., 1.1.

²⁷⁷ Ibid., 1.2.3.

²⁷⁸ Ibid., 1.2.4.

²⁷⁹ Ibid., 1.1.

²⁸⁰ Ibid., 1.2.6.

²⁸¹ Ibid., 6.1.3.2.

²⁸² Ibid., 1.2.6.

²⁸³ Ibid.

²⁸⁴ Aquinas' notion of harmonious inter-connection of moral virtues for the sake of human happiness is possibly the oldest key-theme in the philosophical work of Utz, whose first published book was his university thesis *De connexione virtutum moralium inter se secundum doctrinam sancti Thomae Aquinatis* (Oldenburg: Albertus Magnus, 1937).

²⁸⁵ Arthur F. Utz, *Economic Ethics*, 1.2.4.

²⁸⁶ Ibid.

²⁸⁷ Ibid., 1.1.

²⁸⁸ Ibid., 7.8.6; emphasis in the original.

²⁸⁹ Ibid.

[290] Helen Alford, "An Unusual Animal: A Coherent Economic Ethics", *Oikonomia*, 2(2), 2000, <http://www.oikonomia.it/index.php/en/oikonomia-2000/giugno-2000/53-2000/giugno-2000/155-an-unusual-animal-a-coherent-economic-ethics>.
[291] Ibid.
[292] Arthur F. Utz, *Economic Ethics*, p. 5.
[293] Ibid.
[294] Ibid., footnote included.
[295] Ibid., p. 7.
[296] Ibid., p. 6.
[297] Ibid.
[298] Garrett Barden and Tim Murphy reach the same conclusion in their 2010 book *Law and Justice in Community* (Oxford: Oxford University Press), which too reflects the natural law tradition.
[299] Arthur F. Utz, *Economic Ethics*, pp. 6–7.
[300] Ibid., p. 7.
[301] Ibid.
[302] Ibid., 1.1.
[303] Ibid.
[304] Ibid.
[305] Ibid.
[306] Ibid.; emphasis added.
[307] Ibid.
[308] Ibid.
[309] Ibid.
[310] Ibid.
[311] Ibid.
[312] Ibid.
[313] Ibid.
[314] Ibid.
[315] John Milton, *Paradise Lost*, Book I, verses 258–9 & 263.
[316] Arthur F. Utz, *Economic Ethics*, 1.2.1.
[317] Ibid., footnote included.
[318] Ibid.
[319] Ibid.
[320] Ibid., 1.2.4.
[321] Ibid., 1.2.2.
[322] Ibid.
[323] Ibid.
[324] Ibid.
[325] Ibid.
[326] Ibid., 1.2.3.
[327] Ibid., 1.2.2.
[328] Ibid., 1.2.3.
[329] Ibid., 1.2.5.1.

[330] Ibid., 1.2.3.
[331] Ibid., 1.2.4.
[332] Ibid., 1.2.3.
[333] Ibid., 1.2.5.1.
[334] Ibid.
[335] Ibid.
[336] Ibid., 1.2.5.2.
[337] Ibid.
[338] Ibid., 1.2.5.3. Utz's scepticism *vis-à-vis* the centrally planning State has old roots in his reflection, e.g. *Das Subsidiaritätsprinzip* (Heidelberg: Kerle, 1953) and *Formen und Grenzen der Subsidiaritätsprinzips* (Heidelberg: Kerle, 1956).
[339] Arthur F. Utz, *Economic Ethics*, 1.2.5.3.
[340] Ibid.
[341] Ibid., 1.2.6.2.
[342] Ibid.
[343] Ibid., 1.2.6.3.
[344] Giovanni Bertuzzi, "Non basta il Vangelo a guidare il cristiano?", *Oikonomia* 2(2), 2000, <http://www.oikonomia.it/index.php/en/oikonomia-2000/giugno-2000/53-2000/giugno-2000/150-non-basta-il-vangelo-a-guidare-il-cristiano>.
[345] Arthur F. Utz, *Economic Ethics*, 2.1.
[346] Ibid., 2.1 & 2.2.
[347] Ibid., 2.2.
[348] Ibid., 5.2.6.
[349] Ibid., 2.3.
[350] Ibid.
[351] Ibid.
[352] Ibid.
[353] Ibid., 2.4.
[354] Ibid.
[355] Ibid.
[356] Giovanni Pallanti, "Diritto al lavoro e dignità del lavoro", *Oikonomia* 2(2), 2000, <http://www.oikonomia.it/index.php/en/oikonomia-2000/giugno-2000/53-2000/giugno-2000/147-diritto-al-lavoro-e-dignita-del-lavoro-dalla-globalizzazione-dell-economia-al-caso-italiano>.
[357] Arthur F. Utz, *Economic Ethics*, 3.
[358] Ibid.; cf. also 1.2.1.
[359] Ibid.
[360] Ibid.
[361] Ibid., 3 & 3.1.
[362] Ibid., 3.1. Utz prefers describing the good (aka natural, aka rational) "values" as "teleological decisions based on nature", so as to separate them clearly from mere individual preferences, which can be irrationally subjective (*contra* Max Scheler (1874–1928); cf. also his *Political Ethics*, 6.3).
[363] Arthur F. Utz, *Economic Ethics*, 3.3.2.

[364] Paolo Carlotti, "L'etica economica finanziaria di A.F. Utz", *Oikonomia*, 2(2), 2000, <http://www.oikonomia.it/index.php/en/oikonomia-2000/giugno-2000/53-2000/giugno-2000/148-l-etica-economica-finanziaria-di-a-f-utz>.
[365] Arthur F. Utz, *Economic Ethics*, 3.
[366] Ibid., 3.1.
[367] Ibid., 3.
[368] Ibid., 3.2.
[369] Ibid., 3.3.1 & 3.3.2.
[370] Ibid., 3.3.2.
[371] Ibid.
[372] Ibid.
[373] Ibid., 4.
[374] Ibid.
[375] Ibid., 4.1.
[376] Ibid., 4.2.
[377] Ibid., 4.3.
[378] Ibid., 7.2.2.
[379] Ibid., 4.1.
[380] Ibid., 6.1.3.1.
[381] Ibid., 4.1.
[382] Ibid.
[383] Ibid., 4.3. Communist States and monastic orders are compared and contrasted in Utz's 1982 book *Das Wirtschaftssystem der religiösen Order oder: Ist der Kommunismus möglich?* (Bonn: Institut für Gesellschaftswissenschaften Walberberg).
[384] Arthur F. Utz, *Economic Ethics*, 4.3.
[385] Ibid.
[386] Ibid., 4.2 & 4.3.
[387] Ibid., 4.3.
[388] Ibid., 5.
[389] Ibid., 5.1.
[390] Ibid., 5.
[391] Ibid., 5.2.
[392] Ibid., 5.2.1.
[393] Ibid., 5.2.2.
[394] Ibid.
[395] Ibid.
[396] Ibid., 5.2.3.
[397] Ibid.
[398] Ibid., 5.2.4.
[399] Ibid., 5.2.4 & 5.2.7.
[400] Ibid., 5.2.3 & 5.2.4.
[401] Ibid., 5.2.5.

[402] As cited in Michael Hudson, "Breakup of the Euro?", *Naked Capitalism*, 27th May 2011, <https://www.nakedcapitalism.com/2011/05/michael-hudson-breakup-of-the-euro-is-iceland%E2%80%99s-rejection-of-financial-bullying-a-model-for-greece-and-ireland.html>.
[403] § I.viii.38.
[404] Arthur F. Utz, *Economic Ethics*, 5.2.4.
[405] Ibid.
[406] Ibid., 5.2.6.
[407] Ibid.
[408] Ibid., 5.2.7.
[409] Ibid., 5.2.6.
[410] Ibid.
[411] Ibid., 7.6.2.
[412] Ibid.
[413] Ibid.
[414] Cf. Arthur F. Utz, *Political Ethics*, 4.4.4, 4.4.7, 4.4.8 & 6.2.1.
[415] Arthur F. Utz, *Economic Ethics*, 5.
[416] Ibid., 5.3.
[417] Ibid., 5.4.
[418] Ibid., 5.3.
[419] Ibid.
[420] Ibid., 5.4.
[421] Ibid.
[422] Ibid., 5.3.
[423] Ibid.
[424] Ibid., 5.4
[425] Ibid.
[426] Ferruccio Marzano, "Il punto di vista di un economista keynesiano", *Oikonomia*, 2(2), 2000 <http://www.oikonomia.it/index.php/en/oikonomia-2000/giugno-2000/53-2000/giugno-2000/152-il-punto-di-vista-di-un-economista-keynesiano-2>.
[427] Arthur F. Utz, *Economic Ethics*, 5.3.
[428] Ibid., 5.4.
[429] Ibid.
[430] Ibid., 5.3 & 5.4.
[431] Ibid., 5.4.
[432] Ibid., 5.3.
[433] Ibid., 5.3 & 5.4.
[434] Ibid., 5.4.
[435] Ibid.
[436] Ibid., 6.
[437] Ibid., 6.1.4.
[438] Cf. Ibid., 6.1.3.1–6.1.3.3 & 6.2.3.
[439] Cf. Ibid., 6.2.1.
[440] Ibid., 6.1.4.1.

[441] Ibid., 6.2.2.
[442] Ibid., 6.2.1.
[443] Ibid, 3.
[444] Ibid., 6.2.1.
[445] Ibid., 6.2.3.
[446] Ibid.
[447] Ibid., 6.1.3.1.
[448] Ibid.
[449] Ibid., 7.8.2.
[450] Ibid., 6.1.3.2.
[451] Ibid., 7.8.2.
[452] Ibid., 6.1.3.1.
[453] Ibid.
[454] Ibid., 6.1.1.
[455] Ibid., 6.1.3.1.
[456] Ibid.
[457] Ibid.
[458] Ibid., 6.3.
[459] Ibid., 6.1.3.1.
[460] Ibid. 6.3.
[461] Ibid., 6.1.3.1.
[462] Ibid.
[463] Ibid., 5.2.6 & 7.1.1.
[464] Ibid., 5.2.7.
[465] Ibid., 7.7.
[466] Ibid.
[467] Ibid., 7.
[468] Ibid.
[469] Ibid., 7.6.
[470] Ibid., 7.6.1.
[471] Ibid.
[472] Ibid., 7.8.1.
[473] Ibid., 7.1.
[474] Ibid., 7.1.1.
[475] Ibid.
[476] Ibid., 7.1.1 & 7.1.2.
[477] Ibid., 7.1.1.
[478] Ibid., 7.1.2.
[479] Ibid., 7.1.3.
[480] Ibid., 7.1.4.
[481] Ibid., 7.1.1.
[482] Ibid., 7.1.5.
[483] Ibid., 7.8.2.
[484] Ibid., 7.1.5.
[485] Ibid., 7.3.1.

[486] Ibid., 7.1.5.
[487] Ibid.
[488] Ibid.
[489] Ibid., 7.2.4.
[490] Ibid., 7.1.5.
[491] Ibid.
[492] Ibid.
[493] Ibid., 7.2.4.
[494] Ibid., 7.1.5.
[495] Ibid.
[496] Ibid.
[497] Ibid.
[498] Ibid.
[499] Ibid.
[500] Ibid.
[501] Ibid.
[502] Ibid., 7.2
[503] Ibid.
[504] Utz includes in his bibliography Cornelius Castoriadis, who had similarly argued that "capitalism… inherited these anthropological types from previous historical periods: the incorruptible judge, the Weberian civil servant, the teacher devoted to his task, the worker whose work was, in spite of everything, a source of pride. Such personalities are becoming inconceivable in the contemporary age: it is not clear why today they would be reproduced, who would reproduce them, and in the name of what they would function." ("The Rising Tide of Insignificancy", 137)
[505] Arthur F. Utz, *Economic Ethics*, 7.2.4.
[506] As cited in Jeanne Cummings, "Obama blames 'ethic of greed' for economy", *Politico*, 27th March 2008, <http://www.politico.com/story/2008/03/obama-blames-ethic-of-greed-for-economy-009238>.
[507] Michael Polanyi, *The Logic of Liberty*, Chicago: University of Chicago Press, 1951.
[508] Arthur F. Utz, *Economic Ethics*, 7.3.2.
[509] Ibid.
[510] Ibid.
[511] Ibid., 7.8.5.
[512] Ibid., 7.3.2.
[513] Cf. ibid., 3.1.
[514] Ibid., 7.1.3.
[515] Ibid., 7.3.3.
[516] Ibid. Because of its nefarious psychological, social and political effects, unemployment was the issue that most preoccupied Utz as regards the dysfunctional traits of actual market economies, cf. *Die massive Arbeitslosigkeit und die Wirtschaftsordnung* (Berlin: Duncker & Humboldt, 1998).
[517] Arthur F. Utz, *Economic Ethics*, 7.3.3.
[518] Ibid.

[519] Ibid.
[520] Ibid., 7.5.
[521] Ibid.
[522] Ibid.
[523] Ibid., 7.4.
[524] Ibid., 7.4.1.
[525] Ibid.
[526] Ibid.
[527] Ibid.
[528] Ibid.
[529] Ibid., 9.2.7.
[530] Ibid., 7.4.1.
[531] Ibid.
[532] Ibid., 7.4.2.
[533] Ibid.
[534] Ibid., 7.4.1.
[535] Ibid., 7.4.3.
[536] Ibid., 7.4.1.
[537] Ibid.
[538] Ibid., 7.8.6.
[539] Ibid.
[540] Ibid.
[541] Ibid., 7.4.3.
[542] Ibid.
[543] Ibid., 7.7.
[544] Ibid.
[545] Ibid.
[546] Ibid., 7.8.6; emphasis in the original.
[547] Ibid., 8.1.
[548] Ibid.
[549] Ibid.
[550] Ibid., 8.1 & 8.2.
[551] Ibid., 8.2.
[552] Ibid.
[553] Ibid., 8.3.
[554] Ibid., 4.2 & 4.3.
[555] Ibid., 8.3.
[556] Ibid.
[557] Ibid.
[558] Ibid., 9.1.
[559] Ibid.
[560] Ibid.
[561] Ibid.
[562] Ibid., 9.1 & 9.1.1.
[563] Ibid., 9.1.

[564] Ibid.
[565] Ibid., 9.1.1.
[566] Ibid., 9.2.1.
[567] Ibid.
[568] Ibid.
[569] Ibid., 9.2.2.
[570] Ibid.
[571] Ibid.
[572] Ibid.
[573] Ibid., 9.2.3.
[574] Ibid., 9.2.6.
[575] Ibid., 9.2.3.
[576] Ibid., 9.2.4.
[577] Ibid., 9.2.5.
[578] Ibid., 9.2.4.
[579] Ibid., 9.2.6.
[580] Ibid., 9.2.7.
[581] Ibid., 9.3.1. Utz deals with State capture by private interests, lobbies and pressure groups also in his *Political Ethics* (cf. 2.1.4).
[582] Arthur F. Utz, *Economic Ethics*, 9.3.1.
[583] Ibid., 9.3.3.
[584] Ibid., 9.3.2 & 9.3.3.
[585] Ibid., 10.1.
[586] Ibid.
[587] Ibid., 10.2.
[588] Ibid.
[589] Ibid.
[590] Ibid.
[591] Ibid., 10.3.
[592] Ibid.
[593] Ibid.
[594] Cf. Arthur F. Utz, *Political Ethics*, 3.1.8.
[595] Arthur F. Utz, *Economic Ethics*, 11.1.
[596] Cf. ibid., 11.4.
[597] Cf. ibid., 11.4–7.
[598] Ibid., 11.3.
[599] Ibid., 11.6.
[600] Ibid., 11.4.
[601] Ibid., 11.5.
[602] Ibid., 11.6.
[603] Ibid., 11.1.
[604] Ibid.
[605] Ibid., 11.2.
[606] Ibid.
[607] Ibid., 11.3.

[608] Ibid., 12.3.
[609] Ibid., 12.1.
[610] Ibid.
[611] Ibid., 12.2.
[612] Ibid., 12.2 & 12.3.
[613] Cf. Arthur F. Utz, *Political Ethics*, 1.1.3.
[614] Cf. ibid., 3.1.8
[615] Cf. ibid., 3.2.1.
[616] Cf. ibid., 1.1.3.
[617] Cf. ibid., 1.2 & 2.1.1.
[618] Cf. ibid., 1.1.2.
[619] Cf. ibid.
[620] Cf. ibid., 3.2.5.
[621] Cf. ibid., 5.2.3.
[622] Cf. ibid., 2.1.2.
[623] Cf. ibid., 2.5.2, 3.16 & 3.2.3. Inspired by McMurtry's philosophy and apparently unaware of the jusnaturalist tradition, microbiologist W. Thomson Martin argues that the democratic will is not supreme, if it runs counter to human survival (cf. *From Democracy to Biocracy: Finding the River of Life*, Victoria: Friesen Press, 2016).
[624] Cf. Arthur F. Utz, *Political Ethics*, 2.2.3.
[625] Cf. ibid., 3.1.5 & 3.16.
[626] Cf. ibid., 1.1.6.
[627] Cf. ibid., 4.6.2 & 6.1.
[628] ICESCR articles 11(1) & 12(1).
[629] ICESCR articles 10, 13(1), 15, 7(d) & 7.
[630] Cf. Arthur F. Utz, *Political Ethics*, 4.4.5.
[631] Cf. ibid., 6.2.
[632] Cf. ibid., 6.2.2.
[633] Cf. ibid., 1.1.1 & 1.1.2.
[634] Cf. ibid., 2.4.3.
[635] Ibid., 1.2.1.3.
[636] Cf. ibid., 3.1.7.
[637] Cf. ibid., 3.1.9.
[638] Cf. ibid., 4.2.1.
[639] Cf. ibid., 4.3.5.
[640] Cf. ibid., 2.4.1.
[641] Cf. ibid., 3.1.3.
[642] Cf. ibid., 4.6.7.
[643] Arthur F. Utz, *Economic Ethics*, 6.1.3.2.
[644] Cf. Arthur F. Utz, *Political Ethics*, 6.1.

⁶⁴⁵ SDC began with Leo XIII's encyclical letter *Rerum Novarum* (1891) and had its latest instalment in 2015 with Francis' own *Laudato si'*. The *Compendium of the Social Doctrine of the Church*, issued by the Pontifical Council for Justice and Peace in 2004, makes extensive reference to encyclicals, in addition to Biblical, authoritative (e.g. Augustine, Aquinas) and other Church documents (i.e. constitutions, decrees and declarations by ecumenical and pontifical councils, documents issued by congregations, the Holy See's charter of rights, canon law, the Catechism). Prominent in this respect are *Rerum Novarum*, Pius XI's *Quadragesimo Anno* (1931), John XXIII's *Mater et Magistra* (1961) and *Pacem in Terris* (1963), Paul VI's *Populorum Progressio* (1967), John Paul II's *Laborem Exercens* (1981), *Sollicitudo Rei Socialis* (1987), *Centesimus Annus* (1991), *Veritatis Splendor* (1993) and *Evangelium Vitae* (1995), and Benedict XVI's *Caritas in Veritate* (2009). References to international law are also abundant, i.e. the *Charter of the United Nations* (1945), the *Universal Declaration of Human Rights* (1948), and the *Convention on the Rights of the Child* (1990).

⁶⁴⁶ Cf. Giovanni Franchi, "Arthur F. Utz als Interpret der pluralistischen Demokratie", 2013, <http://www.stiftung-utz.de/file/1/Franchi.pdf>. In *Economic Ethics*, Utz mentions the expression "third way" with respect to OS (7.4.1). Still, on other occasions, Utz used it to describe his own approach in politics and economics as well as the overall stance of SDC, e.g. the 1978 book *Zwischen Neoliberalismus und Neomarxismus: die Philosophie des dritten Weges* and his essay "Das Grundanliegen der Pluralismusidee in der freiheitlichen Gesellschaftskonzeption und der Dritte Weg", included in the collection *Neomarxismus und pluralistische Wirtschaftsordnung* (Bonn: Scientia Humana Institut, 1979, 77–104), edited by Utz himself. Its distinctiveness from both liberalism and socialism makes several public stances of SDC, especially when stated by Popes in the public arenas, sound right-wing at times (e.g. the sanctity of private property) and left-wing at others (e.g. strict environmental regulation), thus drawing praise as well as attacks from both political camps.

⁶⁴⁷ Hans Jonas, *Das Prinzip Verantwortung. Versuch einer Ethik für die technologische Zivilisation*, Frankfurt am Main: Insel, 1979; translated by H. Jonas and D. Herr, *The Imperative of Responsibility. In Search of an Ethics for the Technological Age*, Chicago: The University of Chicago Press, 1984, 140 (hereafter DPV).

⁶⁴⁸ Cf. Fermin Roland Schramm and Miguel Kottow, "Principios bioéticos en salud pública: limitaciones y propuestas", *Cadernos de Saúde Pública*, 17(4), 2001, 949–56.

⁶⁴⁹ Cf. Richard Wolin, *Heidegger's Children: Hannah Arendt, Karl Löwith, Hans Jonas, and Herbert Marcuse*, Princeton: Princeton University Press, 2001.

⁶⁵⁰ Cf. Hans Jonas, *Gnosis und spätantiker Geist*, Göttingen: Vandenhoeck & Ruprecht, 1934–1966.

⁶⁵¹ Cf. Hans Jonas, *Augustin und das paulinische Freiheitsproblem. Ein philosophischer Beitrag zur Genesis der christlich-abendländischen Freiheitsidee*, Göttingen: Vandenhoeck & Ruprecht, 1930.

⁶⁵² E.g. Hans Jonas, *Der Gottesbegriff nach Auschwitz. Eine jüdische Stimme*, Frankfurt am Main: Suhrkamp, 1987; translated into Italian by C. Angelino, *Il concetto di Dio dopo Auscwitz. Una voce ebraica*, Genova: Il melangolo, 1993 (containing "Sul razzismo", 41–9).

[653] E.g. Hans Jonas, *The Phenomenon of Life. Toward a Philosophical Biology*, New York: Harper and Row, 1966; and *Philosophical Essays. From Ancient Creed to Technological Man*, Englewood Cliffs: Prentice-Hall, 1974.

[654] E.g. Hans Jonas, *On Faith, Reason and Responsibility: Six Essays*, San Francisco: Harper and Row, 1978; and his pivotal DPV, which is probably his most famous book.

[655] Hans Jonas, DPV, 2.

[656] Ibid. Cf. also Tomas Domingo-Moratalla, "El mundo en nuestras manos. La etica antropologica de Hans Jonas", *Dialogo Filosofico*, 17(1), 2001, 37–60.

[657] As cited in Benjamin Lazier, "Overcoming Gnosticism: Hans Jonas, Hans Blumenberg, and the Legitimacy of the Natural World", *Journal of the History of Ideas*, 64(4), 2003, 619.

[658] Cf. Christian Wiese, "'Weltabenteuer Gottes' und 'Heiligkeit des Lebens': Theologische Spekulation und ethische Reflexion in der Philosophie von Hans Jonas", *Synthesis Philosophica*, 18(1–2), 2003, 63–81.

[659] Hans Jonas, *Philosophie, Rückschau und Vorschau am Ende des Jahrhunderts*, Frankfurt am Main: Suhrkamp, 1993, 50 (unless otherwise indicated, all English translations are mine).

[660] Cf. Hans Jonas, *Erkenntnis und Verantwortung: Gespräch mit Ingo Hermann in der Reihe „Zeugen des Jahrhunderts"*, Göttingen: Lamuv, 1991; and *Dem bösen Ende näher: Gespräche über das Verhältnis des Menschen zur Natur*, Frankfurt am Main: Suhrkamp, 1993.

[661] E.g. Ulrich Melle, "Responsibility and the Crisis of Technological Civilization: A Husserlian Meditation on Hans Jonas", *Human Studies*, 21, 1998, 329–45.

[662] Hans Jonas, DPV, 140.

[663] E.g. Hans Jonas, *Macht oder Ohnmacht der Subjektivität? Das Leib-Seele-Problem im Vorfeld des Prinzips Verantwortung*, Frankfurt am Main: Insel, 1981; and Hans Jonas and Dietmar Mieth, *Was für morgen lebenswichtig ist: Unentdeckte Zukunftswerte*, Freiburg im Breisgau: Herder, 1983.

[664] Hans Jonas, DPV, 31.

[665] Ibid., 130.

[666] Ibid.

[667] Ibid.

[668] Cf. Lawrence Vogel, "Natural Law Judaism? The Genesis of Bioethics in Hans Jonas, Leo Strauss, and Leon Kass", *Hastings Center Report*, 36(3), 2006, 32–44.

[669] Hans Jonas, DPV, 131.

[670] Ibid.

[671] Ibid., 100–1.

[672] Cf. Chan Wing-Tsit, *A Source Book in Chinese Philosophy*, Princeton: Princeton University Press, 1963.

[673] Cf. Francesca Paola Telaretti, "Vita ed etica in Hans Jonas", *Iride*, 13(29), 2000, 151–69.

[674] Cf. Hans Jonas, *Wissenschaft als persönliches Erlebnis*, Göttingen: Vandenhoeck & Ruprecht, 1987.

[675] Cf. Hans Jonas, *The Phenomenon of Life*.

[676] Hans Jonas, "Ist Gott ein Mathematiker? Vom Sinn des Stoffwechsels", in *Organismus und Freiheit*, Göttingen: Vandenhoeck & Ruprecht, 1973, 138.

[677] Cf. Also Hans Jonas, *Wandel und Bestand. Vom Grunde der Verstehbarkeit des Geschichtlichen*, Frankfurt am Main: Vittorio Klostermann, 1970; and *Philosophische Untersuchungen und metaphysische Vermutungen*, Frankfurt am Main: Insel, 1992.
[678] Hans Jonas, DPV, 168.
[679] Cf. Hans Jonas, *Technik, Medizin und Ethik. Zur Praxis des Prinzips Verantwortung*, Frankfurt am Main: Insel, 1985.
[680] Cf. Fernando Calonge, "Post-humanismo y ética: reflexiones para la reconstrucción de solidaridades en la sociedad moderna avanzada", *Foro Interno*, 5, 2005, 59–83.
[681] Cf. Roman Globokar, *Verantwortung fur Alles, was Lebt: Von Albert Schweitzer und Hans Jonas zu einer theologischen Ethik des Lebens*, Rome: Pontificia Università Gregoriana, 2002.
[682] Cf. Christian Schutze, "The Political and Intellectual Influence of Hans Jonas", *Hastings Centre Report*, 25(7; special issue), 1995, 40–3.
[683] Hans Jonas, DPV, 122; the emphasis on "political" is mine.
[684] Ibid., 22.
[685] Ibid., 32.
[686] Cf. Peter Dews, "Disenchantment and the Persistence of Evil: Habermas, Jonas, Badiou" in *Modernity and the Problem of Evil*, edited by Alan D. Schrift, Bloomington: Indiana University Press, 2005, 51–65.
[687] Hans Jonas, DPV, 36.
[688] Ibid., 204.
[689] Ibid., 145.
[690] Ibid.; emphasis in the original.
[691] Ibid., 185.
[692] Premio Nonino, official website, 2017, <http://premio.grappanonino.it/en/>.
[693] Hans Jonas, "Sul razzismo", 45.
[694] Ibid., 46.
[695] Ibid.
[696] Ibid.
[697] Ibid.
[698] Ibid.
[699] Ibid.
[700] Ibid., 47.
[701] Ibid.
[702] Ibid.
[703] Ibid., 47–8.
[704] Ibid., 48.
[705] Ibid.
[706] Ibid.
[707] Ibid.
[708] Ibid.
[709] Ibid.
[710] Ibid.
[711] Ibid.

[712] Ibid.
[713] Ibid., 49.
[714] Hans Jonas, DPV, 204. Cf. also Jens Kurreck, "Zwischen Technikoptimismus und Kassandrismus: Grundriss fur eine aktuelle Kasuistik der Gen- und Biotechnologie auf der Basis der Verantwortungsethik von Hans Jonas", *Synthesis Philosophica*, 18(1–2), 2003, 245–72.
[715] E.g. R.K. Pachauri and A. Reisinger (eds.), *Climate Change 2007*.
[716] Hans Jonas, "Sul razzismo", 48.
[717] E.g. Dartmouth Common Master Plan, 2009, <http://www.halifax.ca/RealPropertyPlanning/DCMP/documents/DCMPTOC_DraftNov2009.pdf>.
[718] UN, *Charter of the United Nations*, 1945, <http://www.un.org/en/documents/charter/index.shtml>.
[719] Cf. D.J. Whelan and J. Donnelly, "The West, Economic and Social Rights, and the Global Human Rights Regime: Setting the Record Straight", *Human Rights Quarterly*, 29(4), 2007, 908–49.
[720] E.g. L. Arbour, "Economic and Social Justice for Societies in Transition", *New York University Centre for Human Rights and Global Justice*, Working Paper no. 10, 2006, <http://www.chrgj.org/publications/docs/wp/WPS_NYU_CHRGJ_Arbour_%20Final.pdf>; and K. Tomasevski. "Removing Obstacles for the Right to Education", *Human Rights Tribune*, 11(3), 2005, 12–6.
[721] Cf. G. Alfredsson and A. Eide, *The Universal Declaration of Human Rights: A Common Standard of Achievement*, The Hague: Kluwer, 1999; A. Eide, "Economic, Social and Cultural Rights as Human Rights", in *Economic, Social and Cultural Rights: A Textbook*, edited by A. Eide, C. Krause and A. Rosas, The Hague: Kluwer, 2001 (2nd ed.), 10–28.; and D.J. Whelan and J. Donnelly, "The West, Economic and Social Rights, and the Global Human Rights Regime".
[722] Cf. P. Alston, "Putting Economic, Social and Cultural Rights Back on the Agenda of the United States", *New York University Centre for Human Rights and Global Justice*, Working Paper 22nd November 2009, <http://www.chrgj.org/publications/docs/wp/Alston%20Spring%2009.pdf>.
[723] Cf. G. Alfredsson and A. Eide, *The Universal Declaration of Human Rights*, and D.J. Whelan and J. Donnelly, "The West, Economic and Social Rights, and the Global Human Rights Regime".
[724] Cf. G. Alfredsson and A. Eide, *The Universal Declaration of Human Rights*.
[725] P. Alston and G. Quinn, "The Nature and Scope of States Parties' Obligations under the International Covenant on Economic, Social and Cultural Rights", *Human Rights Quarterly*, 9, 1987, 156–229; M.C.R. Craven, *The International Covenant on Economic, Social, and Cultural Rights: A perspective on its development*, Oxford: Clarendon Press, 1995; and C. Scott and P. Macklem, "Constitutional Ropes of Sand or Justiciable Guarantees? Social Rights in a New South African Constitution", *University of Pennsylvania Law Review*, 14(1), 1992, 1–148.
[726] Certification case (*ex parte* Chairman of the Constitutional Assembly. In re Certification of the Constitution of the Republic of South Africa 1996 (4) SA 744 (South Africa)), 1996, <http://www.constitutionalcourt.org.za/uhtbin/cgisirsi/IndU35IdW0/MAIN/108830009/9>.

[727] Cf. G. Alfredsson and A. Eide, *The Universal Declaration of Human Rights*; and D.J. Whelan and J. Donnelly, "The West, Economic and Social Rights, and the Global Human Rights Regime".

[728] Cf. ICESCR, article 2(1), and UN, *International Covenant on Civil and Political Rights* (ICCPR), 1966, article 2 (<http://www.ohchr.org/EN/ProfessionalInterest/Pages/CCPR.aspx>); article 23 applies a "progressive realization" standard *vis-á-vis* equality in marriage since states did not consider themselves able to immediately guarantee this right. This is not to suggest that even today states are successful in fulfilling the ICCPR in its entirety.

[729] ICCPR, articles 14, 18 & 19(2); cf. also C. Scott and P. Macklem, "Constitutional Ropes of Sand or Justiciable Guarantees?".

[730] Cf. OP-ICESCR, *Optional Protocol to the International Covenant on Economic, Social and Cultural Rights* (GA res. A/63/435 (Dec. 10, 2008)), <http://www2.ohchr.org/english/bodies/cescr/docs/A-RES-63-117.pdf>. In July 2010, OP-ICESCR had attracted 31 signatures and 2 ratifications. On coming into force, it will have a competence comparable to that of the Human Rights Committee to consider communications from aggrieved individuals or groups. Noteworthy are also the General Comments by the ESCR Committee, 1989–2009 (cf. ESCR Committee, *Compilation of General Comments and General Recommendations Adopted by Human Rights Treaty Bodies*, 1989–2009 (cited in the present chapter as numbered and dated General Comments), <http://daccess-dds-ny.un.org/doc/UNDOC/GEN/G08/422/35/PDF/G0842235.pdf?OpenElement> & <http://www2.ohchr.org/english/bodies/cescr/docs/gc/E-C-12-GC-21.doc>); and the concluding observations on State reports, included in the Committee's annual reports to the Economic and Social Council (ECOSOC; cf. *Committee on Economic, Social and Cultural Rights: Reports on sessions* (U.N. ESCOR, Comm. On Econ., Soc. and Cultural Rts., various Sess., Supp. No. 2), 1990–2009, <http://tb.ohchr.org/default.aspx>).

[731] Curiously, South Africa is not a party to the ICESCR, having signed in 1994 but never ratified, yet its constitution reflects much of its content, even using the Committee's framework of duties to respect, protect and fulfil human rights (cf. Constitution of the Republic of South Africa, 1996, s7(2); cf. also S. Liebenberg, "South Africa: Adjudicating social rights under a transformative constitution", in *Social Rights Jurisprudence: Emerging trends in comparative and international law 3*, edited by M. Langford, Cambridge: Cambridge University Press, 2009, 75–101). Other countries that incorporated economic, social, and cultural rights in recent constitutions include: Brazil, Bulgaria, Burkino Faso, Congo, Colombia, Estonia, Hungary, Macedonia, Poland, and Turkey (cf. M. Langford, "The Justiciability of Social Rights: From practice to theory", in *Social Rights Jurisprudence*, 3–45, footnote 39 and this collection in general for reviews of over 2000 cases).

[732] For a review of the debate, cf. A. Nolan, B. Porter and M. Langford, "The Justiciability of Social and Economic Rights: An updated appraisal", *New York University Center for Human Rights and Global Justice*, Working Paper no. 15, 2007, <http://www.chrgj.org/publications/docs/wp/NolanPorterLangford.pdf>.

[733] Cf. M. Langford and J.A. King, "Committee on Economic, Social and Cultural Rights: Past, present and future", in *Social Rights Jurisprudence*, 477–516.

[734] Cf. VCLT, *Vienna Convention on the Law of Treaties* (1155 U.N.T.S. 331, 8 I.L.M. 679, entered into force 27th January 1980), <http://treaties.un.org/doc/Treaties/1980/01/19800127%2000-52%20AM/Ch_XXIII_01p.pdf>.

[735] Cf. J. Cordero, "Al menos 34 muertos por las protestas indígenas en Perú. Un proyecto de ley enfrenta a la policía con las comunidades en una zona de la Amazonia", *El País*, 5th June 2009, <http://www.elpais.com/articulo/internacional/34/muertos/protestas/indigenas/Peru/elpepuint/20090605elpepuint_19/Tes>.

[736] Cf. OECD, *Harmonised Unemployment Rates: News Release: August 2010*, <http://www.oecd.org/dataoecd/45/21/46175570.pdf>.

[737] D. Espo, "Republicans find peril and potential as tea party movement reshapes political landscape", *Star Tribune*, 16th October 2010, <http://www.startribune.com/politics/105092684.html>.

[738] Cf. J. Vasagar, "Universities alarmed by 40% cut to teaching budgets", *The Guardian*, 20th October 2010, <http://www.guardian.co.uk/education/2010/oct/20/spending-review-university-teaching-cuts>.

[739] Harvard professor Ralph Barton Perry (1876–1957) argued: "a thing—anything—has value or is valuable in the original and generic sense, when it is the object of interest—any interest." (*Realms of Value*, Cambridge: Harvard University Press. 1954, 2–3) Nicholas Rescher (b. 1951), "champion" of the Anglo-American analytic tradition, rarefied further the notion of value and reduced it to the status of linguistic rationalisation of individual yens: "A value represents a slogan capable of providing for the rationalisation of action by encapsulating a positive attitude toward a purportedly beneficial state of affairs" (*Introduction to Value Theory*, Englewood Cliffs: Prentice-Hall, 1969, 9). Even more abstract was Zdzislaw Najder's (b. 1930) option, whereby: "M is an axiological value if and only if M is a judgement, ascribing the quality of valuableness to objects, properties or states of affairs, and constituting within the given value-system a final justification of other judgements of the system." (*Values and Evaluations*, Oxford: Clarendon Press, 1975, 63–4)

[740] John McMurtry, "What is Good? What is Bad?", § 1.10.4.

[741] Michel Foucault, *The Birth of Biopolitics. Lectures at the College of France 1978–79*, New York: Palgrave MacMillan, 2008, 101.

[742] John McMurtry, "What is Good? What is Bad?", § 1.16.

[743] Ibid.

[744] Ibid., Glossary. A considerable amount of philosophical and socio-political literature has centred in recent years upon "life", yet in connection with the Foucauldian notions of "biopower" and "biopolitics" (e.g. Giorgio Agamben, Homo Sacer: *Sovereign Power and Bare Life*, Stanford: Stanford University Press, 1998; and *State of Exception*, Chicago: University of Chicago Press, 2005; as well as Roberto Esposito, *Bíos: Biopolitica e Flosofia*, Turin: Einaudi, 2004; and "Biopolitica, immunità, comunità", in *Biopolitica: Storia e attualità di un concetto*, edited by A. Cutro, Verona: Ombre Corte, 2005, 158–67). However, no attempt has been made to clearly define "life" and articulate it beyond the juxtaposition of "zoe" (biological life) and "bios" (political and/or fully human life), nor has any objective criterion of value been proposed in this context (cf. M. Nacci, "Su biopolitica, liberaldemocrazia e nazismo si può dire tutto e il contrario", *L'Occidente*, 2009, <http://www.loccidentale.it/articolo/biopolitica, +liberaldemocrazia,+nazismo.0065146>).

[745] John McMurtry, "What is Good? What is Bad?", § 6.2.1.

[746] Ibid., § 6.1.4.

[747] Isaiah Berlin, *Four Essays on Liberty*, 124.

[748] John McMurtry, *Unequal Freedoms*, 164. To avoid misunderstandings, it should be emphasised that: (a) organisms can be harmed psychologically, not just physically; and (b) organisms are not always reducible to individual creatures (e.g. colonial beings, ecosystems, social units and societies at large).

[749] There may be simpler and more complex comparisons of value or evaluations of life-gains and losses. Nevertheless, if McMurtry's axiology is correct, then the preferred option in hard cases should be still the result of comparisons of life-value, e.g. a court's painful decision to separate a child from her cruel parent to foster the former's best interest, or John of Salisbury's (ca. 1115–1180) and John Milton's classic justifications of tyrannicide.

[750] Shue as cited in S.I. Skogly, "Structural Adjustment and Development: Human Rights – An Agenda for Change"*, Human Rights Quarterly*, 15, 1993, 769; emphasis in the original.

[751] It should be underlined that no ontological dualism is implied: "Although we can distinguish the cognitive and feeling capacities of any person, this does not mean dividing them into separate worlds as has occurred in the traditional divisions between mind and body, reason and the emotions. Life-value onto-axiology begins from *their unity as the nature of the human organism*." (John McMurtry, "What is Good? What is Bad?", § 6.3; emphasis in the original).

[752] John McMurtry, "What is Good? What is Bad?", § 6.1.

[753] John McMurtry, *The Cancer Stage of Capitalism*, 206–7.

[754] John McMurtry, "What is Good? What is Bad?", Glossary.

[755] ESCR Committee*, *General Comment No. 3, 1990, § 8 (all General Comments can be retrieved from: <http://tb.ohchr.org/default.aspx>).

[756] Cf. G. Alfredsson and A. Eide, *The Universal Declaration of Human Rights*.

[757] Cf. ICESCR, articles 13(2)(a) and 14.

[758] ESCR Committee*, Report on the Twenty-fifth, Twenty-sixth and Twenty-seventh Sessions*, § 176.

[759] Cf. M.C.R. Craven, *The International Covenant on Economic, Social, and Cultural Rights*.

[760] It follows that, were the privatised civil commons to fail a life-grounded test of success, alternatives ought to be sought promptly, e.g. nationalisation of private companies that are either too small or too big to be able to compete on the market, as also plainly discussed in John Kenneth Galbraith, *The Age of Uncertainty*, London: BBC, 1977.
[761] John McMurtry, "Principles of the Good Life".
[762] Ibid.
[763] "'Major Global Downturn' says IMF", *BBC News*, 8th October 2008, <http://news.bbc.co.uk/1/hi/business/7659086.stm>.
[764] Ki-moon Ban, "UN Secretary-General Ban Ki-moon's message for the World Environment Day".
[765] John McMurtry, *The Cancer Stage of Capitalism*, 243.
[766] E.g. UNESCO, *The Impact of the Global Financial and Economic Crisis on the Education Sector* (ED/EPS/2009/PI/1), <http://unesdoc.unesco.org/images/0018/001836/183667e.pdf>.
[767] Cf. ESCR Committee, General Comment No. 3, § 8.
[768] ESCR Committee, General Comment No. 2, 1990, § 9.
[769] Cf. VCLT, article 18.
[770] Cf. OP-ICESCR, article 18.
[771] ICESCR, Preamble; emphasis added.
[772] Cf. D.J. Whelan and J. Donnelly, "The West, Economic and Social Rights, and the Global Human Rights Regime".
[773] Cf. VCLT, article 13.
[774] ICESCR, article 2(1).
[775] Ibid., Preamble.
[776] Ibid. Non-State actors, as well as states, are prohibited from relying on any of the rights within the ICESCR to deny others the same (ICESCR, article 5(1)).
[777] Cf. Jeff Noonan, *Democratic Society and Human Needs*.
[778] John McMurtry, "Economic Globalization and Ethico-political Rights", in *Encyclopedia of Applied Ethics*, edited by D. Callahan, R. Chadwick and P. Singer, Maryland Heights: Elsevier, 2010, 21.
[779] Ibid.
[780] ESCR Committee, General Comment No. 3, § 10; cf. also M. Langford and J.A. King, "Committee on Economic, Social and Cultural Rights"; and A. Chapman and S. Russell, "Introduction", in *Core Obligations: Building a framework for economic, social and cultural rights*, 2002, Antwerp: Intersentia, 1–20.
[781] ESCR Committee, General Comment No. 3, § 10.
[782] At the implicit heart of biology and medicine there are grounds from which one may deduce universal criteria of planetary and human life-needs, hence guidelines for public welfare too. However, today's so-called "life sciences" epitomise the life-blindness of much scholarship and scientific research, for this term includes life-destructive praxes such as the corporate stipulation of new disorders and the development of biological weapons.

⁷⁸³ Cf. UN, *State Report Guidelines* (compilation of Guidelines on the Form and Content of Reports to be Submitted by States Parties to the International Human Rights Treaties, Chapter I: Harmonized Guidelines on Reporting under the International Human Rights Treaties, Including Guidelines on a Core Document and Treaty-Specific Documents, and Appendix 3, at p. 23, 3 June 2009, U.N. Doc. HRI/GEN/2/Rev.6). The data requests have been criticised for being too detailed and burdensome, in particular for developing states (cf. A. Chapman and S. Russell, *Core Obligations*).
⁷⁸⁴ John McMurtry, *Value Wars*, 156.
⁷⁸⁵ ESCR Committee, *Poverty and the International Covenant on Economic, Social and Cultural Rights* (Statement adopted by the Committee on Economic, Social and Cultural Rights on 4 May 2001, U.N. Doc. E/C.12/2001/10), §§ 7–8, <http://www.unhchr.ch/tbs/doc.nsf/(Symbol)/E.C.12.2001.10.En>.
⁷⁸⁶ §§ 4 & 15.
⁷⁸⁷ Cf. ESCR Committee, General Comments Nos. 12 (1999), § 8, 14 (2000), § 43(b) & (c), and 15 (2002), § 37.
⁷⁸⁸ ESCR Committee, General Comment No. 3, § 14.
⁷⁸⁹ ESCR Committee, General Comment No. 14, § 43(c).
⁷⁹⁰ ESCR Committee, General Comment No. 19, 2007, § 59.
⁷⁹¹ Cf. ESCR Committee, General Comments Nos. 5 (1994), §§ 30–2, and 6 (1995), § 31.
⁷⁹² Cf. ESCR Committee, General Comment No. 14, § 43(a) & (e).
⁷⁹³ Cf. ESCR Committee, General Comment No. 13, 1999, § 57.
⁷⁹⁴ Cf. ESCR Committee, General Comment No. 21, 2009, § 50.
⁷⁹⁵ Cf. ESCR Committee, General Comment No. 18, 2005, § 31.
⁷⁹⁶ Cf. ICESCR, Preamble, and ESCR Committee, General Comment No. 3, §§ 6 & 8.
⁷⁹⁷ Cf. ESCR Committee, General Comment No. 14, § 34.
⁷⁹⁸ In *Democratic Society and Human Need*, McMurtry scholar Jeff Noonan observes that needs balance one another, as, say, the need for liquid fluids is eventually countered by the need to urinate, or the need to be educated, if unrestrained by the needs to properly rest and socialise, will eventually turn into unhealthy ivory-tower bookworm-like existence. Needs, unlike wants, are satiable. However, life-enablement can progress farther than the perfect satisfaction of needs, for it is possible to think of an impeccably sustainable worldwide community of healthy, happy, educated human beings, who test the limits and improve upon athletic ability, explore at ease the pinnacles of aesthetic bliss, and dwell passionately yet wisely the utter depths of learning. Perhaps, this was the ideal horizon towards which the drafters of the ICESCR dreamt for humanity to be able to advance, after experiencing the Great Depression and its most abhorrent child, the Second World War.
⁷⁹⁹ The ESCR Committee's General Comments Nos. 4, § 8(g), 12, § 8, and 14, § 12(c), focus upon the importance of the cultural appropriateness of housing, food and healthcare respectively.
⁸⁰⁰ Cf. Transparency International, *African Education Watch 2010*, <http://www.transparency.org/news_room/latest_news/press_releases/2010/2010_02_23_aew_launch_en>.

[801] Cf. G. Friedman, "Labor Unions in the United States", in *EH.Net Encyclopedia*, 2008, <http://eh.net/encyclopedia/article/friedman.unions.us>.

[802] Cf. Amartya Sen, *Inequality Re-examined*. Oxford: Oxford University Press, 1992; and Gene Shackman, *Understanding the World Today* (Website of the Global Social Change Research Project), 2006–2009, <http://gsociology.icaap.org/>.

[803] Cf. Serge Latouche, *La Mégamachine: Raison technoscientifique, raison économique et mythe du progrès*, Paris: La découverte, 2004; and *Petit traité de la décroissance sereine*. Paris: Mille et une nuits, 2007.

[804] Although the ICESCR and the ESCR Committee are ecumenical regarding the type of economic system employed by a state to realise, progressively, the treaty, the Committee expresses doubts that rights can be fulfilled entirely for all in a wholly unregulated market and recommends that in the case of privatisation, the State ensure some back-up protection for vulnerable groups (e.g. General Comments Nos. 3, § 8, 5, §§ 11–2, 14, § 35, and 18, § 25).

[805] Cf. Worldwatch Institute, *State of the World 2009*, Washington: The Worldwatch Institute Press.

[806] Cf. UNESCO, *Encyclopedia of Life Support Systems*.

[807] Cf. M. Gaggi, "Ibm e i big Usa: chi ha paura del Barack 'statalista'", *Corriere della Sera*, 7th November 2008, <http://rassegna.governo.it/rs_pdf/pdf/JSM/JSMF0.pdf>; and International Labour Organization, *Labour Inspection 2006* (General surveys by the committee of experts on the application of conventions and recommendations), <http://www.ilo.org/public/english/support/lib/resource/subject/labourinsp.htm>.

[808] Cf. D. Leigh, "How UK oil company Trafigura tried to cover up African pollution disaster", *The Guardian*, 16th September 2009, <https://www.theguardian.com/world/2009/sep/16/trafigura-oil-ivory-coast>.

[809] Neither the ICESCR nor the ICCPR contain provisions for denunciation (withdrawal) by their parties, in contrast to the vast majority of treaties in international law.

[810] Cf. General Comment No. 19, 2007, § 11, recognising the need for social security schemes to be sustainable "to ensure that the right can be realized for present and future generations."

[811] Cf. ESCR Committee, General Comment No. 14, §§ 4, 11 & 15.

[812] Cf. ESCR Committee, General Comment No. 15, §§ 7 & 22.

[813] ESCR Committee, General Comment No. 13, § 5.

[814] ESCR Committee, General Comment No. 4, § 8(b).

[815] ESCR Committee, General Comment No. 12, § 7.

[816] Ibid., § 8.

[817] Cf. ESCR Committee, General Comment No. 15, § 11.

[818] Cf. L. Clorfene-Casten, *Breast Cancer: Poisons, Profits and Prevention*, Monroe, Maine: Common Courage Press, 1996.

[819] Cf. ESCR Committee, *Statement in the Context of the Rio+20 Conference on "The Green Economy in the Context of Sustainable Development and Poverty Eradication"* (Statement adopted by the Committee on Economic, Social and Cultural Rights at its 48th Session, 30th April to 18th May 2012, E/C.12/2012/1), <http://www2.ohchr.org/english/bodies/cescr/statements.htm>.

[820] OHCH, Office of the High Commissioner for Human Rights, *Rio+20 United Nations Conference on Sustainable Development*, 27th September 2012, <http://www.ohchr.org/EN/NewsEvents/Rio20/Pages/Statementspeeches.aspx>.

[821] Cf. UN, "Stockholm Declaration on the Human Environment", 11 *International Legal Materials* 1416, 1972, <http://www.un-documents.net/unchedec.htm>; and "Rio Declaration on Environment and Development", 31 *International Legal Materials* 876, 1992, <http://www.unesco.org/education/pdf/RIO_E.PDF>.

[822] Cf. J. Carling, *Indigenous Peoples' Letter to the Incoming President of the World Bank*, 24th June 2012, <http://www.aippnet.org/home/statement/908-indigenous-peoples-letter-to-the-incoming-president-of-the-world-bank>.

[823] The World Bank Group, *Sustainable Development* (official website), 2011–2012, <web.worldbank.org http://go.worldbank.org/57GVYJEEN0>.

[824] Cf. Y.K. Jim, *Reply to the Indigenous Peoples' Letter to the Incoming President of the World Bank*, 6th August 2012, <https://docs.google.com/file/d/0B2Vnefme6P1aUUNKUi1XU3BfUlE/edit?pli=1>.

[825] This consideration is also highlighted by the High Commissioner for Human Rights (cf. *Remarks of High Commissioner for Human Rights Navi Pillay at Rio+social.* 19th June 2012, <http://www.ohchr.org/EN/NewsEvents/Pages/DisplayNews.aspx?NewsID=12254&LangID=E>).

[826] ESCR Committee, *Statement in the Context of the Rio+20 Conference on "The Green Economy in the Context of Sustainable Development and Poverty Eradication"*, § 7; cf. High Commissioner for Human Rights, *Statement of High Commissioner for Human Rights Navi Pillay at the OHCHR-UNEP Joint Side Event on Human Rights in Sustainable Development – Human Rights at the Heart of Sustainable Development: Honouring Principle 1*, 19th June 2012, <http://www.ohchr.org/EN/NewsEvents/Pages/DisplayNews.aspx?NewsID=12255&LangID=e>.

[827] High Commissioner for Human Rights, *Statement of High Commissioner for Human Rights Navi Pillay at the OHCHR-UNEP Joint Side Event on Human Rights in Sustainable Development*, 2.

[828] Cf. United Nations Development Programme, *Human Development Reports*, 2010–2011, <hdr.undp.org http://hdr.undp.org/en/reports/>.

[829] Alan Greenspan, "Economic Flexibility", 12th October 2005, <https://www.federalreserve.gov/boarddocs/speeches/2005/20051012/default.htm>.

[830] Warren Buffet, "Berkshire Hathaway Inc. 2002 Annual Report", 15, <http://www.berkshirehathaway.com/2002ar/2002ar.pdf>.

[831] Cf. T. Petruno, "Mozilo knew hazardous waste when he saw it", *Los Angeles Times*, 4th June 2009, <http://latimesblogs.latimes.com/money_co/2009/06/the-use-of-toxic-to-describe-high-risk-mortgages-has-been-de-rigueur-for-the-last-two-years-now-it-looks-like-countrywide.html>.

[832] E.g. University of Central Arkansas, "Why Study Economics at UCA?", n.d.a., <http://uca.edu/efirm/why-study-economics/>.

[833] Cf. D. Stuckler and S. Basu, *The Body Economic: Why Austerity Kills*, London: Allen Lane, 2013.

[834] G. Katrougalos, M. Figueiredo and P. Pararas (eds.), *Annuaire international des droits de l'homme*, Athens: Sakkoulas, 2014; the actual articles referred to are listed as follows: Christina M. Akrivopoulou, "Eurozone crisis and social rights protection in the south European jurisprudence", 3–13; George Katrougalos, "The crisis of the European social state", 105–23; David Schneiderman, "A New Global Economic Constitutional Order in the Making? The Case of International Investment Law", 243–55; Antonis Bredimas, "État de nécessité, force majeure et dette souveraine en droit international économique avec mention spécifique du cas de la Grèce", 297–329; Marina Calamo Specchia, "La crise économique et l'équilibre budgétaire en Italie. Quel avenir pour les droits sociaux?", 387–404; Ángel Rodríguez, "Sovereign Debt, Decentralization and Fundamental Social Rights After the Constitutional Reform of 2011 in Spain", 445–64; Xenophon Contiades and Alkmene Fotiadou, "The debt crisis proving ground. Social rights theory revisited", 573–82; Stavroula N. Ktistaki, "Les droits sociaux en période de crise économique. Le cas de la Grèce", 615–34.

[835] Cf. D. Stuckler and S. Basu, *The Body Economic: Why Austerity Kills;* and A. Kentikelenis *et al.*, "Greece's Health Crisis: From Austerity to Denialism", *The Lancet*, 383, 2014, 748–53.

[836] Cf. IMF, "Ex Post Evaluation of Exceptional Access under the 2010 Stand-By Arrangement", 2013, <http://www.imf.org/external/pubs/ft/scr/2013/cr13156.pdf>; in it, we read: "With debt restructuring off the table, Greece faced two alternatives: default immediately, or move ahead as if debt restructuring could be avoided. The latter strategy was adopted, but in the event, this only served to delay debt restructuring and allowed many private creditors to escape." (27)

[837] Cf. M-F. Clerin, "What About Greece and Goldman Sachs?", *Diplomatic World*, 26, 2010, <smooz.4your.net/diplomatic-world/files/DW_26_Greece.pdf>.

[838] Life-based metaphors abound in the pundits' descriptions of economic affairs (e.g. "health", "contagion", "metastasis"), which are however conducted in such a way as to cause literal harm to living beings and without taking any noticeable account of them.

[839] Cf. Thorstein Veblen, *Absentee Ownership: Business Enterprise in Recent Times*, New York: Huebsch, 1923. Continuing the classical tradition of Ricardo and Mill, Veblen regarded high finance as a rent-seeking wealth-transferring endeavour, i.e. parasitic upon the real economy, and capable of twisting the constitutionally elected governments' hand in supplying it with public wealth by application or sheer threat of withdrawal of credit from the national economy (cf. Michael Hudson, "Veblen's Institutionalist Elaboration of Rent Theory", 27th July 2012, <http://michael-hudson.com/2012/07/veblens-institutionalist-elaboration-of-rent-theory/>).

[840] I.e. the "Memorandum of Economic and Financial Policies", the "Memorandum of Understanding on Specific Economic Policy Conditionalities" and the "Technical Memorandum of Understanding".

[841] All relevant official documents are available, in English, on the website of the Hellenic Foundation for European and Foreign Policy: <http://crisisobs.gr/en/repository/?ct=98&st=103>.

[842] Cf. "Foreign direct investment - net inflows (% of GDP) in Greece", *Trading Economics*, n.d.a., <http://www.tradingeconomics.com/greece/foreign-direct-investment-net-inflows-percent-of-gdp-wb-data.html>.

[843] Cf. N. Dunbar and E. Martinuzzi, "Goldman Secret Greece Loan Shows Two Sinners as Client Unravels", 6th March 2012, <http://www.bloomberg.com/news/articles/2012-03-06/goldman-secret-greece-loan-shows-two-sinners-as-client-unravels>.

[844] Cf. Joseph Stiglitz, *Globalization and its Discontents*, London: Penguin, 2002.

[845] "Memorandum of Understanding of Economic and Financial Policies", 2, <http://crisisobs.gr/wp-content/uploads/2013/03/Greece+LOI+MEFP+TMU-3__05_20101.pdf>.

[846] IMF, "Ex Post Evaluation of Exceptional Access under the 2010 Stand-By Arrangement", 1–2, <http://www.imf.org/external/pubs/ft/scr/2013/cr13156.pdf>.

[847] Cf. Jubilee Debt Campaign, "Six key points about Greek debt and the forthcoming election", 2015, <http://jubileedebt.org.uk/wp-content/uploads/2015/01/Six-key-points-about-Greek-debt_01.15.pdf>; and J. Zettelmeyer, C. Trebesch and M. Gulati, "The Greek Debt Restructuring: An Autopsy" EBRD, 2013, <http://scholarship.law.duke.edu/cgi/viewcontent.cgi?article=5343&context=faculty_scholarship>.

[848] IMF, "Ex Post Evaluation of Exceptional Access under the 2010 Stand-By Arrangement", 11, 17 & 27.

[849] Cf. D. Stuckler and S. Basu, *The Body Economic: Why Austerity Kills*.

[850] "The Loan Agreements between the Hellenic Republic, the European Union and the International Monetary Fund" (Formerly confidential governmental and inter-governmental documentation, distributed to the participants in the conference "Sovereign debt and fundamental social rights", organised by the International Association of Constitutional Law and held in Athens, Greece, 28–29 June 2013), 58.

[851] IMF, "Ex Post Evaluation of Exceptional Access under the 2010 Stand-By Arrangement", 14.

[852] Andrew Haldane and Piergiorgio Alessandri, "Banking on the State", *BIS Review*, 139, 2009, <http://www.bis.org/review/r091111e.pdf>.

[853] Ibid., 1.

[854] As cited in *The Wall Street Journal*, Streaming *Coverage*, 8th October 2013, emphasis added, <http://stream.wsj.com/story/latest-headlines/SS-2-63399/SS-2-348445/>.

[855] Ellen Brown, "The ECB's Noose around Greece: How Central Banks Harness Governments", 10th March 2015, <http://ellenbrown.com/2015/03/10/the-ecbs-noose-around-greece-how-central-banks-harness-governments/>.

[856] Gérard de Bernis, "Globalization: History and Problems", *ISMEA*, 1999, <http://www.ismea.org/asialist/Bernis.html>.

[857] Cf. N. Ferguson, A. Schaab, and M. Schularick, "Central Bank Balance Sheets: Expansion and Reduction since 1900", 26th May 2014 (Paper presented at the May 2014 ECB conference in Sintra), <https://www.ecbforum.eu/up/artigos-bin_paper_pdf_0551614001400679837-360.pdf>; in it we read: "Measured both by scale and incidence, the post-2007 expansion episode has eclipsed all other historical precedents." (34)

[858] Cf. J. Black and S. Kennedy, "Draghi Commits to Trillion-Euro QE in Deflation Fight", *Bloomberg Business*, 22nd January 2015, <http://www.bloomberg.com/news/articles/2015-01-22/draghi-commits-ecb-to-trillion-euro-qe-plan-in-deflation-fight>.

[859] Cf. Alan Greenspan, "Economic Flexibility"; and M. Sherman, "A Short History of Financial Deregulation in the United States", *Center for Economic and Policy Research*, 2009, <http://www.openthegovernment.org/sites/default/files/otg/dereg-timeline-2009-07.pdf>.

[860] Barack Obama, "Remarks by the President on the Economy", 14th April 2009, <http://www.whitehouse.gov/the_press_office/Remarks-by-the-President-on-the-Economy-at-Georgetown-University/>.

[861] Cf. Q. Chen *et al.*, "Financial Crisis, Unconventional Monetary Policy and International Spillovers", HKIMR Working Paper no. 23/2014, *SSRN*, 18th September 2014; and J.H. Rogers *et al.*, "Evaluating Asset-market Effects of Unconventional Monetary Policy: A multi-country review", *Economic Policy*, 29(80), 2014, 749–99.

[862] Cf. ECB, "Why Has the ECB Introduced Negative Interest Rates?", 12th June 2014, <http://www.ecb.europa.eu/home/html/faqinterestrates.en.html>.

[863] Cf. Ellen Brown, *The Public Bank Solution*, Baton Rouge: Third Millennium, 2013.

[864] As cited in B.E. Brown, "The French Experience of Modernization", *World Politics*, 21(3), 1969, 366–91.

[865] Michael Hudson, "P is for Ponzi", 3rd April 2014, <http://michael-hudson.com/2014/04/p-is-for-ponzi/>.

[866] AID, 10.

[867] Ibid; cf. also 578–9.

[868] Ibid.; cf. also 315–24; unless otherwise indicated, all translations from the French into English are mine.

[869] Ibid., 10–2; cf. also 578–9.

[870] Ibid., 11–2; emphasis added. (All the European countries tackled in this chapter have pension systems consisting of a primary public pension pillar, plus voluntary occupational, personal or profession-based pension saving plans (cf. *Pension Funds Online*, 2015, <http://www.pensionfundsonline.co.uk/>).)

[871] Cf. Matina Yannakourou, "Labour measures of Memorandum II before the Greek Council of State: Decision 2307/2014 (Plenum)", <http://eurocrisislaw.eui.eu/wp-content/uploads/2015/04/Greek-Council-of-State-2307_2014.pdf>.

[872] Cf. Euro Summit Statement, Brussels, 12th July 2015, SN 4070/15, <http://www.consilium.europa.eu/en/press/press-releases/2015/07/pdf/20150712-eurosummit-statement-greece/>.

873 The term "PIIGS" was coined in 2009 by the *Financial Times* (cf. J. Petry, "Constructing the Eurozone Crisis: A Tale of PIIGS, Debt, and Austerity", *Pinpoint Politics*, 8th December 2013, <http://pinpointpolitics.co.uk/constructing-the-eurozone-crisis-a-tale-of-piigs-debt-and-austerity/>). With it, the public authorities and the peoples of few EU countries are mocked for being in trouble, despite their trouble's fountainhead being over-indebted private investment banks. The result is that the public opinion forgets about the private sector's leveraged, i.e. debt-based, bonanza leading to the 2008 collapse, including the notorious "toxic assets", and all that is talked about is instead those countries' "sovereign-debt crisis", as though the States' financial difficulties were the cause rather than the effect of the crisis (cf. John McMurtry, *The Cancer Stage of Capitalism: From Crisis to Cure*, London: Pluto, 2nd revised ed., 2013).

874 All relevant documents are available, in English, on the European Commission's website, <http://ec.europa.eu/economy_finance/publications/occasional_paper/2014/op191_en.htm>.

875 Cf. AID, 7 n12, 575 n8 & 579–81.

876 Cf. Constitution of the Portuguese Republic, 1976, article 18, comma 1, <http://www.wipo.int/wipolex/en/text.jsp?file_id=206670>.

877 Cf. <http://www.tribunalconstitucional.pt/tc/acordaos/20110396.html>; cf. also AID, 7, 578 n13.

878 Cf. <http://www.tribunalconstitucional.pt/tc/acordaos/20120353.html>; cf. also AID, 7–8, 118 n74.

879 Cf. <http://www.tribunalconstitucional.pt/tc/acordaos/20130187.html>; cf. also AID, 8, 119 n75.

880 AID, 578 n13.

881 AID, 118.

882 AID, 118–9. Article 9d of the Portuguese constitution requires the State "[t]o promote the people's well-being and quality of life and real equality between the Portuguese, as well as the effective implementation of economic, social, cultural and environmental rights" (<http://app.parlamento.pt/site_antigo/ingles/cons_leg/Constitution_VII_revisao_definitive.pdf>).

883 Cf. <http://www.tribunalconstitucional.pt/tc/acordaos/20140413.html>.

884 Cf. European Commission, "European Financial Stabilisation Mechanism (EFSM)", 2014, <http://ec.europa.eu/economy_finance/eu_borrower/efsm/index_en.htm>.

885 Cf. European Commission, "Treaty establishing the European Stability Mechanism (ESM) signed", 2012, <http://ec.europa.eu/economy_finance/articles/financial_operations/2011-07-11-esm-treaty_en.htm>.

886 As cited in "Speculation against Italy could destroy euro – business lobby head", *Reuters*, 15th June 2012, <http://in.reuters.com/article/2012/06/15/italy-confindustria-euro-idINDEE85E09220120615>.

887 Cf. <http://eng.forsaetisraduneyti.is/news-and-articles/nr/3037>.

888 On this trend, Spanish jurist Jesús Ballesteros (b. 1943), who speaks of "casino capitalism" (*Globalization and Human Rights: Challenges and Answers from a European Perspective*, Leiden: Springer, 6).

⁸⁸⁹ Cf. J.M. Boughton, "Historical Perspectives on Financial Distress: A comment", *Carnegie-Rochester Conference Series on Public Policy*, 53, 2000, 169–75. It is therefore not surprising that leading statesmen may advocate for a return to the 1946–1972 Bretton Woods system of pegged but adjustable exchange rates and mobile yet not volatile steered capital trade (e.g. former UK PM Gordon Brown, "Bretton Woods Keynote", *Institute for New Economic Thinking*, 2011, <http://ineteconomics.org/video/bretton-woods/gordon-browns-keynote-bretton-woods-conference>).

⁸⁹⁰ Cf. John McMurtry, *The Cancer Stage of Capitalism: From Crisis to Cure*, 176–9, 190–1 & 226–67 explaining how the banking sector can yield power within the EU legislative framework (cf. also H-B. Schäfer, "The Sovereign Debt Crisis in Europe: Save Banks Not States", *SSRN*, 1ˢᵗ May 2012, <http://ssrn.com/abstract=2049299%20or%20http:/dx.doi.org/10.2139/ssrn.2049299>).

⁸⁹¹ Cf. <http://www.giurcost.org/decisioni/2010/0010s-10.html>; cf. also AID, 395.

⁸⁹² AID, 395.

⁸⁹³ Cf. <http://www.cortecostituzionale.it/documenti/download/doc/recent_judgments/S70_2015_en.pdf>.

⁸⁹⁴ Cf. <http://www.inps.it/MessaggiZIP/Messaggio%20numero%2011243%20del%2011-07-2013_Allegato%20n%201.pdf>; cf. also AID, 9 & 395–6.

⁸⁹⁵ Like its Portuguese and Spanish counterparts, the Italian constitution reads (article 3): "It is the duty of the Republic to remove those obstacles of an economic or social nature which constrain the freedom and equality of citizens, thereby impeding the full development of the human person and the effective participation of all workers in the political, economic and social organisation of the country."

⁸⁹⁶ It is also interesting to mention case 223/2012 on Law 78/2010, whereby the constitutional court condemned the pay cuts of the nation's judges as a threat to the constitutionally sanctioned independence of the judiciary power, a violation of the constitutional principle of *equality* (since the judges were being singled out for pay reductions), noting also how judicial pay, given the sensitive role played by judges within the country's institutional set-up, does not stem from standard labour relationships subjected to periodic negotiations (cf. AID, 9 & 579 n19).

⁸⁹⁷ <http://www.giurcost.org/decisioni/2010/0010s-10.html>; cf. also AID, 396; emphasis added.

⁸⁹⁸ AID, 575.

⁸⁹⁹ Isaiah Berlin, *Four Essays on Liberty*: "First things come first: there are situations in which - to use a saying satirically attributed to the nihilists by Dostoevsky - boots are superior to Pushkin." (125).

⁹⁰⁰ Cf. H.Ó. Ágústsson and R.L. Johnstone, "Practising what they Preach: Did the IMF and Iceland Exercise Good Governance in their Relations 2008-2011?", *Nordicum-Mediterraneum*, 8(1), 2013, <http://nome.unak.is/nm-marzo-2012/vol-8-n-1-2013/48-article/354-practicing-what-they-preach-did-the-imf-and-iceland-exercise-good-governance-in-their-relations-2008-2011>.

⁹⁰¹ Cf. Case E-16/11 [2013] EFTA, <http://www.eftacourt.int/uploads/tx_nvcases/16_11_Judgment_EN.pdf>.

[902] Cf. R.L. Johnstone and A. Ámundadóttir, "Defending Economic, Social and Cultural Rights in Iceland's Financial Crisis", *The Yearbook of Polar Law*, 3(1), 2011, 455–77.
[903] <http://www.rgs.mef.gov.it/_Documenti/VERSIONE-I/Utilit/Selezione_normativa/LeggiCostituzionali/LC-20-04-2012.pdf>; cf. also AID, 397–9.
[904] Formally called the "Treaty on Stability, Coordination and Governance in the Economic and Monetary Union", <http://www.consilium.europa.eu/european-council/pdf/Treaty-on-Stability-Coordination-and-Governance-TSCG/>.
[905] Cf. <http://www.rgs.mef.gov.it/_Documenti/VERSIONE-I/Utilit/Selezione_normativa/L-/L24-12-2012.pdf>.
[906] Cf. AID, 398.
[907] All relevant official documents can be found, in English, on the website of the European Commission.
[908] E.g. "In Numbers: How much would we save by abolishing the Seanad?". *The journal.ie*, 20th January 2013, <http://www.thejournal.ie/cost-of-abolishing-seanad-761429-Jan2013/>.
[909] E.g. the Convention on the Constitution, "The Constitutional Convention Votes in Favour of Reforming Economic, Social and Cultural Rights in the Constitution", 23rd February 2014, <https://www.constitution.ie/AttachmentDownload.ashx?mid=adc4c56a-a09c-e311-a7ce-005056a32ee4>.
[910] The Convention on the Constitution, "Convention", n.d.a., <https://www.constitution.ie/Convention.aspx>.
[911] Cf. *Government of the Republic of South Africa* vs *Grootboom* 2001 (1) SA 46 (CC); *Minister of Health v Treatment Action Campaign (No 2)* 2002 (5) SA 721 (CC); and *Khosa v Minister of Social Development* 2004 (6) SA 505 (CC).
[912] E.g. *Hall v Minister for Finance*, where standing was denied; and *Pringle v Government of Ireland*, which was rejected on the merits.
[913] All relevant official documents can be found on the website of the European Commission.
[914] Cf. AID, 451–6.
[915] AID, 455; emphasis in the original. An unofficial 2011 English translation by P. Porta Gracia is available on the website of the Spanish House of Deputies (<http://www.congreso.es/constitucion/ficheros/c78/cons_espa_mod_en.pdf>). For a detailed discussion of the longer and more detailed new article 135 of the Spanish constitution, cf. J.M. Abad and J.H. Galante, "Spanish Constitutional Reform. What is seen and not seen", *CEPS Policy Brief. Thinking ahead for Europe*, 253, 2011, <aei.pitt.edu/32483/1/...Hernandez_on_Spanish_constitutional_reform.pdf>.
[916] Cf. <http://www.tribunalconstitucional.es/es/jurisprudencia/restrad/Paginas/JCC1342011en.aspx>; cf. also AID, 451–3.
[917] AID, 455.
[918] Emphasis added.

[919] Like the Portuguese one, the Spanish Constitution (article 9, comma 2) reads: "It is incumbent upon the public authorities to promote conditions which ensure that the freedom and equality of individuals and of the groups to which they belong may be real and effective, to remove the obstacles which prevent or hinder their full enjoyment, and to facilitate the participation of all citizens in political, economic, cultural and social life." (cf. the official English translation, <http://www.tribunalconstitucional.es/en/constitucion/Pages/ConstitucionIngles.aspx>)

[920] In comparison, Guðmundur Heiðar Frímansson argues that it is precisely because of the lack of large-scale consensus that Iceland's post-crisis constitutional reforms did not bear fruit; cf. his review of *Lýðræðistilraunir. Ísland í hruni og endurreisn*, edited by Jón Ólafsson, Reykjavík: University of Iceland Press, 2014, <http://nome.unak.is/nm-marzo-2012/vol-10-no-1-2015/71-book-review/543-jon-olafsson-ed-lydhraedhistilraunir-island-i-hruni-og-endurreisn-democratic-experiments-iceland-in-collapse-and-renaissance-reykjavik-haskolautgafan-2014>.

[921] Cf. AID, 456–63, and *Consensus Politics in Spain: Insider Perspectives*, edited by M. Threlfall, Bristol: Intellect, 2000.

[922] Cf. "El TC admite a trámite el conflicto en defensa de la autonomía local planteado por 3.000 ayuntamientos contra la Ley 27/2013", *Juridicas*, 11 September 2014, <http://noticias.juridicas.com/actualidad/noticias/4033-el-tc-admite-a-tramite-el-conflicto-en-defensa-de-la-autonomia-local-planteado-por-3-000-ayuntamientos-contra-la-ley-27-2013/>).

[923] All relevant official document are available, in English, on the website of the European Commission.

[924] Cf. Z. Rasnaca, "Constitutional Change through Euro Crisis Law: 'Latvia'", 2014, <http://eurocrisislaw.eui.eu/latvia/>.

[925] AID, 118; emphasis added. Cf. also an unofficial English translation available on the website of the International Network for Economic, Social and Cultural Rights, <http://www.escr-net.org/docs/i/1285934>.

[926] All relevant official documents are available, in English, on the website of the European Commission.

[927] Cf. I. and M. Precupetu, "Growing Inequalities and their Impacts in Romania", *Gini Growing Inequalities' Impacts Country Reports*, 2013, <http://gini-research.org/system/uploads/441/original/Romania.pdf?1370077330>.

[928] AID, 118; emphasis added.

[929] Ibid., 119; emphasis added. Cf. also the original ruling, in German, Hartz IV BVerfGE 125, 175 of 9 February 2010, <http://www.servat.unibe.ch/dfr/bv125175.html>.

[930] E.g. Iceland's Special Investigation Commission, *Report*, 2008–2010, <http://www.rna.is/eldri-nefndir/addragandi-og-orsakir-falls-islensku-bankanna-2008/skyrsla-nefndarinnar/english/>.

[931] Cf. A. Ámundadóttir and R.L. Johnstone, *Mannréttindi í þrengingum. Efnahagsleg og félagsleg réttindi í kreppunni*, Akureyri: Háskólinn á Akureyri, 2011, <http://www.humanrights.is/is/moya/news/mannrettindi-i-threngingum>.

[932] Cf. chapter 7 of *Mortals, Money, and Masters of Thought*, 2017.

[933] Pope Francis, *Evangelii Gaudium*, 2013, §§ 55 & 276, <http://www.vatican.va/evangelii-gaudium/en/index.html>; emphasis added.

[934] Ibid., § 56.

[935] G. Kasimatis, "The Loan Agreement between the Hellenic Republic, the European Union and the International Monetary Fund" (Research paper prepared for Athens Bar Association; English translation by S.G. Vryna), 2010, <http://www.kassimatisdimokratia.gr/index.php/law-science/item/129-the-loan-agreements-between-the-hellenic-republic-the-european-union-and-the-international-monetary-fund>.

[936] As cited in "Hans Tietmeyer, president de la Bundesbank", *L'humanité*, 30th January 1997, <http://www.humanite.fr/node/149752>; emphasis added.

[937] Eduardo Galeano, *Upside Down: A Primer for the Looking-glass World*, New York: Picador, 1998, 151–2; emphasis added.

[938] E.g. AID, 115.

[939] AID, 117 & 243–55.

[940] <https://docs.google.com/file/d/0B52MZ4CG3AqgUUZuZVNLVGo0MjA/edit?pli=1)>, 12.

[941] Ibid., 12–3.

[942] Unlike the crisis-born fascist governments of 20th-century Europe, transnational finance can also be *crueller* than traditional fascism, inasmuch as it does not care for millions of obedient nationals or a select racial group that cuts across classes and nations.

[943] Cf. AID, 755–6.

[944] Cf. <http://www.echr.coe.int/Documents/Convention_ENG.pdf>.

[945] All adjudications are available on the website of the ECHR, <http://www.echr.coe.int/Pages/home.aspx?p=home>.

[946] Cf. AID, 505–13.

[947] "Eventually" is emphasised: it took time before constitutional courts intervened to condemn austerity laws and policies. In Italy, it happened when these could reduce the judges' income and the income of better-off retired citizens.

[948] Marcus T. Cicero, *De Legibus*, ca. 40 BC, 1.III.8, <http://www.thelatinlibrary.com/cicero/leg3.shtml>.

[949] Hannes H. Gissurarsson, "Miracle on Iceland", *The Wall Street Journal*, 29th January 2004, <http://courses.wcupa.edu/rbove/eco343/040Compecon/Scand/Iceland/040129prosper.htm>.

[950] Ibid.

[951] Ibid.

[952] Ibid.

[953] Cf. OECD, *Tertiary Education for the Knowledge Society*, vol. 1, Paris: OECD Publishing, 2008.

[954] Hannes H. Gissurarsson, "Miracle on Iceland".

[955] Ibid.

[956] Cf. R. Boyes, *Meltdown Iceland: Lessons on the World Financial Crisis from a Small Bankrupt Island*, New York: Bloomsbury, 2009; and Á. Jónsson, *Why Iceland? How One of the World's Smallest Countries Became the Meltdown's Biggest Casualty*, New York: McGraw-Hill, 2009.

[957] Cf. H. Horn, "Iceland Is Wrong to Blame Its Leaders for the Financial Crisis, and So Are We", *The Atlantic*, 6th March 2012, <http://www.theatlantic.com/international/archive/2012/03/iceland-is-wrong-to-blame-its-leadersfor-the-financial-crisis-and-so-are-we/254039/>.

[958] Cf. E. Huijbens and H.F. Þorsteinsson, "Letters from Iceland", *Political Insight*, 2010, 21.

[959] Elaine Byrne and Huginn F. Þorsteinsson, "Iceland: The Accidental Hero", in *What if Ireland Defaults?*, edited by B. Lucey and C. Gurdgiev, Dublin: Orpen Press 135–6.

[960] Hannes H. Gissurarsson, "Miracle on Iceland".

[961] In the two editions of his *Cancer Stage of Capitalism*, John McMurtry reviews a large number of these meltdowns.

[962] Cf. S.K. Chand, "The IMF, the Credit Crunch and Iceland: A New Fiscal Saga?", Center for Monetary Economics at BI Norwegian School of Management, Working Paper 3/09, May 2009, <http://www.bi.edu/cmeFiles/wp%2009%203.pdf>.

[963] Elaine Byrne and Huginn F. Þorsteinsson, "Iceland: The Accidental Hero", 135.

[964] Ibid.

[965] Cf. Special Investigation Commission, *Report*.

[966] "The 25 People to Blame for the Crisis. The good intentions, bad management and greed behind the meltdown", *Time*, 13th February 2009, <http://content.time.com/time/specials/packages/completelist/0,29569,1877351,00.html>.

[967] L. Thomas Jr., "A Debate Rages in Iceland: Independence vs. I.M.F. Cash", *The New York Times,* 27th July 2009, <http://www.nytimes.com/2009/07/28/business/global/28iceland.html?pagewanted=all&_r=0>.

[968] Ibid.

[969] Ibid.

[970] Ibid.

[971] Elaine Byrne and Huginn F. Þorsteinsson, "Iceland: The Accidental Hero", 137.

[972] Cf. J.M. Chwieroth, *Capital Ideas: the IMF and the Rise of Financial Liberalization*, Princeton: Princeton University Press, 2009.

[973] Cf. R.L. Johnstone and A. Ámundadóttir, "Defending Economic, Social and Cultural Rights in Iceland's Financial Crisis".

[974] Cf. H.Ó. Ágústsson and R.L. Johnstone, "Practising what they Preach".

[975] Cf. John Kenneth Galbraith, *The Great Crash 1929*, Boston: Mariner Books, 1955 (7th ed. 2009).

[976] Cf. A. Thorvaldsson, *Frozen Assets. How I lived Iceland's Boom and Bust*, New York: Wiley, 2009.

[977] Cf. John Kenneth Galbraith, "The 1929 Parallel", *The Atlantic*, 1st January 1987, <http://www.theatlantic.com/magazine/archive/1987/01/the-1929-parallel/304903/>

[978] This was not the only peculiar, highly revealing statement that I came across in conversations with local business experts. Another, whose name I also omit for reasons of professional courtesy, told me that some of the scholars in his university department had concerns about the country's boom, but kept quiet: "we did not want to rock the boat and, above all, we did not want to be taken for leftists". Ideological self-censorship runs deep in academia.

[979] John Kenneth Galbraith, "Interview", *The Progressive*, 2000, <http://www.progressive.org/mag_amitpalgalbraith>.

[980] Cornelius Castoriadis, "The 'Rationality' of Capitalism", 82.

[981] Cf. Elaine Byrne and Huginn F. Þorsteinsson, "Iceland: The Accidental Hero",

[982] Cf. P.L. Young, "Iceland's economic thaw a thorn in EU's side", *RT News English*, 1st May 2013, <http://rt.com/op-edge/iceland-parties-crisis-eu-685/>.

[983] Cornelius Castoriadis, "The 'Rationality' of Capitalism".

[984] John McMurtry, "Behind Global System Collapse: The Life-Blind Structure of Rationality", *Journal of Business Ethics*, 108(1), 2012, 49 & 59.

[985] Cf. S. Motesharrei, J. Rivas, and E. Kalnay, "Human and Nature Dynamics (HANDY): Modeling Inequality and Use of Resources in the Collapse or Sustainability of Societies", 2014, <http://www.atmos.umd.edu/~ekalnay/pubs/2014-03-18-handy1-paper-draft-safa-motesharrei-rivas-kalnay.pdf>.

www.ingramcontent.com/pod-product-compliance
Lightning Source LLC
Chambersburg PA
CBHW052054230426
43671CB00011B/1898